SIMPSON AGONISTES

SIMPSON AGONISTES

A History of a Crime

Robert Metcalfe

iUniverse, Inc.
Bloomington

Simpson Agonistes
A History of a Crime

iUniverse books may be ordered through booksellers or by contacting:

iUniverse
1663 Liberty Drive
Bloomington, IN 47403
www.iuniverse.com
1-800-Authors (1-800-288-4677)

ISBN: 978-1-4697-8308-6 (sc)
ISBN: 978-1-4697-8307-9 (hc)
ISBN: 978-1-4697-8309-3 (e)

Printed in the United States of America

iUniverse rev. date: 04/12/2012

In Memoriam

Benjamin Metcalfe-Marshall

April 19, 1981–November 23, 2001

Contents

PREFACE

This book began as a letter to Marcia Clark (the main attorney for the prosecution in the O. J. Simpson criminal trial), which I wrote at the urging of several friends and sent off about six weeks after the murders occurred. In it, I outlined a viable scenario that had dawned on me soon after the details emerged for what was then still a central mystery in the case—the uncut left-hand glove, the cuts to Simpson's left hand, and the absence of any of his blood on the manhandled victims. It also included a connected explanation for the mysterious thumps on Kato Kaelin's guest house wall. Not surprisingly, since I've no background in, much less reputation for, forensics, it got no response. But at least I'd done my duty, I felt. Murder offends against us all.

The eventual civil trial would conclude in February 1997, with Simpson convicted this time around, but with these mysteries still unresolved. By then I had finally completed my thesis on Herodotus and graduated from the University of Toronto with a doctorate in classics. However, I didn't find, nor even really seek, a position in that field—jobs were scarce—but returned full-time to advertising and a secure income.

I continued, though, to stay interested in Simpson and to bounce my theory off others from time to time—they would invariably say,

"That works." I also read the main books on the case as they came out: by Clark, of course; and Daniel Petrocelli, who headed the plaintiff team in the civil trial; by the initial lead investigator, the now-infamous Mark Fuhrman; and Lawrence Schiller and James Willwerth's coverage of both trials from the standpoint of the defense. And I kept a file of newspaper clippings on O. J. as he'd sporadically make headlines.

I had, meanwhile, long been interested in doing some writing—of the nonacademic variety—and these two interests coalesced one day into a decision to advance my theory in print. So I carefully reread and made notes on the main sources—especially what they had to say regarding the physical evidence from the crime scene and Simpson's home—as well as all testimony concerning the timeline and Simpson's known whereabouts that night. I also used the Internet to review key testimony, especially regarding the cuts to his left hand. I even read the pertinent section on sharp-force injury in Dr. Werner Spitz's classic textbook on forensics. From this I compiled a thoroughly researched paper that now took into account certain issues I'd not been aware of when I first wrote to Marcia Clark. The paper was long, however, thus difficult to market—and compounding that, I still had no qualifications in forensics.

So the project languished once more for a few years, though from time to time I'd show my manuscript to any friend who'd expressed interest, and again I'd get a thumbs-up on my theory. But what I also got now was the suggestion that I expand on the few classical references I'd made, in particular on my discussion of the notion of *nemesis*, or retributive justice, with the idea that this was something people would find informative and intriguing. Eventually the penny dropped, and I decided to revise my text into a book-length study in nemesis, with the Simpson saga as a modern case in point. This was something I *did* have the credentials for, especially since my thesis dealt with this very theme in Herodotus's *Histories*, indeed, with nemesis as the proper theme of all true history—and, by implication, tragedy, its dramatic extension (whether fact- or fiction-based). The resulting text—the book that follows—is intended, quite literally, as a "tragical history" in the truest sense of those terms.

CHAPTER 1

PERSPECTIVES LOST

It was called the trial of the century—the century, that is, that's now a decade past. But its impact has reverberated well into this one as its protagonist continues to make headlines, often on slight pretext. And many of the other participants long continued to make news as well: on talk shows, for instance, or in the courts on other cases, or as author or actor (in no matter how minor a part), or as crusading detective trying to retrieve a tattered reputation. Indeed, in the case of the central figures—(like Johnnie Cochran, the lead defense attorney in the criminal trial, who died in March 2005), or even of those in significant minor roles (like the accused's too-faithful friend Robert Kardashian, who died the year before)—their eventual obituaries, even decades hence, will no doubt get wide mention as the media seizes on their passing to recall its and our fascination with the case. This won't be hard to do: Orenthal James Simpson was—and remains, if infamy be a mode—a celebrity. His guilt to most seems patent and his crime "most foul" or, as it were, archetypally offensive because of its classic motivation: obsessive jealousy and the need to tyrannize or control, its cold premeditation, and the brutality or fury with which it was dispatched. This was unmitigated murder "as in the best it is."

And he got away with it, at least in the criminal trial, thanks in large part (as most of us saw it) to the race card played by the defense and to a jury that couldn't or, more likely, wouldn't draw the distinctions that would dismiss as irrelevant most of the defense arguments. Their reasons, while understandable, are not wholly pardonable. Those like me who believed him guilty were either outraged by the eventual acquittal or resigned to it, our outrage long since spent on seeing what the defense was getting away with on a regular basis throughout the course of the trial. But, resigned though we may be or have been—Simpson's recent reversal of fortune may satisfy some—there remains for many, I think, a lingering bad taste and something akin to that crisis of faith that a Greek chorus, concerned spectators like ourselves, would feel when they saw injustice apparently triumphant, with no redress in sight.

That's where I come in—in more ways than one. I was, of course, part of that chorus, composed of most everyone else not directly involved, who viewed with mounting dismay the trial's unfolding. But I was also, to modify Horatio, more the antique Greek than all but a few in this troupe. When the murders occurred (June 12, 1994), I was immersed in a doctoral thesis in classics at the University of Toronto, though soon less immersed than I had been. For I was straightway absorbed by all that ensued—the car chase, the criminal trial with its various stages, the civil trial—which together effectively delayed by months the completion of my thesis. I was absorbed by the same things as everyone else: the grisly details, the celebrity aspect, and the mounting body of evidence, including the indications of a very clever plan that went awry due to unforeseen developments. But what was also interesting was the way passion warped the judgment of so many people. I had been a fan of Simpson's too, at least in his playing days, and had even gone down to see some Bills' games when he played there. (Buffalo's roughly a ninety-mile drive from Toronto.) But it wasn't hard to separate the killer from the football hero: I mean, my world didn't collapse when I learned the guy that I'd once cheered for could do this (though how I would have reacted in my sports-mad teen years might have been a different story).

Nor did my world collapse later on when the verdict of innocence was returned. That's the way the world often works, as the authors I was studying well knew. Ancient Greece is often celebrated for the gift of democracy it bestowed upon the world. What is no longer so well known is that some of its greatest thinkers (e.g., Plato and Aristotle) were at best lukewarm in their attitude to this form of government since they had a healthy fear, based on experience, of how easily major segments of the general populace (the *demos*) could be manipulated by ad hominem tactics—appeals to passion rather than reason—particularly by anyone who had the credentials of a military hero or who could list Olympic victories on his résumé. And this point is also driven home in the writings of Herodotus, the Greek historian who was the subject of my thesis, as a series of ambitious men (rogue aristocrats in all cases) succeed in duping the Athenian people and thereby gaining despotic power. This, by the way, has nothing to do with the title of this chapter (though lately you might wonder). That democracy—or popular opinion—can have its dark side too, its potential for being abused, was until not too long ago a fairly widely held perspective. Edmund Burke, perhaps the greatest spokesman for true liberalism, warned against the power of the demagogues. He pointed out how it was the same men who flourished under monarchies as flattering courtiers that throve in different guise in a democracy, posing as the people's champion and friend while manipulating them to their own ends. And Mark Twain was pretty much on the same wavelength with his Dauphin and Duke of Bridgewater characters—the Dolphin and Duke of Bilgewater as mangled by Huck—who demonstrate with ease how fertile a ground is mainstream America for con men and smooth talkers of every stamp; or when he reported how some said of Tom Sawyer, the quintessential American marketing genius/entrepreneur, that "he would be president, yet, if he escaped hanging." Fooling people—if not all of the people, then at least a majority for a period of time sufficient to get you, or your man, elected, your guilty client acquitted, your stock price up, or your worthless product off the shelf—is in practice an unwritten right in a democracy, as is proved every day in America.

Herodotus, for those who have never heard of him or know little more than the name, is the so-called Father of History. In part he has earned this title because he wrote the first history in anything like the modern sense of the term. It was a narrative of what happened *and why*, as opposed to a bare chronicle of royal births and deaths, wars and conquests, along with any natural disasters or remarkable meteorological or astronomical phenomena that may have occurred. Specifically, he sets out to put on record the story of the wars between the Persians and the Greeks in the generation previous to his own (early fifth century BC), as well as what led up to them. But his narration of these events, including the defeat of Darius's expeditionary force at Marathon in 490, and then that of Xerxes's vast host at Salamis (480) and Plataea (479), takes up only the last three of his *Histories'* nine books. The first six are all background, of vastly different kinds, as Herodotus ranges freely over virtually all the then-known world and over many prior generations, some of them quasi-mythical, as the digression-laced thread of his narrative leads him. Much of what he writes is ethnographic, regarding the various customs, or *nomoi*, of the peoples his narrative comes into contact with, and much of it geographic. Indeed, one book, the second, is entirely about Egypt, as occasioned by the Persian king Cambyses's decision to add her to his empire, which Herodotus relates as he traces the course of Persian expansion. But prior to the conquest proper, we get a lengthy excursus on Egyptian geography and customs, including religious beliefs and practices, for which Herodotus is our main literary source in antiquity; we then get a history from the earliest times down to the Persian invasion and occupation. Much in the *Histories*, too, is *fabulous* in the original sense of that term: that is, like a fable or (better, given their pointed nature) like a parable or monitory tale. This latter matter, by the way, is almost always something he reports on secondhand, something he got from someone else and cannot personally vouch for. Indeed, he expressly asks his reader not to assume he believes any of what he reports (at least literally) unless he confirms it or it's his own firsthand testimony. It's in this way, however, that he's able to introduce so many keys to the interpretation of his text or, indeed, to the meaning of *history* as he sees it—for the point, or paradigmatic value, of these stories is what matters, not whether they actually happened.

This brings me to the other reason why Herodotus is called the Father of History, which is that the term *history* was, if not coined by Herodotus, first applied by him in this context when he chose to call his work the *Histories*. Prior to that it did not at all mean "a record of the past," but rather an "inquiry" or, more precisely, "a learning by inquiry" or "finding out" or "coming to know"—with the emphasis on the result and not the process. And this is in accord with the word's essential meaning, which—no offense to the feminist movement—has nothing to do with "*his* story," apt pun though that may be (and though *story* does, in fact, derive from *history*, as *squire* does from *esquire*). In Greek the word looked like this: ἱστορία; and this, when transliterated, comes out as *historia*. But the *h* sound is actually indicated in the Greek not by a letter but by the mark like an initial curly single quotation mark above the first *i*, which indicates that this *i* (or iota) has a "rough" or aspirated pronunciation.[1] Moreover, this particular "rough" breathing also represents one of the many instances in ancient Greek where a *w* sound once stood. But the *w* sound, as represented by the letter digamma, *F*, which is found on ancient inscriptions, had disappeared from most Greek dialects (and from the alphabet where it had been the sixth letter) by the time of the classical period.[2] So, had the Greeks not dropped their *w*'s, the word that we now use would not be *history*, but *wistory*. And this word would have recognizable and valid English cognates (words that derive from their common Indo-European ancestor), for instance, the now almost-obsolete verb *wit* (as in *to wit*), with present tense *wot* ("know"), and *wist* for past tense and past participle ("knew" and "known") as well as words still current, such as *wise, wisdom, wit* (the noun) and, from *wit*, *witness*.

This connection with English words having to do with knowledge or cognition is hardly fortuitous. The Indo-European root, or primary semantic element, underlying both the Greek and English terms is *wid*—for the ancient Greeks, *id*, since they'd dropped the *w*. Literally it means "see," which sense, along with the *wid*-root, is particularly well preserved in the Latin verb for "to see" *videre*.[3] But *seeing* and *knowing* are, obviously, closely related. Thus the *e·vid·ence* is the means by which we prove something to be true (or not) or from which we draw conclusions. And *witnesses* know what it was they saw (or heard etc.), at least superficially. In Greek this connection was

1 An inverted apostrophe means the reverse: a "smooth" breathing. All initial vowels and diphthongs in ancient Greek have one or the other of these markers; and initial *r* (*rho*) always has a "rough" marker.

2 It's called digamma because its upper case looks like a gamma, Γ, with two horizontal strokes. And, if it looks to us like our sixth letter *F*, that's no coincidence: Roman *F* derives from Greek digamma with a slightly altered pronunciation. The ultimate source is the Phoenician letter *waw*.

3 Latin is also an Indo-European language. The Romans pronounced *v* as we do *w*.

even more semantically secured: for what was originally the present perfect tense of "see," *oida* ("I have seen"), became, without any change of grammatical form, a simple present with the meaning "I [have seen and thus] know." This *[w]id* root, then, underlies *historia*, which, thanks to its deriving directly from *historein*, "to inquire" (or "look into"), may, as indicated, be loosely translated as "inquiry." But both words derive from the noun *histor* (*wistor* with the *w* restored), which does not mean, as you might suppose, an "inquirer"; rather, it retains its *[w]id* root origins in its sense: "a wise man, one who knows right, a judge."[4]

As a writer and native speaker of a language still alive to its underlying semantic roots, Herodotus would have entitled his work advisedly, knowing full well what his word choice implied. His reader should thus be aware that there is more than mere information or a dead record of the past in the *Histories*. By implication, there is some form of enlightenment as well; hence, he'll be the wiser for reading them, assuming he sees what Herodotus means, that is, assuming he sees the causes not just of what *has* happened, but of what, given the nature of things, will still happen. A *histor*, to be worthy of the name, should have foresight, should know the future too, not in detail, of course, but in essence, since he grasps the *id*·ea (note again the *[w]id* root) or essential form and nature of his field of inquiry. This idea of history is never formally expounded in Herodotus, despite the odd maxim or terse observation. Instead, he prefers a deceptively naïve exterior, choosing, as stated, to convey his essential message simply but succinctly in the parables or monitory tales that weave their way in and out of his narrative. There are various themes and various illustrative tales in the *Histories*, but the central theme, which is introduced in the very first parable, is, as I'll now demonstrate, that

4 The third so-called classical language, along with Latin and Greek, is Sanskrit. There the *wid* root gives us *veda*, "knowledge, sacred knowledge, sacred book."

of crime and punishment—or folly and fiasco. Herodotus, above all, is about crime and its requital, wrongs done or mistakes made, and their inescapable payback, however long delayed. It's not that his text doesn't end with wrongs not righted, but the pattern is established and the message is clear: they will be, somehow, some day.

The initial parabolic insert, sometimes called *The Tale of Candaules's Wife*, is, conveniently, fairly well known to a modern audience, thanks to its inclusion in a popular novel of recent date, *The English Patient*,[5] as well as in the Oscar-winning movie adaptation. More conveniently still, the author, Michael Ondaatje, left out certain elements that did not suit his purpose, but which I'll here reinsert, since several of these bear precisely on my own. The story is also apt in our larger context, the Simpson case, since it treats of a woman wronged by her husband, though in Candaules's case, it is he who is killed in consequence, not she. And it is, of course, apt in *The English Patient,* when the tale is read aloud at a campsite in the Egyptian desert by the heroine, Katherine Clifton, to her husband and Almásy, the titular hero and her soon-to-be lover; for her husband has himself been waxing overly enthusiastic in praise of his new bride.

This, too, is Candaules's mistake. King of Lydia (in present-day western Turkey) and the last of the Heraclid line, he has, as Herodotus puts it, become erotically obsessed with his own wife. Fixated as he is on his wife's external charms, and feeling the need to impress on someone else how fortunate he is, he keeps extolling her beauty to his most trusted retainer, Gyges. Unfortunately, words will not suffice: he can't be sure that Gyges truly appreciates his good fortune without he sees for himself the naked queen. Gyges protests: this will be a violation of her modesty; it will run counter

5 (Toronto: Vintage Canada, 1993), 232–4.

to time-honored rules of good behavior, which bid with the voice of experience that a man always mind his own affairs; finally (and this is the only plea Ondaatje includes) it will be a lawless act (*anomos*), and thus by implication (in Herodotus) will fly in the face of our innate sense of right and wrong. But Candaules insists, and says he has a way whereby Gyges may see her undetected. Candaules will hide Gyges behind the bedroom door, near a chair on which his queen will place her clothes as she disrobes prior to joining him in bed. Gyges thus may gaze upon her beauty at his leisure and then slip out undetected as she walks toward her husband. So Gyges, when he cannot dissuade the king, complies with his lawless behest. All goes according to plan, save that when he exits the room the queen catches sight of him and realizes instantly just what is going on. But she retains her composure and joins her husband in bed. Then, the next day, having readied loyal retainers of her own within her chamber, she summons Gyges and presents him with two alternatives: either kill her offending husband and reign with her in his place, or be put to death on the spot. Again Gyges pleads his case in vain; then, when he sees there's no way out, he chooses (somewhat basely) "to survive." So he slays Candaules in the way the queen has devised and takes over his throne (1.7–13).[6]

This is the point where *The English Patient* essentially leaves off; I'm not saying that it distorts the story, but it does leave out (in addition to those mentioned) certain elements that are fundamental to an understanding of Herodotus—and to my revisionist *History*

---

6 The bracketed information lets you know that this material is to be found in Book One, chapters seven through thirteen. Note, however, that Herodotus's chapters are extremely short as a rule, so that there are usually two or more per page: they won't take long to read. Since I'll be citing him quite frequently, and since a fair part of what I cite might seem far-fetched, I thought it best to help you find the source in each case, lest you think I'm making it up. And, if you take a liking to the *Histories* and want to read more, so much the better. He's an author that more people ought to know.

of the Simpson affair. The first is within the framework of what's already been related. The queen, when Gyges consents to kill her husband, goes on to explain just how this is to be done. Gyges is to launch his attack on her sleeping husband from "the *very place* where he displayed me naked," meaning from behind the same bedroom door whence Gyges had beheld what he should not have. Candaules's punishment will thus be poetically just: it will suit the crime by underlining in some way (here by analogy) why it's been incurred. Then a further dimension is added to the story, one that will link us to both the larger framework of Lydian history (pre-Persian conquest) and, more important, to the overarching thematic framework of the text as a whole. Most of the Lydian nobility revolt when they learn of the murder of their king. But to avert bloodshed, they agree with Gyges's supporters to arbitrate their dispute not by arms but by the verdict of all-knowing Delphi, Apollo's oracular shrine. Delphi sanctions Gyges's rule and the new Mermnad ruling house. But the case is complex: there are derelictions of duty on all sides, and in the strict scales of heaven, a better man than Gyges would not have killed his king. So Delphi, whose authenticity per se is never questioned in Herodotus, advises that the dethroned Heraclids will have "requital" *(tisis)*, or satisfaction of some kind, in the fifth generation of the Mermnad line. Everyone, Herodotus says, forgot this prophecy, and his readers—thanks to him—soon do so too, as his narrative wends its meandering way through the successive Mermnad kings. It is in chronicle style, but interrupted by these beguiling digressions—all ostensibly inserted on purely tangential grounds—as the mention of this or that figure reminds him of some remarkable incident that occurred in connection with them *and* makes us forget where we set out from.[7] In such fashion,

[7] By no coincidence perhaps, it was a Greek, Daedalus, who gave us the labyrinth—or so the myth goes.

then, we arrive at the reign of Croesus, which was where we were when the Gyges tale began, at the outset of a digression that at first seemed only meant to explain how the Mermnads came to power.

The ensuing story of Croesus, the fifth and last Mermnad king, and a man fabled for his wealth and power, is one of the *Histories*' most famous episodes. It is also what the academics like to call programmatic, since it sets the pattern for all that is to follow. It is too long to deal with here, and anyway, the point I want to make is made at its outset, as Croesus repeats the mistake of Candaules after his fashion. In his case he is so besotted by the spectacle of his own wealth and power as to be proof against all advice to the contrary. When Solon, the wise Athenian lawgiver, arrives at his court in the course of a ten-year grand tour, Croesus gives him a "grander" tour of his bulging treasuries. Then he asks him, given his reputation for wisdom and his wide-ranging travels in quest of knowledge, who is the most blessed man he ever has seen. Solon's answer fails to please: for he names a certain Tellus, an Athenian of comfortable means, who lived to see his sons all married and with children of their own and then died a glorious death defending his homeland. Croesus is quietly irked, but, controlling himself, asks whom he would accord the second place. When Solon again disappoints, by citing an even starker example involving two Argive youths whose lives were cut short at an acme of honorable achievement, Croesus can't contain himself and chides his guest for so scanting his manifest good fortune as not even to compare him with men of the common sort. Then, in a lengthy response, Solon explains that one must always look to the end and count no man as blessed, but merely lucky, until he has finally escaped life's myriad pitfalls with his good fortune still intact. Croesus fails to comprehend, and he dismisses Solon with cold indifference, thinking him a fool who says such things and who looks at an abstract end as opposed to present prosperity. So Solon departs from the stage, and in his place enters *ek theou nemesis megalē*[8] or, as I'll somewhat loosely translate, "a divine nemesis of great magnitude," which seizes on Croesus for presuming himself—or so Herodotus supposes—the most blessed of all men (1.30–4).

The rest need not be recounted. Suffice to say that Croesus is chastened by fate—he loses all his wealth and power, but he emerges a wiser man who counsels others, as Solon once did him. What I want to focus on here is the concept of nemesis, which was fundamental to the Greek world view and which is the "lost perspective" par excellence that I'll be applying in this revisiting of the Simpson saga. Formally, the word occurs but once in Herodotus, as quoted above. But otherwise, where it might be expected, he uses the more prosaic (or less metaphysical) *tisis*, "recompense" or "payback," as already seen in the eventual *tisis* promised the Heraclids by Delphi as satisfaction for Candaules's murder. Their *tisis*, however, coincides precisely with the nemesis, or divine retribution, visited on Croesus: they are two sides of the same coin and are accomplished with one fell swoop. And nemesis, though it thereafter goes unuttered, remains suspended over the whole of Herodotus's text, like an unseen but inescapable dimension in the presence of which all human crime and folly are played out.

A word, therefore, on *nemesis*, especially since, as popularly used today, it is rapidly losing any vestige of its original sense. For some time now, when we hear someone described as someone's "nemesis," we understand by that a very persistent or frequent rival, such as that other high school's team you love to hate, the one that always seems to stand between you and a championship season. Or it's used

8 The *ē* is there to facilitate pronunciation and indicates a long vowel; here properly *ay* as in "say", though *e* as in "he" will do. I'll only be using it for end vowels of some Greek words (including names).

humorously but with the same sense of a "fatal" weakness we're always overthrown by (e.g., her nemesis was chocolate chip cookies), in which case it's synonymous with "Achilles' heel." More recently it's become a favorite of the sci fi/horror and video-game crowd, as attested by such titles as *Star Trek: Nemesis* and *Nemesis Game.* In this perfervid, adolescent world it conjures up, besides an unbeatable foe, that hint of lurking menace—that *frisson* that they all crave—for the sake of which mythology and language are ransacked for fresh foes with sinister-sounding names to replace whatever's just been worked to death. No sense of right or wrong survives, although there is still, even in the first example given (that other high school's team), a certain supernatural overtone: the notion that it's somehow in the nature of things that we forever be balked of what we most wish for, and the bitterest blow, just when it seems within our grasp.

What *nemesis* properly means, however, is "an apportioning or distribution of what's due." It comes from the same root as the verb *nemein*, meaning "to deal out" or "apportion," and also that of the already encountered noun *nomos*, meaning "law" or "custom," including the "set of laws" apportioned any branch of the physical world—like the stars and planets, which are governed, as well as studied, by astro·*nomy*. As such, *nomos* (and by extension, nemesis) is not unlike the Hindu dharma, the "decree" (or "decreeing") by which each particular thing, or category of things, must be what it must be. Indeed, it could even be called the more comprehensive precursor, or archetype, of DNA (the determiner of the determiner or, qua "decree," the fiat DNA), since it extends through and determines *all* realms of existence, moral and cultural, as well as physical (and, in the latter case, both animate and inanimate).

In the moral realm, however, things happen which should not: people, for one ill-advised reason or another, commit crimes and misdemeanors or just have a bad attitude. And it's here that nemesis, in the traditional sense and as the Greeks generally understood it, comes in. It is the due assignment of (righteous) wrath or indignation at evident wrongdoings or injustice by men as they experience it, are wronged, and then are actuated by it—they are prompted to right wrongs, to themselves or others, and to punish the guilty. (By extension, *nemesis* also came to mean the offense seen as an "occasion for just resentment" or "call to arms"—at any rate, for those with an unimpaired sense of right and wrong.) Meanwhile, as on earth so in heaven: Nemesis with a capital *N* is "the divine wrath" personified, or the goddess of Retribution. Then by extension (and this until fairly recently was the normal English sense), it is the retribution that results—in all cases, but especially when that retribution is conspicuously heaven-sent, by which I mean accomplished by an agent that is unaware that it is serving as an instrument of the divine wrath. This might be a storm or drought, for instance, or a plague or, in Croesus's case, the rising power of Persia, which he seeks to quell and by which he's overthrown, thanks in large part to his habitual complacency. Finally, and to come full circle, nemesis is not restricted to the wrath or indignation aroused by the offenses of others. It includes our indignation at our own misdeeds: the realization we've done wrong and the sense of sin, with its attendant shame and remorse. This is another mode of retribution, heaven-sent from a most unlikely source, at least with respect to the state of mind we're in when we transgress. For it's our self that comes back to haunt us; our *real* self, that is, the one we thought we'd got rid of (or "outgrown") when we first chose to cross the line. Thus it is that some (the more fortunate) confess of their own accord and take the consequences or seek to make timely amends. In the *Histories* a frequent reason for going to Delphi is to enquire after a means of expiation, which the oracle then prescribes.[9] But others harden themselves against themselves, become deaf to the voice of

9 The Catholic sacrament of confession comes to mind.

conscience, and thus expose themselves to the full fury of heaven—to what you might call a category-five encounter with nemesis, such as Croesus incurred.

Nemesis then, as described, can be seen as an all-encompassing continuum (like that of time-space), at least so far as human affairs are concerned; its several elements, both subjective and objective, readily pass into one another, since they're facets, or phases, of one and the same thing. In a certain sense, it is coextensive with, or is an aspect of, fate. But it is fate with a purpose, which purpose is the maintenance of a kind of equilibrium: the kind, namely, that crime and presumption (that arrogance the Greeks called *hubris*) temporarily overthrow. In this respect it's like another Hindu-Buddhist doctrine, that of karma—save that karma refers to the effects of all our actions, both good and bad, whereas nemesis in the sense of retribution (which is really a restorative quid pro quo) is called into play by bad conduct and attitude only (their opposites avert it). Of course, no one believes in nemesis today (in retributive justice as a constituent part of the nature of things) or at least not officially. I mean, the whole notion has to be anathema to academics. Though privately, of course, I'm sure many of them, like the rest of us, entertain the possibility that some of the contretemps we all incur are payback somehow for something we shouldn't have done, or even have thought, and often for something that only we—and an all-seeing God, if there is one—could possibly know about. These are fantasies, no doubt, of a guilty conscience—excuse me, of a culturally imposed sense of shame—but sometimes so perfectly justified that you can't help but wonder.

In any case, I'm not writing for academe—at least, not any longer; nor for that matter am I asserting anything, in this realm at least, with certainty. In what follows I will simply be applying, among other things, Herodotus's (lost) perspective. This is not to say that I won't be relying as well on logic and the physical evidence;

much of what Herodotus himself wrote is a rational analysis of cause and effect or of what's probable and what's not. But he has, as well, this other dimension to his methodology, for which in my thesis I coined the term *nemesiology* (on the analogy of *kinesis* and *kinesiology*), since it is quite patently and unabashedly the attempt to discern the operations of nemesis and its intrusions in human affairs. Indeed, there are moments in his narrative when he actually speculates, in the case of multiple offenders, on what offence it was of theirs that brought down a specific chastisement. And in making this determination, he always looks, among other criteria, for a certain aptness, symbolic or otherwise, in the punishment inflicted.

Thus, in analyzing why it was that Cleomenes, the recreant king of Sparta, was driven mad and ended his life by hacking himself to pieces with a knife, he lists the explanations offered by others. Most Greeks—nemesiologists all, as most people were in an age of faith—think it was because of the sacrilege he had committed when he bribed the Pythia, the Delphic priestess, to deliver a false oracle that would help him oust the other Spartan king, Demaratus, with whom he reigned in a dual kingship, or diarchy. The Athenians and Argives, on the other hand, think it was punishment for sacrileges he committed that affected them. The Spartans, meanwhile, opt for the rational explanation that he had picked up the habit of drinking unmixed wine (the Greeks used to dilute their wine with water) from consorting with the wild Scythian nomads. But Herodotus rejects all these and simply affirms, without explanation, that he believes Cleomenes met the end that he did on account of what he did to Demaratus, that is, the wrong done to his fellow king as distinct from the attendant sacrilege at the Delphic shrine (6.84). His reasoning though—or rather, symbolic logic—is clear: Cleomenes, by attacking another legitimate king (they were constitutional monarchs), thereby attacked his own royal raison d'être. Self-slaughter was his due and apt reward.

What's past is prologue. Our "hero" cut himself as well, though not on purpose, which circumstance, and how it came to pass, shall figure largely in my *History.* Without giving anything away, I believe there was something about the way things unfolded that night, something that tripped up O. J. Simpson's almost-perfect crime in such a way as to smack of divine intervention, of the *peripeteia* or sudden "reversal of fortune" that's always pivotal to Greek tragedy. It has to do mainly with the cuts to his hand and how they really occurred, for which I have a radically different explanation from any that's been offered before. It also has to do with the glove that was found on the walkway back at his home, the one that was a virtual compendium of all the evidence pointing at him. For this and how it got there—a major bone of contention in both of his trials—I have a much different explanation, one which again sorts well with the notion of an inescapable nemesis holding all the cards in its hand and easily tripping us up just when we think we've gotten away. Meanwhile—to stray somewhat from the notion of nemesis, though not from the context of perspectives lost—there is that in what little we know of his movements of that night that could indicate he was given a chance to relent before crossing the line—that "heaven" didn't simply intervene to expose him after the deed was done but that complications arose as he approached the fatal point of no return, complications that amounted to so many (unheeded) warnings to turn back.

If this all sounds overly dramatic, that's intentional—and in keeping with the *agonistes* in my title, which word I'll next explain. Despite Milton's *Samson Agonistes,* it never really became English, either as a foreign borrowing or as *agonist,* its anglicized form (though the latter now serves as a technical term for certain muscles). We do, however, have it in compound form in *protagonist,* the "first" or "lead" actor in a drama—and *that* O. J. Simpson certainly was.[10] And, of course, there's the even more common *antagonist* (the word most responsible, probably, for keeping *agonist* out as redundant). Milton chose the term in the first place to signal to his educated readership (*educated* then meant learning the classics virtually by heart) that he was reformatting the biblical story as a classical tragedy, though as a poem and not as a play (as a Puritan, he could hardly write for such a lewd institution as the public stage[11]). And we will be doing much the same: reviewing (and reworking) the Simpson case in the context of classical tragedy or as seen through classical eyes. More specifically, we will look at it through Herodotus's eyes, the eyes of truly ancient Greece, the eyes of a world that was swiftly passing away and yielding to the "modern" rationalist spirit, especially in Athens, even as he wrote. This was, essentially, the world of Homer and that of Aeschylus and Sophocles, the first two of the three great Attic tragedians (Euripides is harder to gauge but certainly is more modern in his outlook). Sophocles, according to tradition, was a friend of Herodotus, and there are several passages in his plays that allude to passages in the *Histories*. And Herodotus, as should be evident already, was not that far removed from being a dramatist himself, though he wrote in narrative mode. Nor, for that matter, was he that far removed from the outlook of those who originally recorded the history of Samson (Judges 13–16), save that he spoke of gods in the plural (though also of *to theion*, "the divine," as a single entity). Indeed, he narrates certain events (in his Egyptian

10 There are also the terms *deuteragonist, tritagonist,* and even *tetragonist*, which refer to the second, third, and fourth actors with a nonchoral speaking part in ancient Greek tragedy. Originally, though, there would just have been the protagonist and chorus (indeed, in the rites from which drama evolved, just the chorus); the others were added later one by one.

11 The Puritans closed the theaters, but they were open again when this poem was first published in 1671. It may, however, have been composed much earlier, possibly during the Puritan interregnum (1642–60).

section, for instance) that the Bible narrates too. And his conception of nemesis, as should also be clear, is essentially in keeping with Biblical views, which latter still obtain in traditional schools. Witness the retribution prophesied some years back by a leading rabbi for Madonna—of all people!—for her dilettante Kabbalism and, more specifically, for writing a song, "Isaac," about a certain Renaissance era adept, thereby trying to turn a profit from what's holy.[12]

Getting back to Milton, his other major reason for choosing the term *agonistes* was to conjure up the notion of a contest, one that's for the highest stakes. For him this would have been victory in the Christian sense: spiritual recovery or salvation, as is (for Christians) prefigured in the blind and captive Samson's ultimate victory over the Philistines and over his nemesis, Delilah. An *agonistes* was, in its primary signification, a rival or competitor—an *antagonist* in its original sense of "one who competes *against* others for a prize." But it especially meant a competitor at one of the four great pan-Hellenic games periodically held in ancient times: the Pythian, Nemean, Isthmian and, most famously, the Olympic Games. These games, all of them, were for the Greeks as much, or more, a religious rite as a sporting event (an offering of the first fruits, as it were, of athletic achievement and physical excellence to the gods[13]). They were termed *agons* (or, to pluralize more Greekly, *agones*), which word, despite the evident connection to our *agony* or *agonize*, originally had nothing to do with the duress or anguish these words now convey. The related verb *agein* simply means "to bring" or "convey," and an *agon* was an assembly "brought" together for some reason (cf. *ag·ora*, the Greek town center or marketplace, so-called because public or private business "brought" people together there). But, since nothing brought people together (then as now) like sporting events for the

---

12 The offense is called *simony* in a Christian context; it means "trafficking in sacred things."

13 Contests in music and poetry were also held.

highest stakes, these games monopolized the term. Thereafter, by a natural progression, *agon* was extended to mean both the venue, or arena, and the contest itself—running, boxing, wrestling etc. Then it was further extended to mean any kind of struggle, trial, or danger, including a military battle or an action at law or legal trial; and, in the latter application, the more appropriately the greater the stakes became, culminating in a capital charge.

O. J. Simpson never was, strictly speaking, on trial for his life, though the charge in the criminal trial was first-degree murder. Still, consideration was given to asking for the death penalty, and though that was eventually rejected as being likely to undermine the prosecution's chances for conviction, he was exposed for a time in pretrial preparation to the real possibility of capital punishment. Even without that, however, if you glance back over all that *agonistes* conveys, you will realize that there are few in our generation this word would more aptly describe; in one form or another, Simpson has been one all his life. First it was as a football star, the greatest running back of his era, the guy the other team always had to key on, the guy all eyes were on from the stands that he helped pack or at home watching television. Then, when he retired and traded on his accumulated celebrity, it was as part-time actor, Hertz pitchman, or football commentator. It's not that he excelled in these later roles, but that wasn't why they used him. No, by this point he was simply a featured "attraction," someone who could bring people into the theater, or to your rent-a-car operation, or who could keep them from changing channels during lulls in the action. He was an *agonistes* in the (here "revived") root sense of "one who draws [a crowd]."

All of this paled, of course, beside what came next: the "trial of the century" and what led up to it, starring O. J. Simpson. In point of scale this was probably the greatest legal *agon* that any of us have ever, or will ever, see (the hearings that led to Nixon's resignation are the nearest equivalent I can think of). Thanks in large part to television, a nation-wide electronic arena or theater was instantly assembled. Some ninety-five million Americans tuned in to watch the slow-speed car chase that preceded Simpson's arrest, and about one hundred fifty million were watching when the criminal verdict finally came down. Meanwhile, there was an even larger global arena. Here in Canada, for instance, we followed CNN's coverage just as intensely throughout the entire proceedings, and this ongoing involvement was matched to some extent, no doubt, throughout the English-speaking world, if not well beyond. Certainly the verdict was read out to what amounted to a global audience. Then came the civil trial, still compelling though it wasn't on television and though the stakes were greatly reduced: damages if guilty but no jail time. On the plus side, however, was the unearthing of new evidence, especially the photographs of O. J. in the Bruno Magli shoes (the ones we know the killer wore). And he had to take the stand, which *agon* he'd declined in the criminal trial. Best of all, he was convicted and ordered to pay damages—sort of. Unfortunately, this penalty was really only nominal, since—as was foretold us, and depending on how you look at it—he's to this day avoided paying one red cent.[14]

His *agons*, then, at least as regards the murders of Ron and Nicole, would appear to have long since ended. And, inasmuch as he evaded any real penalty and has the criminal verdict on his side, you could say he emerged victorious. But emerged into what?—a world where most people are either convinced or strongly suspect

14 He did, of course, finally have to pay up at least in part, in the form of the proceeds from the sale of his pseudo-confession *If I Did It*, which the Goldman family was awarded the rights to. But, given that he was paid an advance of reputedly more than a million dollars—which he kept—and that he clearly indicates in the book he's not really confessing (more on this later), the net result is that he actually profited hugely from his crimes—and got away with murder all over again.

that he did it. In 2005 he tried attending a couple of Bills' home games, against Miami on October 9 and the Jets on October 16; at some point during the second of these, security had to escort him out, because nearby fans were showering him with beer.[15] So much for returning to the scene of former glory! By then ten years had passed since the first verdict and more than eleven since the crime. I guess he was hoping that things had *died* down, so to speak, or that we'd got over being mad and that he could come home, as he would to Nicole after a suitable amount of time had elapsed since he last punched her out. Didn't he realize he can never come home again—at least as things now stand? That he kept trying, however, speaks volumes for how lonely he must feel. He's been like a dead man walking in our midst, looking back with longing at his former life, at what he used to be, at all he's lost. He's been like Tantalus in the nether regions, allowed to look on all that he desires, remember even how it once in fact was his, but doomed to see it snatched away each time he reaches for it. So there is—or was, while he was still at large—one *agon*, the public's indignation and rejection, that he still endured, though he pretended it didn't faze him; this is (a degree of) the first form of nemesis as I've defined it.

In this respect, the Vegas incident of September 13, 2007 (where he, with several associates, forced his way into a hotel room and, at gunpoint, "reclaimed" memorabilia he thought was his that was about to be auctioned), might be said to sum up neatly his futile situation hitherto, with the memorabilia he was trying to retrieve ironically and banally mirroring the reputation he has almost certainly lost forever. Only this time he wasn't just rebuffed; he was sentenced to prison for a minimum nine years for armed

---

15 See the October 22, 2005 edition of the *Toronto Sun*, S10, which cites the *Buffalo News* as the source.

robbery and kidnapping, an even starker confirmation of his outcast state. Not that this sentence (which may yet be reduced on appeal[16]) amounts to the overdue, but adequate, payback for Ron and Nicole, loosely connected though these crimes are and satisfying though his sentence be. Nor does it close the case on that earlier crime. Different crimes, different histories, as we saw with Spartan Cleomenes earlier on. And, as we also saw, some crimes have, for discernable reasons, a greater claim on the involvement of nemesis in all its modes. Simpson, no doubt, will long be kicking himself for his stupidity in Vegas, and he might learn his lesson on that score. But will that at all quiet the furies aroused by the slaughter of Ron and Nicole? That crime was of a completely different order, and the requital required must be of a matching degree. That is a crime whose *full* history still begs to be told.

There remains, then, one further *agon* that's bigger in its way even than the vast audience assembled by his criminal trial. It is bigger in that it's all-enveloping and never-ending (or at least coterminous with life). Because there's also *himself* he has to deal with—now more than ever, since he has so much time alone; and *that* he can't run away from, try though he might. This is the third form of nemesis as I've defined it: namely, our own sense of right and wrong, and how we steer the course we do through life, how we handle the cards we're dealt and the challenges we face. This is the fundamental and, in a way, the only *agon*, and it takes place in the arena that is the mind or soul, where we confront ourselves and existence and what it all might mean. This is the true location of every tragedy, and we, the audience, are like flies on the wall of what is at heart an inner dialogue—a soliloquy—in which the protagonist, with whom we naturally identify in some way, is forced to come to terms with himself and with his situation. And this latter,

16 It certainly seems way out of proportion to the offense.

in essence, is a function of himself, of who he really is, for as the Greeks used to say, "character is destiny." This maxim can equally mean that our situation is subjectively induced by the choices that we make, or objectively by a "system" of rewards and chastisements that seamlessly incorporates the role our choices play.[17] This qua "system" is essentially the same as nemesis in the second or objective sense that I described: the impersonal outside power. But, as can be seen, it's continuous (it works glove on hand) with the internal dimension, our own subjectivity, and our choices. In a certain way, nemesis, like destiny (of which it is one face), is really us. Our final opponent or antagonist is ourselves.

Meanwhile, the lesson the protagonist either learns or teaches by where he goes wrong, is feelingly imparted to the audience to the extent that they're engaged by and identify with his *agon*, and they either embrace (the noble) or reject (the base) course he chooses to take. More concretely, they either join the "flights of angels" that "sing [Hamlet] to [his] rest," or fervently part company with Macbeth. But in the latter instance, which obviously is more relevant to my theme, they do so only *after* tasting what it is to sink where he has sunk. For it is not Macbeth's heinous crimes that they're engaged by; it's their consequence: an indelible sense of guilt, self-disgust, and moral and spiritual desolation. They descend, if briefly, into that same hell that he inhabits—the better to reject utterly the state itself and all that that way leads.[18] This, in either form, is the experience called *catharsis*

17 Thus the "sea-change[d]" and in-step-with-destiny Hamlet acknowledges that "there's a divinity that shapes our ends, rough-hew them how we will" (act 5, scene 2, 10–11). He later adds: "the readiness is all" (act 5, scene 2, 223). We have to watch for our cues and rise to whatever it is the occasion should call for.

18 See Martin Lings, *Shakespeare's Window into the Soul* (Rochester, Vermont: Inner Traditions, 2006) 93–5, for a fuller discussion of the purgatorial dimension of *Macbeth*.

or "cleansing."[19] Few, I'm sure, would willingly identify with O. J. Simpson, especially with his state of mind on the night of June 12, 1994, or think that they would somehow find this cleansing; quite the reverse is true, I'm sure. But that is exactly what I'll be doing here for much of what follows: trying to get inside a murderer's mind and undergo his *agon* of that night; identifying with, but not embracing, his point of view as he copes both with what confronts him and with what urges him on.

He, of course, wasn't thinking of right and wrong. He was intent on killing her—*and* getting away with it. I said he was never officially on trial for his life. From the moment, however, that he began to plot his ex-wife's murder, but especially during that brief but intense span of time when he was putting his plan into action, he must have been very conscious of the fact that *his* life, too, was at stake if he were caught; capital punishment was a real possibility. He was thus on various levels an *agonistes* or contestant in the trial that took place that night, though in an otherwise empty arena with himself alone, or so he thought, an audience of one. The "prize" or *athlon* he competed for (that's how *athlete* derives[20]) was revenge or satisfaction, something to appease his jealous rage and sense of rejection. And his sole anticipated opponent or rival wasn't the surprised and much weaker Nicole, who virtually had no chance; it was chance itself, incorporeal and impersonal chance, or all that could go wrong. At least, that's how he would have seen it.

---

19 What Aristotle meant by this term in his sketchy remarks in the *Poetics* is in dispute. Most take it as little more than a (salubrious) workout of the emotions of pity and fear. The loftier version given here is based on Martin Lings's discussion of Shakespeare (see previous note). Though Lings uses such terms as *purification*, *Purgatory,* and *atonement* in his analysis of this dramatic effect, he makes it clear (*ibid.* 198) that he intends the same thing as, in his view, Aristotle did by *catharsis*.

20 It's also connected to the closely related *athlos*, a "contest for a prize."

What I am arguing, however, using Herodotus's point of view, is that that was not blind chance that Simpson had for "witness" and opponent on that night (and has had ever since) but rather all-seeing nemesis, a "witness" that the courts can never call—or the guilty, short of making atonement, ever have called off. His *agon*, then, the fundamental one, the one we all have, the only one that really matters, isn't over—far from it! And, as things now stand, he's losing if not lost. In my final chapters I intend to look at Simpson's present sorry state, which has basically not changed one iota since he took that fatal step. (Not even his incarceration changes that; it only makes transparent what he's always been: a prisoner of himself.) I'll even suggest a way out of his woes, a way to retrieve, albeit in a different mode, something like the stature that he's lost, to become someone that people's hearts go out to, even given what he's done, such a catharsis as would include *him* among the cleansed. I do not think there's any realistic hope he'll take it, but I just want to complete the picture, to fill in all of the lost perspective I am claiming to revive. Christianity didn't introduce redemption; the classical world had a fully developed notion of it, too. The afflictions nemesis deals us have a purpose, which is to make us understand what brought them on; and this we cannot do without self-knowledge. "Know thyself." This was the message every visitor encountered who entered Delphi's shrine. It was inscribed above the gate. This is the final victory and the end of all our *agons*—be they never so herculean.

CHAPTER 2

WHAT CAN'T HAVE HAPPENED

When Herodotus (and whatever forerunners he may have had[1]) began to write what we now, thanks to him, call history—as opposed to the bare bones chronicles of previous ages—and to determine the true causes of complex events that took place in prior generations and in far-flung locales, he encountered a problem that the chroniclers had not, which is separating fact from fiction, or the possible from the impossible, or assessing degrees of probability. For there are competing versions of the truth: it's been exaggerated over time, or covered up, deliberately garbled, or simply confused by fond or faulty memory. And this was nowhere more true than in Greece itself, where each city-state had its own more or less partisan view of what had taken place in the great events of time gone by;

1 There were a few writers, such as Hecataeus of Miletus, who prior to Herodotus had begun to go beyond mere chronicles by writing accounts of foreign peoples, or of the geography of the then-known world, sometimes with a little history thrown in. They were referred to collectively as logographers, which may be roughly translated as "prose writers." What Herodotus gave the world was, as history and as literature, of a different order altogether.

each would exaggerate its own services to the national cause while traducing those of its neighbors, especially if they were involved in a current quarrel.

In addition, there were the theories of one's own colleagues, or at least the prior attempts by others to explain "objectively" what exactly had taken place and why. Granted, one didn't have too many colleagues to take into account—whereas today they're never-ending—but one had to take cognizance of whatever interpretations were in circulation (whether published or not) of events that one was interpreting afresh. This is what I am about to do now regarding the Bundy portion, as it were, of a closely connected set of circumstances that was from the outset one of the most intriguing aspects of the entire Simpson case. I am referring to the murderer's gloves, probably the most dramatic piece of evidence in the trial; to the cuts on O. J. Simpson's left hand; and to the sequence of actions that caused the left glove to be dropped, along with a knit woolen cap, at the murder scene at 875 South Bundy Drive and the right one to turn up on the narrow walkway beside and toward the rear of Simpson's house. This was at 360 Rockingham Avenue, just outside the semidetached quarters of Kato Kaelin, the "world's most famous house guest," at the point approximately where he, Kato, testified that he heard at discrete intervals three heavy thumps directly against the wall on that side. These thumps, which I'll discuss in due narrative course, are themselves a part of the mystery; as Kato describes them, they don't correspond well with any attempt ever made by the prosecution or the plaintiff lawyers to explain how they could have occurred. What I want to dispense with here, and prior to my reconstructed narrative of that night, is the explanation of the cuts and how they occurred—or better, how they didn't. This way the story that follows—what I think *did* happen—will flow more smoothly.

A troubling weakness of both the prosecution's case in the criminal trial and that of the several plaintiffs in the civil suit, on an issue that perplexed one and all from the moment the details of the murder began to emerge, was the want of a plausible theory or scenario to explain how the left glove had come off at the crime scene so as to allow for the ensuing cuts to Simpson's left hand. It must have been removed, since it had no slices anywhere on it; had it stayed on, it should have been sliced through at points corresponding to the cuts he received on that hand. These cuts are as follows: a moderately deep one about a half inch long that left a permanent scar, atop and across the second knuckle of his middle finger (this cut, as captured in a widely shown police photo of the back of his hand taken the following day, from an angle directly above, was at first thought to be the only one he'd sustained); a shallower, inch-long crescent-shaped flapping gash on the medial or inner side of his ring finger (the side nearest the thumb and, in this case, adjacent to the middle finger), extending from near the tip to the second knuckle; and a third one, three-eighths of an inch long and even slighter and harder to discern, near the tip of the lateral or outer side of the middle finger. The latter two cuts were opposite to and contiguous with one another; they were also so situated that he could conceal them both by keeping his fingers pressed together.[2]

The police photos also showed seven small, faint, curved abrasions on the back of his left hand, which in the civil trial were identified by Dr. Werner Spitz, a leading forensic pathologist, as fingernail marks or gouges, which the victims would have inflicted

---

2 For a more detailed description of these cuts, see the transcript of Dr. Robert Huizenga's civil trial testimony (available online at http://walraven.org/simpson/nov07-96.html). Dr. Huizenga, who worked for the defense in the first trial, examined Simpson both on Wednesday, June 15 (three days after the murders) and on Friday, June 17.

as they defended themselves. These, however, are not cuts and do not necessarily require that the glove was off; they could have been inflicted by pressure upon and through the cashmere-lined, thin leather material of the gloves the murderer wore. As stated in the *Medicolegal Investigation of Death*, the definitive textbook on forensic pathology that Dr. Spitz coedited and was the chief contributor to, "Fingernail marks and abrasions that are produced by the tugging and rubbing of clothing occur in many instances of hand-to-hand combat and most commonly in stabbing cases."[3] And the fact that neither victim in this case was found to have blood or tissue from their assailant on or under their fingernails argues that the gouges were made through the leather and cashmere. Ron's nails, in fact, were too short to allow for clippings to be afterward taken or for him to puncture the skin (though he still could bruise and abrade it). But Nicole's certainly weren't, so if she inflicted any or all of these minor abrasions, the wonder is that in her desperation she didn't break the skin much more severely and retain traces on her nails—unless, of course, the glove prevented this.

Interestingly, Dr. Spitz seems to have been prepared to allow that the cuts, too, were caused by the victims' fingernails. But this is even harder to credit, especially in the case of the deep slice across the middle knuckle. The plaintiff lawyers, who otherwise relied so heavily on his testimony, were evidently not wholly convinced themselves. For, while not discounting this, they also suggested to the jury a likelier scenario involving the knife, which I'll shortly discuss. Meanwhile, I repeat: none of the murderer's blood or tissue was found on or under the victims' fingernails, which is even more

---

3 Werner U. Spitz and Russell S. Fisher, eds., *Spitz and Fisher's Medicolegal Investigation of Death: Guidelines for the Application of Pathology to Crime Investigation*, 2nd edition (Springfield, IL: Charles C. Thomas, 1980), 167. Dr. Spitz, in fact, wrote the chapter "Sharp Force Injury" that I'm quoting from here.

incredible in the case of these deep cuts—that is, if we're to assume that their nails inflicted them.

One could, of course, theorize that the gouges occurred while the left glove was still on and that the cuts were unintentionally self-inflicted with the knife during some later phase of the struggle—after the glove came off, though without any further damage from the victims' nails, which would at this point pierce the skin and take away blood and tissue. At best it's a very awkward scenario, and it still leaves the nagging question: How exactly did the glove come off? This puzzle, till now, has had to be resolved by our assuming, as both the prosecution and the plaintiff lawyers would have us do, what has heretofore been the only apparent viable option: that the left glove was somehow pulled off by one of the victims as they fought for their lives. Thus, in the criminal trial, the prosecution, led at least de facto by the plucky and ever-quick-on-her-feet Marcia Clark, theorized that the gloves came off in the struggle between Simpson and Ron Goldman (the likelier of two unlikely scenarios, since he was much the stronger of the two victims). They theorized that at some point Simpson was holding Goldman from behind while he was trying to pry Simpson's left arm from around his throat and that in this attempt he pulled off the glove, thus allowing for Simpson to be cut in what remained of his exertions without there being corresponding cuts to the glove. Daniel Petrocelli—the adroit and superbly prepared lead attorney for Ron's father, Fred Goldman, and who spearheaded the plaintiffs' case in the civil trial—is more cagey and noncommittal. Quoting his own summation to the jury, he writes: "They [Ron and Nicole] managed to get a glove pulled off, a hat to drop off; they managed to dig nails into the left hand of this man, cause other injuries to his hand, forcing him to drop his blood next to their bodies as he tried to get away." Then he inserts the following revealing comment on his tactics here: "I was careful throughout the argument never to commit to any specific, precise version of how this happened. I didn't say who pulled off the glove or how the hat dropped. I didn't have to."[4]

He was right, obviously, because he won the case. Because there was by this time an even bigger mountain of incontrovertible evidence—most notably the pictures of Simpson in the Bruno Magli shoes—than had been amassed in the criminal prosecution. And, to be sure, because he had the kind of jury, and trial, that enabled him not to "have to." After the initial jury selection, there were nine unhyphenated white jurors and only one such black, and she was dismissed during deliberations and replaced by an Asian man. Meanwhile, the bar for conviction in the civil trial was not unanimity, but only nine votes "for." And the standard of proof that had to be met was not "beyond a reasonable doubt" but rather "the preponderance of the evidence"—in other words: Is it likely that he did it? With all the other evidence, the civil jury could brush aside, and justifiably I think, any doubts they might have had as to just how the glove came off. Though doubts they still must have had. We all recall that pivotal moment in the criminal trial when Simpson, at the ill-considered insistence of certain of the prosecution team, tried on the leather gloves, the extra-large brown Aris Isotoner Lights that matched one of the two pairs (the other was black) that a Bloomingdale's receipt proves Nicole had bought him back in December 1990 and which numerous photos showed him wearing since. They didn't fit—at least not in the circumstances, that is, in their somewhat shrunken condition (due to their having being moistened with blood that then dried and to not having been worn for over a year), with the latex gloves he was allowed to wear when putting them on, and with him no doubt splaying rather than relaxing his hands, thus preventing a fit.

---

4 *Triumph of Justice: The Final Judgment on the Simpson Saga* (New York: Crown Publishers Inc., 1998), 602.

But even though we didn't buy his act—and "we" included the jurors in the criminal trial, some of whom later said in interviews that none of them were taken in by that—there was no doubting that the gloves fit "tight and snug," as they were supposed to according to the Bloomingdale's buyer Brenda Vemich, who testified at the trial. So it is highly unlikely one would just slip off when tugged on by a victim, even in the course of a violent struggle. For Simpson's powerful hands, those of a running back rarely known to fumble, would be even more tautly set than in the courtroom that day. And he had an interest in keeping them on: to avoid leaving damning evidence, which was why he wore gloves in the first place. Moreover, the struggle had to be brief, maybe no more than a minute or two; on the one hand for the prosecution's tight, and the plaintiffs' even tighter, timeline to work[5] and on the other to account for the almost total absence of human sounds heard by the neighbors, who were probably all still awake. This can only be explained, or so you would think, by the victims', or more likely, Ron's (since Nicole was likely quickly rendered unconscious) not having the time to collect himself and to start shouting for help as he fought with the killer. That would be the natural thing to do—especially in such surroundings: a quiet condominium-lined residential street, with neighbors well within earshot. There was no time, then, for the glove to be worked off gradually in an extended phase of the fight. And, given the physical dynamics of the situation and the wounds we know he sustained, Ron Goldman was likely facing his killer while he still had strength to fight, desperately trying to ward him off and concentrating especially on the knife-wielding hand rather than

5 These and their rationales will be discussed later. Briefly, the prosecution worked with a timeline of approximately 10:15 to 10:40 p.m. as the period within which the murders must have taken place; the plaintiff lawyers went with roughly 10:32 to 10:40 p.m.

pulling at the other.[6] It was only when he was too weak to defend himself and had perhaps sunk to the ground that his right-handed assailant got behind him and inflicted wounds from there: to the right side of his chest and to his jugular, which he severed with a complex stabbing and cutting motion.

Moreover, Simpson had no bruises the next day, which he should have sustained had they been wrestling for a time in the manner suggested above by the prosecution, with Ron trying to pry his left hand away as Simpson gripped him from behind, which is just about the only conceivable scenario in which he would be pulling on Simpson's left hand.[7] Granted, a cashmere fiber from the lining of one of the gloves was found on Ron's shirt, which Marcia Clark cited as proof that the left glove came off in their struggle, the theory being that fibers left on the murderer's bared hand were then transferred to his shirt as the struggle continued.[8] But that could have easily resulted from either glove's more loose-fitting cuff rolling back a bit at some point while in contact with Ron, so that the edge of the exposed lining rubbed against his shirt, thus leaving the fiber. And, according to DNA scientist Gary Sims in his criminal trial testimony, the lining of the Rockingham glove (the right-hand one, from the uncut hand that held the knife) shows blood that is likely Ron's, which would have been transferred when it, the lining, came in contact with him.

---

6 Compare the expert opinion of Dr. Spitz, who ascribes the many superficial wounds Ron received to his trying to protect himself at the outset with his arms and presenting alternately the right and the left to an attacker he was facing (*Triumph of Justice*, 431).

7 The physical dynamics of this scenario have been thoroughly dissected by Richard Wagner, a retired (and now deceased) engineer, on his website http://www.wagnerandson.com/oj/lefthand.htm. He demonstrates conclusively how there was no way it could have led to the glove's ever being pulled off.

8 Marcia Clark with Teresa Carpenter, *Without a Doubt* (New York: Penguin Books, 1997), 416.

The foregoing is based on a kind of common sense, that is, on the natural, almost involuntary aptitude we all have for projecting ourselves into the physical dynamics of a struggle such as this, so compelling and dramatically charged in the relation, as we try to follow it in imagination and as we empathize with the horrific plight of the victim. And in this, as well as the normal acceptation, the jurors in the first trial did show common sense when they rejected the prosecution's explanation, or lack thereof, for how the glove came off. Something was amiss. In Lawrence Schiller and James Willwerth's *American Tragedy*, which (mainly) covers the criminal trial from the defense's perspective, Barry Scheck is quoted as follows from a discussion with fellow Dream Team members about how jurors make up their minds: "What people really do is listen to testimony and turn it into a story that makes sense to them."[9] Unfortunately—for the prosecution, that is—the scenario they vaguely suggested for how the glove came off never made narrative sense to the jury, especially in the context of a necessarily brief struggle and the absence of cries for help. And the fact that there was "something wrong," or insufficiently convincing, about this one aspect of the prosecution's reconstruction of the events of that night, and on a point connected with the vital question of how Simpson's blood, the most incriminating evidence against him, was found at the crime scene, played nicely into the defense's police conspiracy argument. It was a hole of sorts in the people's case, that is, a weakness or gray area which didn't invalidate the rest, but which gave those predisposed to acquit some justification for rejecting it. In the civil trial, with the virtually all-white jury, this issue was simply glossed over: the glove just somehow came off. But, as I recall, in the post-trial media interview with the jury, a black woman who was an alternate juror cited this very inadequacy as grounds for her

9 (New York: HarperCollins, 1996), 417.

dissenting opinion. Had she been empanelled, and won over three others during deliberations, O. J. Simpson would have gone scot-free—de jure as well as de facto.

But that's only part of the problem, because it isn't just a question of common sense regarding the physical dynamics of these murders and our being unable to envisage realistically how the glove came off. There *is* physical evidence as well: to begin with, the *absence* of any of his fingerprints at the crime scene. As Henry Lee, the renowned forensic scientist retained by the defense, observed, "The more bloody the scene, the better for the defense. One glove was dropped. One of the killer's hands was bare. But there were no bloody fingerprints"[10]—or unbloody fingerprints either. This, while it raises serious doubts, can be explained as the luck of the draw, or by supposing he kept his left fist clenched after losing the glove to avoid leaving prints. There remains, however, an even more serious problem with the physical evidence, although it's one that to my knowledge has never been remarked on, let alone adequately addressed. And this is the location of Simpson's blood at Bundy, the pattern the drops describe, which would seem to refute any scenario, however vague, in which the glove comes off and cuts to that same hand ensue in the course of the actual commission of the murders. This, more precisely, would seem to show that the cuts at least did not occur during Simpson's struggle with the victims and that the glove, therefore, need not have been removed then either, which, for the reasons just given, would have been highly unlikely. For if Simpson had been cut deeply during the struggle with Ron Goldman or, the less likely scenario, as he viciously stabbed and slashed the more helpless Nicole, his blood should have been found at the crime scene in far greater quantities than it was, especially given his violent exertions—not to mention in other locations, especially on the bodies of his victims.

10 *American Tragedy*, 590.

As it is, however, all we have are three drops to the left of the murderer's footprints as he walks away, another on the side walkway beyond where the footprints fade out, and then a smudge on the latch of the rear gate, drops on the lower rung and the gate's center mesh, and a final drop on the driveway.[11] Something is clearly wrong, although none of the lawyers in either trial—*or* on either side—seems to have taken sufficient notice. Of course, neither set of Simpson lawyers would have been theorizing as to how he accomplished the murders; thus they had less reason to come up against this issue. And in the criminal trial, though the prosecution advances a theory (discussed above) for how the glove came off, even they leave everything vague as to when and how after this the cuts could have occurred. After all, his left glove was there, uncut, on the ground beside the victims, drops of his blood led away from the scene, to the left of his footprints, and he later turned up with cuts to his left hand. The dots suffice; you don't need to fill in exactly what lay between. At some point *after* he lost the glove and *before* he finished stabbing his victims and turned to leave, he cut himself with his knife. Whether they were skirting the issue of why there wasn't more of his blood and in more places at Bundy is unclear.

In the civil case, however, the plaintiff lawyers, somewhat contrary to their usual "less is more" approach, attempted at least to suggest to the jury a viable (and alternative to the victims'-nails) scenario in which the cuts could have occurred during the commission of

---

11 There is also the bloody fingerprint on the brass deadbolt knob of the lock of this same gate that Mark Fuhrman says he and his partner Brad Roberts saw in their initial investigation of the crime scene. This fingerprint is detailed in the notes he handed over to the two detectives who soon afterward took over the case, Tom Lange and Phil Vannatter. But, for some reason, it was never recovered at the time with the rest of the evidence. It was destroyed not long thereafter when Nicole's father, Lou Brown, had all the Bundy locks changed. See Mark Fuhrman, *Murder in Brentwood* (New York: Kensington Publishing Corp., 1997), 52–5.

the murders. This is convenient for my argument, since it illustrates how, once you try to do so, you've got a problem. In examining one of their expert witnesses (the aforementioned Dr. Spitz), one of the plaintiff team, Ed Medvene, had the doctor play the killer while he himself substituted for Nicole. Dr. Spitz then demonstrated a scenario in which the killer, with his left hand, would have grabbed the fallen and face-down Nicole by the chin, then concluded his assault by slitting her throat from left to right. Petrocelli comments: "As he [Spitz] pulled his hand from left to right across Ed's throat, the jury could see how close the blade would come to the fingers on the killer's [now bare it's assumed] left hand, the fingers on which Simpson had his cuts."[12]

As mentioned, this is just suggestion, not actual argument. It's of a piece with their general strategy for dealing with this sort of hard-to-determine aspect of the case—the less definitive the better. In the criminal trial, the prosecution theorized that he grabbed her by the hair when slitting her throat. This theory makes more sense, since it keeps his left hand away from the spurting blood, something he'd want to avoid all the more if it were bare, and from the possibility of being bitten if she's conscious. But, to get to my point, if he did cut himself deeply in the way suggested above by the plaintiff lawyers, which would have his knuckles facing down, to boot, why is his blood not mixed with any of hers at the crime scene? That is, why is it not on her person, or pooled with hers on the ground beneath, which it should have been if he had cut himself on the hand with which he held up her jaw? This would also be the case if he had her by the hair, for that matter—if we follow the prosecution team, whose scenario would likely assume he's already cut himself when he was disposing of Ron—for then it should have been found in ample quantities in her hair. And, if they decide that

12 *Triumph of Justice*, 430.

it must be Ron he finishes up with, and that he's cut while fighting with him, why isn't his blood on Ron, along with the cashmere fiber and several hairs from his head—and again, in significant quantities? No, in the absence of Simpson's blood on at least one of the victims, or on the ground where their struggles occurred, any scenario that has him getting cut while committing the murders, on the hand he was gripping them with, simply makes no sense.

What does, I think, make sense with these givens is this: Simpson was not cut until *after* the murders were finished and after he had *himself* removed his gloves. How I believe this occurred I'll now narrate, beginning with the situation that led up to that night. For what first needs to be established is how thoroughly premeditated these murders were, or rather Nicole's murder, along with getting away with it, and how carefully plotted out the exit strategy was. It is in this context, or so I'll argue, that we'll find how it was that the cuts were incurred.

CHAPTER 3

A TANGLED WEB

So far as we know, Herodotus wrote the *Histories* only; it was his great lifework. But the scope of this one work is almost inexhaustible, taking in as it does virtually all the then-known world, and that from almost every angle or disciplinary approach: sociological, geographical, scientific, literary, historical, et cetera. And the *Histories*, which runs to some six hundred typed pages, has itself been divided into nine books, though likely not by Herodotus. Scholars believe that this was probably done by the librarians at Alexandria in the early third century BC (more than a century after his death). These books were also at some point given individual names, though again likely not by Herodotus. But whatever their provenance, these titles are a particularly "inspired" choice: for starting with Clio (History) and ending with Calliope (Epic), they're the names of the muses nine, the daughters of Mnemosyne ("Memory") and Zeus, who were imagined as residing on Mount Helicon, whence they presided over the various (mainly) literary modes we mortals essay. And they're inspired, too, in that together they so perfectly express the richness that is Herodotus, whose text in its own fashion runs the gamut of literary modes and their corresponding emotions, from comedy to tragedy, from the lyric to the epic.

The muses, of course, like the rest of the Greek deities, have long since ceased to be accorded their meed of worship, though they lingered in the arts, at least formally, till not too long ago. But we all still know just what it's like to muse, if only when we're trying to compose something cleverer or more personal than "All the best!" when that birthday or farewell card's being passed round at the office for everyone to sign. We all know, too, that wistful or abstracted look that comes over people's faces when they truly muse: that inward meditative cast that changes their expression and commands (or should) a strange respect. And, while the act of musing is ultimately all one (as the nine muses were just one to start with), there are shades of mental focus and their concomitant reflections in our faces. For instance, our features take on a somber hue when we're waxing elegiac, while a faint smile plays upon them when our aim is mirth and wit. In either case—and indeed, in all cases where the motive of our musing is positive and generous, where it seeks to express something that, we hope, will be welcome unto some other or others, be it simple affection, or sympathy, or ardor whether passionate or holy—the effect upon our features is becoming, ennobling, even, for certain aspirations, though there's no one there to see. It's as if we were already savoring what we seek; as if we were emotionally there and waiting for conception to catch up.

This catching up can take some time. Anyone who's truly courted inspiration and who won't settle for the first semipassable approximation of what it is he or she wants, knows that that "great" idea often comes when least expected and when one is occupied with something else. But it comes precisely because he or she has started searching, gap though there may be between conscious effort and its eventual reward. It's like those occasions when you're struggling to remember something (Mnemosyne *is* the muses' mother, you'll recall) and it won't be fetched until you've given up; at some point after that it pops into your head. Only with creativity what you're trying to "recall" is not some particular name or fact but rather a certain quality or degree of excellence, anything less than which you won't accept. And that, too, is essential to the process: you staying true to the standard you would meet.

The process just described and its becoming transformation of our features is, of course, mostly a private affair, with just ourselves to witness (and we're preoccupied). But there's a variation of it that is more readily on display—at Christmas, for instance, in the stores and among the female shoppers in particular (because, let's face it, they're by and large much nicer than the guys). We guys are usually just trying to come up with something adequate at the last moment, and we look frazzled and impatient. The women, on the other hand, are so often really seeking to please; they are imagining the recipient's hopefully delighted reaction to the gift whose purchase they now ponder, as they hold it up for study in their hands. And this love and generosity of spirit is plain to see in the expression on their faces, which are rendered even prettier—nay, angelic—by their thoughts.

This makes me wonder: Did Nicole Brown Simpson look this way in Bloomingdale's that day in December of 1990, in the glove department where she did some Christmas shopping and sought a pair a cut above the rest, a pair that O. J. would be sure to like? Did she have that soft, attentive gaze as she searched for something special? Were there several pairs that caught her eye and made it hard to choose? Or did those Aris Isotoner Lights, so sleek and snappy, make deliberation easy? Did her eyes light up when she saw them on the counter, and did she know at once that they were just the thing—they would suit so well his stylish winter coat and look so good on camera as he held the mike, during a sideline interview, in some late-season game, in chilly weather, in a place like Buffalo? Did she picture all of this? So very pretty as she was, she would have looked prettier still, her face unclouded by any apprehension of the role they'd one day play. It can't have crossed her mind, as she caressed the soft, smooth leather, that it would one day wield the weapon that would take her life.

On what, one also wonders, does a murderer muse? Where does he search for inspiration or with what powers commune? I don't mean, of course, your spur-of-the-moment offender who goes over the edge at some provocation and whose hurt and angry impetus is etched upon his face. Nor do I mean your professional assassin, your Mafia hit man, for instance, for whom killing's usually not personal, but rather a condition of his cold-blooded profession or of ruling the underworld. No, I mean premeditated murder of a certain stamp—where it's personal, and you have, for some reason, an overwhelming emotional need that someone else should cease to exist, and where, for instance, you can't bear to see this person getting over you and on with her life. And, it's not just her death that you require; though, if you want to get away with it, you'll sometimes have to settle for "mere" murder, without any prolonged sadistic trimmings. Ideally, however, you want to hurt this person as much as she has you; you only get one shot at it, and you want to do it right.

What is it like to be in that frame of mind for an extended period, when you're brooding on how you'll do it and anticipating, indeed already savoring, the result? The closest most of us get to experiencing something even remotely like this is when we see that look that comes over the face of someone with a penchant for vicious remarks: how the eyes get hard and narrow or glaze over to conceal the motivation, just *as* he or she is about to strike. But malicious sniping is a far, far cry from premeditated murder, and that difference should surely be reflected on the face. How dark, then, the face of a murderer must look—how cold and inhuman! How cruel must be the smile that forms when a killer finally hits on how he'll do it or nods approval as he solves an obstacle in his way! He would have what used to be called an "abandoned look": the look of one who has totally surrendered to the influx of evil, who has severed all contact with his conscience and become open to every infernal suggestion. He would have the look of the beast thereby released.

One of the (many) annoying things about the original trial was the inept and shallow comparisons drawn by some of the media between Simpson and Othello, simply because both were black and, out of jealousy, killed their white, much-younger wives—or so most of us thought in Simpson's case—and maybe subconsciously because each of their names features at least one conspicuous *O*. But, if you've read or seen *Othello* and paid even minimal attention to what's being said, you'll know that O. J. Simpson's no Othello. The latter was the soul of modesty and his soldierly career a litany of hardship and peril in loyal service to the Venetian state. It's this which wins the love of Desdemona—inadvertently, on his part, at the outset—as she hears him recount his life history and bold exploits, at her father's urging, while a frequent guest at their home. As he says: "She loved me for the dangers I had pass'd, And I loved her that she did pity them" (I, iii, 167–8). It is only after being wrought upon by the invidious machinations of Iago that he comes to believe, wrongly, that she has betrayed him for the younger, handsomer Michael Cassio. So he kills her, not furtively with the intent to escape detection, but in pursuit of an "aggrieved" revenge and with no intent to deny or run from a deed he thought was done "upon just grounds."

O. J., on the other hand, was his own Iago, possessing an unquenchable ego that could never have enough recognition, especially from his wife, whom he abused verbally and physically in his many darker moments, so that her terror and abasement might make good the respect he craved and forfeited. To the world at large, however, he was "honest, honest" O. J., at times an overly ingratiating professional public persona who, despite the violence of his original career, didn't seem to have a mean bone in his body. It's not that this persona was threatened by Nicole's ultimate rejection; the celebrity-besotted public would still be fooled. It was his gnawing insecurity, as massive as the ego it was spawned with, that couldn't endure this threat to its self-assumptions. So it was him or her. If she were really going to leave him for good, as was becoming increasingly apparent in the months and weeks leading up to the murder,[1] he'd have to show her once and for all just who was the boss. If he didn't, he would not be who he was in his own estimation—which for him would have been crushing. Moreover, he had to kill her *and* get away with it and thus prevent her "filching from [him his] good name"—for, failing that, she'd win.

He had, then, been pondering her murder for some time—which, of course, is nothing new. Premeditation, in some degree at least, was argued very effectively by both the prosecution and the plaintiff lawyers in the respective trials. And necessarily, since *without* premeditation the circumstances of the timeline are just too tight and fortuitous, while *with* it there emerges a very clever, if patent, attempt to create a virtual alibi or, to translate the Latin, an all but certainly "elsewhere" for himself when the murder's

---

1 They had tried to reconcile beginning in April 1993; and Simpson even split up with his girlfriend, Paula Barbieri. Things didn't work out, however, and Nicole called it off in April of 1994. Simpson went back to Paula. Nicole, meanwhile, confided to certain intimate friends that she was finally done with O. J. for good.

to take place.[2] For instance, take his schedule that weekend. On the day of the murders, Sunday, June 12, 1994, there was a 5:00 p.m. dance recital in which Simpson's then eight-year-old daughter, Sydney, would participate. Simpson—uncharacteristically, in view of his past history of being somewhat negligent with his kids—had flown in on Friday from New York to attend the recital, while at the same time scheduling a red-eye back to Chicago at 11:45 that Sunday night (1:45 a.m. Chicago time), where he was to play golf early Monday morning. According to Alan Austin, one of Simpson's long-time golfing buddies, in an interview with Petrocelli,[3] this was unlike O. J. He wouldn't have put himself out like that. If he had to be in Chicago Monday morning, he would normally have either stayed back east or, if he felt he had to be both at the recital in LA and in Chicago the next morning, he would have flown out immediately after the recital (to give himself more time to sleep before his early-morning game). So the demanding crisscrossing of the country was highly unusual, while the late departure left open a window, one that occurred after dark (sunset was at approximately 8:07 p.m.).

Then there are his dealings that Sunday, indeed that weekend, with Kato Kaelin, who lived rent-free in a guest house at the back of his property. Prior to that, Kato had rented a guest house from Nicole when she lived on Gretna Green in the expensive townhouse condominium she had moved into after divorcing Simpson in 1992. But when she had moved to her smaller, cheaper Bundy condo in January of 1994, during the period of their attempted reconciliation, Simpson had thought it inappropriate that Kato live with her there

---

2 The cashmere-lined winter gloves alone, it should be added, prove premeditation on "someone's" part. We're in sunny LA: there would not be a glove at a murder scene in January, let alone June, unless it had been worn to prevent leaving evidence.

3 *Triumph of Justice*, 221–3.

under the same roof, so he offered the guest house, which offer Kato accepted. Shortly after returning home from Sydney's recital—where Nicole wouldn't let him sit beside her nor talk with Sydney and pointedly excluded him from the family celebration at the nearby Mezzaluna restaurant (fresh proof that she was through with him for good)—Simpson initiated a conversation with Kato, hailing him as he headed to his quarters around seven o'clock in the evening. It was the third time that weekend he'd done that, prior to which he'd always paid scant attention to Kato. Simpson was wearing a dark sweat suit, though he'd later deny ever owning such an outfit. They talked for about an hour as Simpson complained at length about Nicole's skimpy dress and her playing hardball with him with the kids. Kato was uncomfortable with this. Eventually he escaped the conversation by asking to use the Jacuzzi. A little later, Simpson showed up at his door to reprimand him for not turning off the Jacuzzi jets—a further oddity, since he'd never come to his room before. Then came another surprise: he was back again after five or ten minutes to borrow some money. He said he needed some cash to later give the airport skycap, as he only had hundreds; then he added that he was going out for dinner (thus, you'd think, obviating any need for getting smaller bills from Kato). Kato gave him a twenty, but then he suddenly invited himself along to dinner. Simpson mumbled, "Sure," and Kato sensed he'd overstepped his bounds. It was the first of several unforeseen developments to upset Simpson's plans—not that Kato would have been a necessary part of the original plan; rather, he was one of the variable components. After all, he could have been away that night. In that case, Simpson would have had to conscript someone else as a witness to his being elsewhere and going about other innocuous business at as late a point as possible—at some fast-food restaurant, for instance, which he could have gone to without involving Kato and where he could have easily made sure that he was recognized.

Meanwhile, there was by then at least one other such variable component, or witness, already in place. At 9:00 p.m., just prior to going back to Kato's room to borrow money, Simpson placed a call to Christian Reichardt, at the time Nicole's friend Faye Resnick's fiancé. Reichardt was not a particularly close friend of Simpson's, and there was no apparent point to the call. Simpson just chatted away about how great things were with his girlfriend, Paula Barbieri, and casually indicated he was packing to go to the airport. Hardly the sort of conversation you'd expect from a man about to murder his wife, which of course was the point of the call. Moreover, what he said about his and Paula's relationship was a lie, since she had dumped him by a lengthy voice-message left that morning. They had fought the previous night at a dinner party they'd attended, which party, or rather his escorting her to it, was part of his alibi too, for it was his emotional "elsewhere," proof that he had a love interest in his life and was over Nicole. Unfortunately for Simpson, they had had a falling out because he'd told her she couldn't accompany him to Sydney's recital the next day, and she had left by herself. Phone records, which were not properly interpreted until the civil trial (and which, like the photos of Simpson in the Bruno Maglis, gave a major advantage to the plaintiff lawyers in that trial[4]) prove that he listened to it pretty well in its entirety at 6:56 p.m.—and probably not for the first time—right after the embarrassing rejection he'd endured at the recital and before he accosted Kato.

By his own admission, Simpson also placed a call at about this same time to Nicole at Bundy—whether before or after the call to Reichardt is uncertain, since the phone records for these were never retrieved. Petrocelli believes that a heated exchange ensued and

4 It was a well-earned advantage, I should add. Credit for noticing and deciphering this portion of these records (where Simpson dials his message manager) goes to Daniel Petrocelli's colleague Peter Gelblum (*Triumph of Justice*, 473–4).

that this was what finally pushed him over the edge. Simpson says he merely asked to speak to Sydney, whom Nicole then put on the phone. Personally, I suspect this *is* what occurred: he'd already made up his mind and he had no compunction about involving his (and Nicole's) own daughter in the façade of normalcy, so integral was it to the alibi that he was constructing. (The call could also have served to let him know when she and her brother, Justin, would be going to bed). Moreover, he would have enjoyed being unexpectedly, if coolly, civil to Nicole—faking her out, as it were, and giving her a false sense of security for the few remaining moments of her life.

There were, then, the fixed components to Simpson's plans, such as the flight arrangements and the method, still to be discussed, of disposing of the weapon and bloodied clothes (as will be seen, his elaborate preparations here are an even starker proof of lengthy premeditation). But there were also the impromptu elements, like Kato and Reichardt, and perhaps even his daughter, to be worked in as opportunity presented.[5] Marcia Clark asks at one point: "Was this murder the result of a long-standing plan or one formulated on the night it was committed?"[6] If she ever decided, she doesn't say so in her book. But I would say it was both, just as the motive was both one of long standing and one of fresh provocation. For it is one thing to create the opportunity for murder, another to actually do it. Unfortunately, fuel had been added to the fire all that day: first by his girlfriend, Paula's, dumping him and then by the rebuff from his ex-wife at the recital, which occurred in the presence of friends. Finally, there's the strong possibility that he knew who Ron was, though he since denied it, and suspected him and Nicole of having a

---

5 His live-in maid, Gigi Guarin, who'd been away since Friday, called Sunday and got permission to stay away another night. Had she not, she too would likely have been used in some way to shore up his alibi.

6 *Without a Doubt*, 241.

relationship.[7] In that case, as proved by his previous obsessive interest in Nicole's relations with other men during their frequent separations and when they were later divorced, he would have almost certainly taken the pains to learn more about Ron. He should then have found out without much difficulty that he was a waiter at Mezzaluna, where, as Simpson may have learned at the concert or prior to it, from Sydney or Justin or someone else, she was headed that night without him. All in all, it was the perfect storm.

After Kato had invited himself along, he and Simpson headed off in Simpson's Bentley at around 9:10. About ten minutes later, they turned in at a McDonald's and ordered from the drive-through. Simpson ate his burger on the way home, quickly. Kato held off until they got back. Once there, Kato headed toward the main house, thinking Simpson would follow and keep him company while he ate. But when he saw Simpson hanging back, he changed course and returned to the guest house, food in hand, while Simpson lingered by the car. It was about 9:46, and Kato was the last person to see O. J. Simpson until after the murders. Simpson didn't go into the house. He was last seen lingering by the Bentley, still dressed in that dark sweat suit, either black or navy blue.

When he was next undeniably accounted for, it was approximately 10:56 p.m. as he finally responded to the intercom buzzer from airport limo driver, Allan Park. He'd come to fetch him for his flight and had since 10:40 been pressing intermittently at his driveway's Ashford gate. In the meantime, the murders had taken place, somewhere between about 10:15 and 10:40. The former is the earliest approximate time by which Ron Goldman could have arrived (he

7 Faye Resnick describes an encounter at a Starbucks restaurant, where she and Nicole were talking to Ron and some of his friends. Simpson, she says, pulled up in his Bentley, got out, walked up to Ron, and said "This is my wife!" (*Triumph of Justice*, 188). Simpson, when deposed by Petrocelli, denied all knowledge of Ron. (*Ibid*, 136).

had left Mezzaluna with Nicole's mother's glasses, which she'd left behind about an hour before, at around 9:50, and had stopped off at his apartment to change before dropping them off at Nicole's). The latter, on the assumption that Simpson is guilty, is the latest approximate time by which he would have had to leave Bundy (about a three-mile, or five-minute, drive from Rockingham) in order, first, for him to have caused the thumps on Kato's wall at around 10:51 or 10:52 and then, about four minutes later, for the six-foot-tall, two-hundred-pound African American to loom out of the dark, cross the driveway, and enter Rockingham under the gaze of Allan Park, who then got out of the limo and buzzed the house once more. A minute later Simpson answered the phone. He said he'd been sleeping and had just woken up. He said he'd be down in a minute to go to the airport for his 11:45 flight.[8]

8 If you do the math, he could have left as late as 10:45 p.m., as Mark Fuhrman says (*Murder in Brentwood*, 182). The time of 10:40 p.m. allows him to get back *comfortably* in time for the above sequence to take place. As will be seen, 10:40, or even earlier, works better for me as the time by which the murders themselves were concluded—because I don't think he exited Bundy right after that.

CHAPTER 4

A GAP IN CRIME

I haven't read all of the O. J. literature—far from it; life's too short. But I have, of course, read the main sources, and in none of them has there been much concern or speculation as to what he was up to in the interval between when Kato last saw him, at 9:46 p.m., and when his assault most likely (for reasons still to be given) began, at approximately 10:30 or 10:35 p.m. (though possibly, if slimly, as early as 10:15, the earliest time by which Ron could have arrived). That's mainly because there's almost nothing to go on: no one saw him at any point in this interval, and he hadn't yet swung into action or started to make his presence felt forensically. The one thing we know for sure, from phone records, is that he was trying to reach Paula Barbieri on his cell at 10:03 p.m., so that he was, therefore, almost certainly in his car at this point, where the cell was usually kept. He was also almost certainly—unless he was riding around aimlessly for a while—by this time parked a short walk away from Nicole's home on Bundy; indeed, he had been parked there for a while; either in the back lane or in the deserted parking area across from where the lane ended at Dorothy, the first cross street to the south. The drive from his place to hers, as stated, was about three miles and took no more than four to five minutes. And he likely set out no more than a minute or two after Kato and he parted company and the former went back to his room; in which case he was parked near Bundy by no later than about 9:55 p.m. This raises the question: Why didn't he strike right then—and save himself the problem of dealing with Ron?

This hesitation on his part, if that it was, is made all the more curious if one recalls that he had clearly intended to leave Rockingham at around 9:10 p.m. when he went to Kato's room to borrow some cash for his restaurant meal. But when Kato invited himself along, under the mistaken impression created by Simpson's unwonted familiarity that weekend that they were now pals, he was forced to delay his departure until they returned, thus losing some thirty-six minutes from his carefully constructed window of opportunity (though part of that would likely have been *conspicuously* spent in some fast-food restaurant, to validate his statement to Kato that he was heading out to get something to eat). His plan was probably to be back home from his murderous errand by no later than 10:00 or 10:15 p.m., well in advance of the airport limo's expected arrival at 10:45. That way he'd have plenty of time to cool down, clean up, and then, say, be out in his yard chipping some golf balls when the limo arrived. That was the explanation he eventually settled on for what he was doing at the time Nicole was murdered, a better excuse than the (probably impromptu) claim about sleeping that he'd made to the limo driver—because why would you take a short nap when you're about to board a red-eye flight, when the wearier you are the more likely you'll sleep on the plane? Meanwhile, he'd have had time to place at least one more call from a landline in his home—ideally as soon as possible, so before he even began to clean up—to another acquaintance, perhaps, like Reichardt earlier on, laughing and joking, talking about golf and about Paula. Such a call would both narrow considerably the time in which he could not be accounted for at home, and, maybe, further pad the list of demeanor witnesses who would later attest that one and the same man could never have, let alone just have, committed a brutal murder.

Meanwhile, he must have had a plan in place for getting his deuteragonist, Nicole, out of her house as part of the overall scheme. He could hardly just loiter outside like lovesick Romeo, hoping his lady'd emerge from her chamber and stroll within striking distance. No, he'd have to get her to come out, and quickly; and the likeliest way was this: The front gate at Bundy is not immediately adjacent to the public sidewalk, but inset some ten or twelve feet up the condo's cobblestone walk. Within the gate is another few feet of cobblestone before you reach the four steps that bring you adjacent to the front landing, or porch, that's on your left. The front door faces the street. To your right, meanwhile, is a narrow garden that runs from the gate to a point in line with the door; what little space it has is made still more cramped thanks to a fair-sized tree. The steps lead directly onto a raised walkway that runs between the porch and garden and then continues along the north side of the condo, the side to a visitor's right. The rear gate is located a little beyond where the walkway descends and a few steps in from where it ends, at the side of the garage. There is a parking area beyond the garage and then the back lane.

Simpson's planned approach, of course, would be from this back lane; it wasn't that late, most adults were still awake, and he didn't want to be seen. As well, he had a key to that rear gate. Six days before her murder, Nicole had complained to her friend Cora Fischman that her spare gate key, which she always kept in one specific place, was missing. She had also told her mother. How long it had been missing isn't known; its absence, presumably, had just come to her notice. This key was found in Simpson's travel grip when he was brought in to the Parker Center, the LAPD's downtown headquarters, on the day after the murders. But the police didn't know what it opened, since Nicole's father, Lou Brown, had had all the locks at Bundy changed shortly after her murder. Fortunately, Nicole had given another set of backup keys to Cora. Tom Lange, one of the lead detectives on the case (along with partner Phil Vannater), commissioned a locksmith to fashion a lock around Cora's key. And the key Simpson had in his bag opened this lock.

Meanwhile, conveniently for O. J., there was a problem with the front gate: the buzzer wasn't fully operational. A visitor could signal his arrival, but you couldn't use the intercom to buzz him in; you'd have to go out and open the gate in person. And Simpson would surely have known about it, either from experience—his own visits during reconciliation attempts or when picking up the kids—or from quizzing one of the kids when he had them with him. This was an opportunity while it lasted, for Nicole might get it fixed, so a reason not to put things off.

The plan for getting her out, then, would be this: He'd enter stealthily through the back gate, go along the walkway to the front and, reaching over from inside the gate, buzz the intercom to be let in. He could also have opened the gate himself to make sure that she ventured out of the house to shut it. This gate was open following the murders, though we know from his footprints that the killer left by the back. It's usually assumed that the gate had been opened by Nicole to let Ron in. But he may, in fact, have come upon a murder in progress, at a point where Simpson had knocked her out but not yet slit her throat. He could then have rushed in to defend her or to see why she was lying there, with Simpson having hidden in the shrubs to the side of the steps when Ron approached. Or Ron could have arrived to find the gate open, with Simpson still lying in wait. He might have used the buzzer anyway, to announce his arrival, or gone to the door to knock—though the latter scenario is unlikely, given the location of Nicole's body at the foot of the walkway steps. She seems to have gone out either to meet him or to check the front gate.

Whether Simpson's plan was to open the gate or not, after pressing the buzzer he would have retreated back up the steps and along the walkway beyond the door, or to the porch area to the right of someone exiting the condo. And when Nicole came out he'd kill her, either right away when she first came within reach, or after letting her go down to the gate to close it or simply to check things out. It's some form of the latter scenario that Marcia Clark favors, and I think she's right, at least as far as how he planned to do it. That way he would get the maximum effect and get to savor the moment, as at first she's puzzled that there's no one there, and then her horror when she turns and sees it's him, "dressed for silent combat, dark sweats, knit cap, gloves … come to take her life."[1] Their eyes would meet for one last time, and he'd know *she knew* who'd won.

What actually happened is moot, however, because we don't know when exactly unscripted tritagonist Ron Goldman made his entrance, or how—through an open gate with her murder underway, or as let in by Nicole to share her fate? It's possible then that Simpson was balked of the crowning reward of his intricate machinations: that parting look of terror in her eyes, assuming this refinement entered his plan. But whether it did or not, the real point is that he *had* a viable plan for getting Nicole outside, and one that worked the better the earlier after nightfall it was tried. He didn't know Ron was expected, but he did know that the later he buzzed the intercom the more leery she would likely be about opening the door or walking outside. So why then, to return to our original question, was he still sitting in his car at 10:03 and calling Paula? And, more inexplicably still, why is it that Nicole's dog did not start barking until roughly 10:15 or 10:20 p.m., thus possibly *marking* the commencement of

1 *Without a Doubt*, 104.

his onslaught, but much more likely *heralding* his fell approach. As stated, 10:15 or 10:20 would probably have been the absolute latest time he'd originally hoped to be home by (if carried out with hit-man expedition, the whole operation, door-to-door, shouldn't have taken more than twenty minutes, plus another ten at most if he stopped at a fast-food restaurant), and he still could have been home by 10:15 if he'd gone about his business right away when he reached Bundy.

At the close of forensic expert Werner Spitz's testimony in the civil trial, Ed Medvene had him mark off sixty seconds on his watch while the court fell silent. This was the length of time that Dr. Spitz, perhaps the foremost authority in his field, had said was needed for a man of Simpson's size, strength, and athletic abilities, with the element of surprise on his side, to inflict the numerous knife wounds suffered by Ron Goldman. And the point of this mute demonstration was to impress upon all present just how long sixty seconds really is when we're not distracted—as we usually are by various mostly trivial things—and simply focus on time passing. As Daniel Petrocelli describes it, "One minute seemed like an eternity."[2] More important, it was ample time for the infliction of all Ron's wounds. Imagine, then, if the court had been asked to wait silently while twenty minutes ticked off (or maybe twenty-five), or try the experiment yourself, *if* you can do it: that is, sit still and hear yourself breathe for twenty minutes. It will seem to take forever. Yet this is approximately the time that Simpson spent parked near Bundy, between the time he arrived around 9:55 and when the dog was first heard barking at 10:15 or 10:20 p.m., which, as stated, likely coincided with his approaching or opening the Bundy back gate. Why was he hanging fire all this while? Why did he hesitate and not get down to business?

---

2 *Triumph of Justice*, 439.

As mentioned, the one thing we know for sure is that he called Paula Barbieri at 10:03 p.m. on his cell phone, the last of several attempts he made that day to reach her after receiving her voice message of that morning announcing they were through. This call must have been placed from inside the car—because he would hardly have been taking his cell phone with him to a violent crime scene, and assuming she answered, he didn't want his voice to be heard by someone in the vicinity (a quiet neighborhood now even quieter since most of the kids were in bed). But why was he still in his car a full eight to ten minutes after coming to Bundy? Or why had he perhaps returned to his car to make this call after aborting his first approach? Why, too, was he putting what remained of his emotional alibi at risk? If Paula answered and repulsed his attempts to win her over, then there would be a witness that he was aware he no longer had a love interest to replace Nicole—that he'd been jilted, and knew it, just prior to her death. He would later deny ever receiving Paula's call, but this latest attempt to reach her, though futile, could only compromise further such an intended claim. Indeed, it seems he had blown the Paula angle from the get-go on that weekend. As mentioned, they had fought the night before at a dinner party on the issue of her attending the next night's recital. She had left the party early by herself and then phoned the next morning to call it quits. On the one hand, this reluctance to include Paula in a family function can be taken as proof that Nicole was still the one—as, of course, she was. But Simpson still might have been comfortable with Paula's attending the recital under normal circumstances—when she was not going to get in the way of his tight post-recital schedule for killing his ex-wife, or of giving her one last chance to relent and take him back with open arms (thereby saving her life). Paula's insistence on being included, and the breach it precipitated that blew his emotional alibi, was perhaps the true first untoward circumstance of that weekend to snarl his careful plans. He miscalculated, just as he always did with Nicole, and took her too much for granted.

Simpson's hesitation once *at* Bundy, and his telephoning Paula, can only be explained by his having had second thoughts of some kind. Despite the premeditation, despite the virtual alibi that had now been put in place, this was still a crime of passion, and that passion may have wavered or needed further fuel. There he was, sitting in silence in the dark, and given the moral crossroads that he'd come to, the razor's edge he was on, it truly was the "witching time of night." You would think the enormity of the "bitter business" that he was there on, the "contagion" he was about to "breathe out to this world," would have started to dawn upon him now, if ever—or maybe just the risk. He must have wondered: *Can I really pull this off?* A play could be written just on this one phase of his activities that night, a one-man play, of course. It would be one long soliloquy or internal monologue, though punctuated, perhaps, with Nicole's voice heard offstage, on the phone maybe, or shouting something motherly from downstairs to one of the kids. But whether or not her voice ever reached his ears and gave him pause, the call to Paula suggests a reaching out for help, for some kind of positive reinforcement, a sign perhaps to stay him as he approached the point of no return (which he'd maybe neared before)—some sort of external stimulus, or salve for his ego, to give him the equivalent of the moral strength his conscience couldn't provide. So, if Paula had answered and returned into the fold, Nicole might be alive today or at least have gotten a stay of execution.

She didn't, of course, having already hied herself to Vegas and a tryst with singer Michael Bolton. Simpson was left to his own counsel, never a good idea at the best of times, and least of all now, after that "bitch" Paula had ditched him too. So it was not their good times that he thought of—his and Nicole's, that is. And it was not their kids, Sydney and Justin, and how awful it would be for them to lose their mother—at any time—but especially now, so early in their lives. No, whatever review he conducted of his reasons for coming there would have been severely edited, would have been determined solely by such "search" emotions as bitterness *and* jealousy *and* rage. He would have reminded himself of how much he'd been wronged and how she had it coming; he'd have remembered every slight, real or imagined, that Nicole had ever done him; he'd have thought of her affairs, real or imagined—indeed, of every other guy she'd ever looked at or who'd looked at her. And then he'd think of all he'd done for her, and how she'd be nothing without him. What thanks had he gotten for that? None! Just the opposite: disrespect and humiliation, as at the recital earlier on. It was the ego *in extremis*, wallowing in self-pity, stoking the fires of rage. It was still another twelve to seventeen minutes before the dog would be heard barking, and by then O. J. had got his game face on. Only it wasn't a game, and any motivational pregame shouts like "kill" and "take no prisoners" weren't overstatements anymore.

What Simpson looks like when incensed is on the record, as told by Nicole to the police when she summoned them to her home in October 1993 (during the period of their attempted reconciliation) on account of one of his rages. They had taped both her and him surreptitiously, and she had said, "When he gets this way, I get scared ... He doesn't even look like himself. All his veins pop out, his eyes are black, and he's just black and cold, like an animal. I mean very, very weird." She added that she'd called the police as a "precaution, more than anything ... I just got scared. I don't totally think I believe it would happen, but I get scared. I think if it happened one more time it would be the last time." Her apprehension was vindicated only eight months later.

This description of Orenthal *furioso* is corroborated by Nicole's friend Faye Resnick in her civil trial deposition. She had been with the two of them at a restaurant when, after Nicole's simply mentioning the name of a man she once had dated, Simpson had snapped and started screaming at her in front of their friends and the other patrons. "It was as if a different person just took over … it was like watching a man possessed … His jaw would protrude, his teeth would clench, sweat would come pouring from his head … He would perspire through his clothing. His eyes would get narrow and black. He became—the only way to describe it is—animalistic when he would become angry at Nicole."[3] Meanwhile, for those who have their doubts about anything connected with the so-called "world of Faye Resnick," her description, and Nicole's, is borne out by what you'd think is in this context a completely unimpeachable source: Johnnie Cochran, Simpson's lead attorney in the criminal trial. During a jailhouse visit with Simpson late in the trial, he pressed him—too closely, as he quickly learned—for some kind of reasonably credible and consistent explanation for how he got the cuts to his hand. Simpson suddenly snapped, his face going dark with rage, and he started screaming at him, "I'm paying you guys! You guys listen to me, listen to me!" Indeed, his manner was so threatening, his mood swing so instantaneous and extreme, that when Johnnie was relating the incident the next day to some fellow Dream Team members, among them Carl Douglas, as they were driving in to work, he admitted, "He scared me, Carl. It's a good thing I didn't have blonde hair."[4]

If O. J. gets this ugly, this quickly, when his kids are around, or in a public restaurant, or with his lead attorney when the latter won't just be the pliant mouthpiece that he's paid to be, imagine how he looked that night as he exited his car, when he'd steeled himself for the murderous business now at hand or surrendered fully to his darker side. Not, of course, that he's raging openly: he

---

3 *Triumph of Justice*, 187.

4 *American Tragedy*, 842.

knows he has to perform semicoolly in a dicey situation. But he's seething all the same, a cold fury coiled and ready to strike. He's about to cross a line he's never crossed, save in imagination, and to begin an onslaught unlike any that preceded, where no punches will be pulled, and where a knife will add a grisly new dimension to his knuckles' normal work. One climactic outburst of rage will consummate their relationship, one last slashing touch, and then she's *it*, forever. And he's aroused. He can almost taste it. His mien exudes his murderous intent, his every fiber's instinct with the urge to kill; he is quite literally oozing harm from every pore. Cue the barking dog.

Nicole's Akita, which, by an odd coincidence, went by Kato too, was normally kept outside in the walkway area, either having the full run of it or confined to the portion at the rear. This cannot have been for Simpson an unforeseen development. He was very familiar with the dog and must have known that he'd encounter it when he entered; he must have been confident that after an initial and unremarkable bark or two the dog could be calmed down.[5] This mistake was inversely parallel, perhaps, to the one he had made with Rockingham Kato, where his change in behavior on this weekend, the sudden calculated familiarity to help set up his alibi, had made Kato think that he'd be welcome company on the announced trip to the restaurant. This time, however, I don't believe it's false friendship that causes untoward delay; it's what he dissimulates, or tries to: his menacing intent beneath a would-be casual surface calm. This likely

5 They owned Kato prior to their divorce, as well as a Chow named Chachi. After the divorce, Nicole got Kato and Simpson Chachi; but they would often look after each other's dog when the other was away. Interestingly, Simpson, in his interrogation the day after the murders, goes out of his way to show what pals he was with Kato, what familiar terms he was on with the dog.

would have worked on house-guest Kato, but a dog's a different story and its sensory apparatus of a different order. It smells such things as fear and, maybe, murderous intent. Shortly after the murders, Simpson would take a lie-detector test, as arranged by his then-lead attorney Robert Shapiro. He failed abysmally; indeed, so badly as to make you wonder how he ever could have thought he might succeed. I suggest he failed too with the dog, and for a similar reason: a total inability to appreciate how when we cross a certain line we change, and palpably so.

The dog would never testify, of course. Its story had to be told by those who heard it or who later found it running loose, bloodstained and frantic, in the neighborhood. But it figured prominently in both trials, at the outset in each case, as the prosecution and then the plaintiff team used it to try to establish what had happened that night at Bundy. It began with Pablo Fenjves, Nicole's neighbor, who heard the dog's "plaintive wail" commence at around 10:15 or 10:20 p.m. This barking would continue for over an hour. At around 10:30 or 10:35 p.m., a more-distant neighbor, Robert Heidstra, came within earshot of the noise. He had been walking his dog by his usual route and at his usual time, and as he neared Bundy, he recognized the sound of Nicole's large Akita "barking like crazy, like he was confused and panicky." To avoid a dogfight, he took a different route, up an alley. It was about two minutes later that he heard two male voices, apparently arguing, which likely marked the onset of their fatal struggle.

The Akita was first sighted roaming the streets at around 10:45 or 10:50 p.m. by Louis Karpf, Nicole's next-door neighbor. It was "barking profusely" and frightened Karpf. Another neighbor, Steven Schwab, ran into the dog at 10:55 p.m. He patted it, saw it had a collar, and then noticed the blood on its legs and paws. He brought the dog back with him to his apartment on Montana Avenue, about two hundred yards from its home, and was sitting outside with the dog when his downstairs neighbors, Sukru Boztepe and Bettina Rasmussen, came home at around 11:40 p.m. They offered to keep the dog till the next morning and then take it to a shelter. But the dog's nervous behavior in their apartment, along with the blood on its legs, soon prompted them to see if they couldn't find its owner. They took it outside and let it lead them. The animal headed straight toward 875 South Bundy, straining against its collar as it came near. When they got there, it turned right and looked up the walkway. They turned too—and saw a woman slumped on the lower front steps in a pool of blood. It was shortly after midnight.

Such are the canine contours of the crime—some audible, some mute. The dog beheld its mistress's murder, saw it coming too, perhaps, and tried to let her know. It saw Ron enter, try to save her, and lose his life in the attempt. It saw the killer turn and leave when all was done; maybe it followed, barking at his heels, as far as the back gate. More likely, though, it lingered by its mistress—licked her face and tried in vain to bring her back to life. All this the neighbors heard, like fans outside a stadium who've arrived late for Sunday's game. They hear the roars, of exultation or dismay, and surmise accordingly if the home team's doing well or the reverse. In this case, though, the nature of the contest—indeed, that there *was* a contest—was only known in hindsight. The dog had seemed more agitated than normal, but that can sometimes happen over nothing, some stranger or a passing dog it particularly dislikes or even likes. It was only later that they knew that what had reached their ears had been a long and futile cry for help.

The dog's part in this drama—he'd be the tetragonist, I suppose—conjures up a well-known feature of Greek tragedy, for it mimics, if unconsciously, that convention of the genre whereby horrific and bloody deeds are deemed too repugnant and shocking to be enacted on the stage. Instead, they occur offstage and must be recounted by a convenient witness, who is usually (but not always) in the play for this sole purpose. Thus his wife/mother's suicide and Oedipus's self-blinding is related by a messenger; it is a messenger too who describes how Antigonē's Haemon killed himself after finding his beloved dead within the tomb where she'd been placed alive. But the most apt comparison, perhaps, to the situation here—especially to the first ten to fifteen minutes or so of the dog's barking, when the murders are almost certainly (especially if we believe Robert Heidstra) not yet underway—is with Cassandra, King Priam's youngest daughter, in Aeschylus's *Agamemnon*. Following Troy's fall, she's brought back home spear-captive by Agamemnon, king of Argos and leader of the Greeks, to be his concubine. Cassandra, having formerly caught Apollo's eye, was gifted by him with prophetic power, but when she then denied him her sought favors, was cursed in that she'd never be believed. Proof of her strange plight had already been given at Troy, where she warned in vain against the wooden horse. And yet more tragic proof awaits at Argos, where Clytemnestra, Agamemnon's vengeful wife, and her lover Aegisthus have plotted his demise. The plan is first to welcome him home with flattering pomp and splendor and then to stab him unsuspecting in his bath. When Agamemnon, at his wife's cajoling, enters his palace, treading on the fair-seeming tapestries she's laid out, Cassandra, who is with him, won't advance. Instead, a prophetic trance descends upon her, as she sees—indeed, virtually experiences—the bloody scene that lies in wait for her as well as him. But it's to no avail. As always, she's ignored; she's then forced to enter, where with Agamemnon, she meets the gruesome fate she's just foreseen. The audience, meanwhile, is given a description—albeit in disjointed, raving mode—of the horrors that will next take place offstage.

There are various parallels, inverse and otherwise, between Argos and its ruling House of Atreus and Brentwood and the Simpsons:

intramarital reprisal, careful plotting, assault from well-laid ambush with a knife—even two surviving children not yet mentioned: Orestes and Electra, boy and girl, offspring of the killer and the killed. Cassandra, meanwhile, is a little bit like Ron, in that her involvement is more circumstantial, though it was part of the plan that she be killed. More to the point, though, she's the counterpart to Nicole's unheeded hound, who was for maybe as long as fifteen minutes trying to warn her of an imminent threat—and the while, perhaps, keeping her killer at bay. Not that Simpson would have feared Kato per se, with whom he was quite familiar. The dog was examined later by police canine experts who concluded that Kato had a "very nice disposition … [but] inadequate instincts or courage to protect his territory, owner, or himself," which Simpson must have known. He must have pondered the possibility of the dog's coming to its mistress's aid. As far as his success in killing her, this posed no problem: Ron certainly did not enter his calculations, and with a knife in hand he could easily dispose of both Nicole and her (not-so-) little dog, too. But he had to get away with it. There's the rub: if the dog should surprise him and suddenly attack, he might well be bitten before he could react, especially if he was preoccupied with Nicole. And that bite could convict him if he were suspected and examined for any injuries by the police. For all he knew, they could even match the bite marks to the animal's dental pattern. Moreover, if the dog went into attack mode, the sounds it emitted would be quite different, and far more alarming, than the usual barking, however incessant that might be. And so would its death yelps, if he had to finish it off. His kids would surely come running—and maybe the neighbors, too.

So he must have been virtually certain that the dog would do no more than bark in the usual way. And what would have given him this certainty? Obviously, that the dog had been present during some of his previous acts of battery on Nicole and had barked anxiously but done no more; it had not tried to defend her. So if all wouldn't be as quiet as he'd like it on the canine front, at least it would only be noise he'd have to deal with. But again the question is raised: Why did he once more take so long? Why this second phase of hesitation? Why did a further ten to fifteen minutes elapse from the time the dog started barking to when his attack began, approximately when Robert Heidstra heard the two male voices? Sure, a minute or two might have gone by while he tried to calm the animal down and cocked an ear to see if this unexpectedly frantic barking elicited any response from inside, which it apparently didn't. But then you'd think he'd have gotten down to business. But he didn't, and with each passing minute the gap in time he was going to have to explain, between when he last was seen and when he later resurfaced, grew wider. As well, it was getting nearer to the time when (approximately 10:45 p.m.) the regular airport limo driver could be expected to show up and buzz to be let in. And he had to clean up and regain his composure. For purely tactical reasons, then, you'd think he would've started to reconsider and maybe postpone his plans for a while; but this he also didn't do—at least, not decisively. This all suggests that there was something about the way the dog reacted that took him by surprise or gave him pause, and not just for caution's sake: he was confused as well, or even paralyzed for a time, struck by something strange about the animal's behavior that he'd never seen before.

In Rabbinical literature it is written, "If the dogs howl, the angel of death has entered the city." And a similar view obtains among Muslims: one reason given for why contact with a dog renders believers unclean and in need of renewed ablution is that dogs see the angel of death, or at least that's the metaphysical reason, for the source in question was some Sufi author I once read. People of a certain age are reminded of a scene in the classic western *Shane*, where hired gun Jack Palance makes his entrance at the local saloon. A dog that had been sleeping by the bar suddenly cocks his head anxiously and then, seeing Jack come through the swinging doors and sensing his grim purpose, slinks away in fear. Old wives' tales perhaps, and Hollywood melodramatics, but there is abundant evidence to suggest that animals possess a kind of sixth sense when it comes to danger in the offing. Indeed, remarkable anecdotal evidence of this was fairly recently provided by the devastating tsunami of Christmas 2004 in Southeast Asia, where tales are told of elephants and other animals making a beeline for the interior and high ground long before any humans, excepting some primitive tribesmen, had any inkling of the wave's approach. And the squirrels will always know when a hard winter is nigh. To return to the species at issue, dogs have a strange, but proven, faculty that allows them to sense and warn against a coming epileptic seizure. And tests have likewise shown that they can detect tuberculosis, coming heart attacks, and certain kinds of cancer.

I suggest it was an intuition of this kind that Simpson encountered. Interestingly, he had expected the dog would know him, indeed had banked on it—and it did, but not in the way he expected. Rather, it knew him for exactly what he was; it knew in essence what had brought him there. I suggested earlier that Simpson had called Paula in search of a sign: if she'd answered and they'd made up, he might have called things off. It would have been a temporary solution at best, one that catered to his ego but did not confront his dark side and the unresolved issues that had brought him to the brink. Of that he's always been in full denial. What Simpson saw, then, in the dog's reaction, in its frantic barking, was an honest opinion: the truth about himself he couldn't, and still can't, face. It was directed at the beast that was approaching, at the beast that he becomes whenever his bloated ego is affronted, when he's in the grip of uncontrollable jealousy and rage. As such, it was the perfect mirror of his soul and fittest manifestation of the sign he sought, that is, the one true antidote to his sick condition—assuming he's able to accept the lesson being taught and able to admit the painful truth that brings self-knowledge and release. He couldn't and didn't, as is proved by the event. Instead, the reverse psychological process would have necessarily ensued: an even greater hardening of his attitude, an even greater fury at the dog's implied rebuke *and* at being thwarted in any way.

Decline and Fall

In Herodotus's *Histories*, as in Greek drama, which shares its views on fate and the human condition, those who are approaching a line they shouldn't cross are always given a warning. It may be a literal warning by some "warner-figure" wiser than themselves, or it may be in the form of a sign, or it may even be both; in any case, it gives them a chance to wake up from their complacent or egotistical delusions and see things as they are (witness Cassandra and Agamemnon). Thus is Darius I of Persia saved from annihilation at the hands of the nomadic Scythians, whose land he's invaded (the present-day Ukraine). Just as the decisive battle's about to be joined, a hare darts forth between the marshaled hosts, and the entire Scythian cavalry, heedless of discipline, impetuously spur their steeds in hot pursuit—thereby demonstrating how little they are in awe of Persian arms. This immediately causes Darius to reconsider his vain interpretation of the cryptic Scythian present he'd been sent. It consisted of a bird, a mouse, a frog, and five arrows, whose meaning the deliverer refused to explain, saying that the Persians should be clever enough to figure out what they meant. Darius takes the gifts as signifying surrender: the mouse and frog standing for land and water, and the birds and arrows for the horses and weapons of the Scythians, their mode of combat, which they were now putting under his command.

But Gobryas, one of his nobles and a man of proven valor, cautions otherwise and reads the gifts to mean, "Unless you Persians turn into birds and fly up in the air, or into mice and burrow underground, or into frogs and jump into the lakes, you will never get home again, but stay here in this country, only to be shot by the Scythian arrows." His advice is rejected for the moment, but when Darius sees the Scythians' impromptu demonstration of utter contempt for his army, he comes to his senses and realizes Gobryas was right. They then succeed in extricating most of the army under cover of night and avoid impending calamity (4.131–5).

Unfortunately, by the next generation the Persian royal ego is so swollen that it can no longer be disabused of its delusions of grandeur by even the starkest of warning signs. Thus Xerxes, son of Darius, refuses to learn the lesson taught by the storm at the Hellespont, which destroys the first awe-inspiring pair of bridges he's constructed across its seven-furlong width.[6] The Hellespont, by which the gods have seen fit to divide Europe from Asia, represents a limit he ought not cross (though it's hardly the first that he's ignored); and the storm, as all of Herodotus's contemporaries knew, was heaven's way of warning Xerxes that despite the millions of men he commands he, too, is just a man; there are forces more powerful than he that he cannot control; the route ahead to Greece, which he means to conquer, is fraught with unforeseen dangers; and it's still not too late to abort his plans and avoid the potential catastrophe that awaits. But rather than be humbled, Xerxes waxes yet more proud: in a famous gesture indicative of his ever-more-towering megalomania, he orders the obstreperous seaway to be given three hundred lashes and rebuked for defying its master, namely him (7.33–4).

6 They were boat-supported suspension bridges, one made of papyrus, the other of flax.

One wonders what Simpson would have done to the barking dog had circumstances allowed or he had not had to worry that its death yelps would be heard. Perhaps nothing; perhaps it only further fueled his wrath against Nicole. He must have sensed the animal's unwonted hostility toward him, but that doesn't mean he recognized the implied rebuke or accepted any blame. Or, if he did, he might have transferred it to Nicole: it was all her fault; it was she who made him this way. But, however he processed things—that is, to what conclusion—he seems not to have done so right away. Many minutes went by, and with each passing moment success became less certain and the need to strike more urgent if he wanted to get home and clean up in time for the limo. This suggests that he once again wavered, that some form of internal debate took place: due to his fear of detection, no doubt, but also perhaps due to a faint stirring of conscience, some recoil from the loathsome depths to which he'd sunk. But if it were the latter, then *faint*, unfortunately, is the operative word. Whatever lukewarm pricking of conscience he may have felt only delayed his onslaught; it didn't make him leave. He now either hardened himself to the task—psyched himself up in the way described before—and completed what he'd come for, or his chance to turn back was squandered and came to a close. Heaven loses patience, as it were, when its warnings aren't truly heeded, when our relenting is too tepid and impure, and we can't escape the grip of darker forces. To repeat the Greek maxim: "character is destiny," and Simpson's character is fixed. So heaven forsook him—after its fashion. In Herodotus, when warnings are ignored, our punishment is always the more deserved. And heaven hastens this by substituting for its former warnings positive inducements to do wrong. It is as if it were saying, "If there's no other way, and you absolutely must, then don't hold back; rather vent your fury [or whatever] to the full." Thus opportunity passes by: his chance to turn around and leave. Then Ron arrives to see Nicole, and Simpson loses all control.

This, of course, is only a possible scenario, since it's equally possible that Ron arrived with Nicole's delayed murder finally in progress or a fait accompli. Only one person knows the exact sequence of events, and he isn't (really) telling. Meanwhile, even if the sequence is as I've described, at least circumstantially, it's long been out of fashion to read into circumstance, as Herodotus once would have, a kind of authorial intent: here, heaven's eleventh-hour intercession, its vain attempt to communicate in some way with Simpson's conscience, and then its abandoning him to his chosen fate. Cynics and pragmatists, I'm sure, are completely unimpressed, and not just with the idea of divine intervention: the conscience itself, the supposed recipient of this admonishment, is for them a figment of our conditioning or upbringing. I'll resume this theme—the part that "conscience" plays—in the final act (my closing chapters) in studying Simpson's behavior since the trials. But, in what comes next, it *has* all too clearly left the stage.

CHAPTER 5

AN (ALMOST) IMMACULATE DECEPTION

The actual sequence in which Nicole and Ron were slain cannot be determined with certainty by forensic pathology. We know, of course, what wounds each victim suffered, but not necessarily in what order their combined wounds occurred, though the order of their individual wounds, especially Nicole's, seems fairly clear. The biggest mystery, perhaps, is the possible scenarios, already discussed, in which the onslaught started. Did Ron arrive before the attack began? If so, how were the three positioned relative to one another when Simpson struck? Whom did he assault first? Only the last question is, to some degree, inferable. Four torn fibers from Nicole's black dress were found on Ron Goldman's shirt, which suggests that she was assaulted first. It's possible, however, that they were together, even embracing, with her head on his shoulder (twenty-five of her hairs were also found on his shirt) and that Simpson first drove hard into Ron, stabbing him at least once as he did, and maybe knocking him (or both of them) down; he then quickly turned, grabbed Nicole—tearing her dress in the process—and knocked her out, or at least stunned her, with a blow to the head. After that he would dispense with Ron and then return to finish her off. Still, it's likelier even with this scenario that he'd strike her first so as to prevent a shrill and spontaneous scream that his kids or the neighbors might hear. And nobody heard a woman's scream that night.

Nicole's injuries consisted of: a bruise to her scalp, which indicates that she was struck and knocked out, or at least dazed, for a time; three cuts to her hands, sustained as she tried at some point to defend herself (either at the outset or when she lay facedown and he was about to slit her throat); a total of seven stab wounds, four to the back of her neck and three to her scalp, which would have been delivered in a rapid and frenzied manner as he held her down from behind—like something straight out of *Psycho*, only she's not in the shower—and, finally, the one fatal wound, the gaping, left-to-right slash to her throat, so deep that it almost severed her head (the blade, in fact, did nick her spine). All of these wounds, as the forensic experts agreed, probably took no more than fifteen seconds to inflict, but not necessarily fifteen continuous seconds. As I've stated, Ron could have arrived at a murder in progress—at some point or other in the foregoing (most likely) progression—and caused a brief delay in these proceedings. Or he could have been there when the attack began and forced a scenario like that described above, where she's knocked out first and then Simpson takes care of him. He could even have arrived with her already dead. The hairs on his shirt would then have come from Simpson's gloves (one or more of her hairs was found on each). There are assorted horrific tableaux that Ron may have stumbled on, but the worst are those evoked by the criminal trial testimony of FBI footwear and tread expert Bill Bodziak. He had found an "impression" on the "center front" of Nicole's black dress as well as a heel print on her back. As Marcia Clark observes, this "conjured up a chilling image. Simpson planting his foot on Nicole's chest to make the first cut, then stepping on her back and pulling her head back to deliver the cut that nearly decapitated her."[1] Or maybe Ron was spared this dolorous sight. Maybe the dog alone was witness to these horrors—the dog and whatever power it is that gave it its uncanny instincts.

Ron's wounds were even more numerous. Many were defensive wounds: abrasions and sharp-force injuries to his palms and forearms that were likely incurred at the very outset, as he tried to ward off his attacker and still had strength. There were also about a dozen stab wounds or, in some cases, stabbing/slicing wounds to his face, scalp, and neck. Many of these were on the right side, which would indicate that his right-handed assailant was at some point, probably near the end, controlling his weakened victim from behind as he stabbed away. And the face wounds, so unnecessary otherwise, suggest a frenzied and jealous motivation, a desire to mutilate. There were also five stab wounds to his torso: three to the right side of the chest, two of which punctured a lung and were potentially fatal; one to his right flank; and another, very deep, one to his left flank, also potentially fatal (as will be discussed more thoroughly later); on top of these there was a stab wound to his upper left thigh. Finally, Ron's throat was cut open on the left side by a complex stabbing and cutting motion that severed his jugular vein. In the criminal trial, both sides assumed that this last wound was the one that killed him. And so their respective expert witnesses testified: Dr. Lakshmanan Sathyavagiswaran, the Los Angeles County coroner, for the prosecution, and Dr. Michael Baden, the former medical examiner for the city of New York and a man of considerable renown within and beyond his field, for the defense. He had long since parlayed his medical reputation into a lucrative second career: as a kind of well-paid celebrity witness in high-profile cases (he reputedly got a hundred thousand dollars for his services here). And, when

1 *Without a Doubt*, 412.

he wasn't testifying, he was a regular on the talk-show circuit, on shows such as *Larry King Live*, commenting on sensational cases such as this.[2]

Though Dr. Sathyavagiswaran did argue in his testimony that all Ron's wounds could have been, and likely were, inflicted within a few seconds, *his* expert opinion was effectively neutralized, if not trumped, by that of his more-famous colleague, Dr. Baden, the defense's hired gun. Baden argued that the struggle between Ron and Simpson would have been protracted, even after the fatal wound to his neck, which he would have received early on and while still standing. His reasoning, which held up in the criminal trial (at least so far as the neck wound's having occurred early on), was that this would explain why there was so little blood in Ron's lungs, despite the two potentially fatal chest wounds he received. According to Baden, this could only be accounted for by too much of Ron's blood having already bled out from his neck wound, drenching his shirt and spattering his shoes. There was, then, not enough blood pressure remaining to force much blood into his lungs when the chest wounds occurred. He also argued that, despite his fatal neck wound and the bleeding that ensued, Ron would have been able to continue on his feet for another five to ten minutes at least—or even fifteen!

Baden's testimony, and their lack of a forensic expert of sufficient stature to counter it (they tried repeatedly to get Dr. Spitz, but he declined), was a major problem for the prosecution's de facto timeline. Though they allowed in principle for a 10:15 p.m. to 10:40 p.m. window of opportunity for the murders to take place—from

2 Dr. Baden, it should be noted, has the reputation of being an honorable man: he doesn't lie to protect the guilty. But, as Marcia Clark and Daniel Petrocelli both point out, he's unavoidably beholden to the clients who are paying him so handsome a fee and thus predisposed to do all in his power to interpret the evidence in the way that is most beneficial—exculpatory or doubt-sowing—to them.

when the dog started barking to when Simpson would have had to depart Bundy to be the one who caused the thumps on Kato's room at 10:51 p.m.—in practice they had to lean toward the front end of this window and the theory that the commencement of the dog's barking coincided with the commencement of the crime. Thus they had to try to discredit any witnesses, but most notably Robert Heidstra, whose testimony, already touched on, would indicate too late a start time for the attack for Simpson to have done it; that is, if we also assume that Ron kept fighting for at least ten minutes.

Heidstra, as mentioned, testified that on June 12 he was walking his two dogs as per his normal routine. At around 10:30 or 10:35 p.m., as he approached Bundy on Gorham, the first cross street to the north, he heard Nicole's Akita, with which he was familiar, barking frantically. Fearing a dogfight, he changed course and cut south through the alley that ran parallel to Bundy on the side opposite to Nicole's. Two minutes later, he heard "a clear, male, young adult voice say, 'Hey, hey, hey!'" Then he describes that a deeper male voice replied "very fast; sounded like an argument." This exchange lasted about fifteen seconds,[3] after which he heard "a gate slamming." He continued walking, and a few minutes later he saw "a white kind of Jeep with tinted glass" stop briefly under a street light on Dorothy and then speed away south on Bundy.

This testimony is compelling, and the problem for the prosecution is this: if Heidstra is correct about the time, approximately 10:32 p.m., at which he heard the two men arguing—which exchange, by its tenor, would seem to indicate when Ron's deep-voiced assailant first sprang into action—and Baden is right about the ensuing struggle taking at least ten minutes, then Simpson (almost) certainly couldn't

3 These are the only human sounds heard by anyone. Significantly, there are no cries for help, which would indicate, as discussed (see above, 33), that the attack was swift and overwhelming.

have done it for the reason cited above.[4] Though I would add that this still leaves Heidstra's testimony in contradiction with Baden, in that he, Heidstra, says that he heard a brief struggle (or at least fifteen seconds' worth of arguing) and saw a white Jeep (Simpson's Bronco?) only a few minutes later, easily in time for Simpson to be outside Kato's room at 10:51 p.m. This would seem to mesh perfectly with Dr. Sathyavagiswaran's theory of a brief physical encounter (not to mention that there wasn't a lot more yelling on Ron's part[5]), and you wonder why the prosecution didn't use Heidstra as their own witness. The problem, I assume, had more to do with Baden's stature and, especially, with a jury bent on acquittal: he was their expert pretext for ignoring the facts.

One of the main advantages enjoyed by the plaintiffs in the civil trial, in comparison to the prosecution earlier on, was the services of the aforementioned Dr. Werner Spitz, probably the foremost forensic pathologist in America (not to mention a friend of Dr. Baden's, with whom he worked on the committees investigating the assassinations of President Kennedy and Martin Luther King Jr.). As well, he was, like Baden, an experienced and formidable courtroom witness. Thanks to him they were able to show that both murders, Ron's as well as Nicole's, took place very quickly; indeed, that Simpson's struggle with Ron, as Dr. Sathyavagiswaran had already argued, probably lasted no more than sixty seconds. Interestingly, though, it wasn't just the stature and gruff but likeable demeanor he brought to bear that proved decisive. He was also able to demonstrate very convincingly that the effective cause of death in Ron's case was not

---

4 See *Triumph of Justice*, 428, for a discussion of this issue.

5 Baden, interestingly, does in his civil trial testimony remark on the surprising absence of any yelling and screaming on the victims' part and then tries to infer from this that there was more than one assailant (*Triumph of Justice*, 570). But this still doesn't explain why Ron wasn't crying out at some point or points during a desperate ten-minute fight for his life.

the neck wound that cut through his jugular, as previously thought by both sides in the criminal trial; rather, it was the deep wound to the left flank I called attention to earlier. This wound severed the aorta, a much more capacious conduit even than the jugular, and this severing would have occurred, Spitz argued, early on in the struggle. As he observed, all of Ron's other wounds combined bled very little (for wounds, that is, of their respective types). And this includes the neck wound that, in Dr. Baden's interpretation, had caused such a loss of blood and consequent drop in blood pressure that the chest wounds discharged far less blood than they normally would have into Ron's lungs. Granted, Ron's shirt was drenched in front, but had the neck wound truly been the fatal stroke, the ground around him, too, should have been soaked in blood—much as was the walkway beneath Nicole—but it was not.

According to Dr. Spitz, the truly massive bleeding occurred through the severed aorta, from which, when punctured, "the blood gushes out at fantastic speed." For the most part, however, this blood did not escape Ron's body; instead it drained into "a space in the lower back called the retroperitoneum." Thus the absence of anything like a fatal flow from the wounds later inflicted to Ron's chest and neck, which last may still have been, with Ron as with Nicole, the intended coup de grâce—that is, with Ron already inert and on the ground, Simpson severed his jugular to make sure he died. Spitz then went on to argue that this gushing flow of blood from the aorta would have been so rapid as to cause a near-immediate drop in blood pressure, with the result that not enough blood would reach the brain. "A person loses ability to stand up, loses ability to think, becomes woozy, and, in very short order, disabled."[6]

Baden, who testified again on Simpson's behalf in the civil trial, never backed off his diagnosis that it was the neck wound that did

---

6 *Triumph of Justice*, 431–2.

Ron in. But he effectively undercut the exculpatory value of even this interpretation of Ron's wounds when he admitted under cross-examination that after receiving the wound that he did to his neck Ron could have remained standing for at most five minutes longer but, equally likely, for perhaps no more than three. Moreover, this considers the neck wound in isolation, but if the other wounds were occurring in short order, as is likely the case, the additional flow from them would hasten Ron's collapse. In any case, gone are the ten to fifteen minutes needed for Simpson to be (all but) excluded as the killer.

So the bottom line is this: the assault likely commenced at around 10:32 p.m. when Heidstra heard what he says sounded like two men arguing—though the first words he heard, the "Hey, hey, hey," sound more like an alarmed reaction to some kind of attack. Or, it could have commenced slightly before these sounds were heard, if Simpson had already started in on Nicole. What followed was an overwhelming onslaught, due both to the pent-up fury of an extremely powerful assailant now at last unleashed and to his being well aware he had to move quickly—to prevent his victims' crying out; to allow him to get back home in time to preserve his alibi; perhaps even to reduce the chance of his kids' waking and coming downstairs with him still there. (How, you wonder, would he have dealt with that?) A minute or two after it started, everything was over. Simpson was breathing heavily, and the dog was still frantically barking, but otherwise, as the intervals in the barking would confirm, the only sound was the soft romantic music Nicole had put on, which drifted through the open front door. Simpson's victims were lying inert at his feet. Ron was on his back in the small garden, his torso turned slightly to the right, his right leg bent, his left stretched out toward the walkway, his head propped up against a palm stump by the fence. His eyes were open but empty, encased in the glaze of death. Nicole was in a fetal position, her left hip on or against the lowest of the four steps leading up to the porch, her legs and arms curled by her side on the cobbled sidewalk, her bloody hair tumbling down over her face and wounds. A large pool of blood had spread beneath her and was flowing down the grout lines toward Bundy. While Ron wasn't visible from the street, she was virtually framed against the steps rising behind her, as seen through the open, or soon-to-be-opened, front gate—pushed by the dog as it left. So there was one thing the Akita accomplished by its actions of that night: it spared its mistress's children the "backstage" view of this grisly tableau.

The foregoing contains nothing of note that hasn't already been said. Where I part company with my predecessors—or rather, what I challenge—is their various attempts to explain, or avoid explaining, the circumstances under which Simpson's left glove came off at the crime scene (along with a woolen cap) and the cuts to that same hand ensued. And I want to explore how premeditation—including the obvious, but still worth stressing, intent to get away with it—would have conditioned what he did, and wore, at Bundy as much as it did the alibi he set up. Clearly, one of the things he most had to worry about, especially given his record of spousal abuse, which would make him a natural suspect, was how to prevent any trace of Nicole's blood from getting into his car. After all, this is the age of DNA evidence, isn't it, as just about everyone knows? If some of the victim's blood leads back to you, it's a virtual confession—or so you would think. And there was going to be blood, lots of it, by his deliberate choice. This was a rage killing, with rage's ideal instrument, a knife, and as such it was intended to be the final, emphatic assertion of his power and control. Granted, if he did it right and slit her throat from behind, her blood would spurt away from him. But there were no guarantees. She could twist in some way that sent her blood toward him, or he could stumble as they struggled and somehow brush against it; even if only a little got on him, that could be enough. Plus it would be dark and he'd be wearing dark sweats (for the obvious reason), so that when he was done and set to return he wouldn't be able to tell if all was well, if his clothes were still unstained. And the stakes were as high as could be, with capital punishment a real possibility.

Moreover, even without that or *any* official retribution, there were the needs of his ego. Any lingering widespread suspicion, or conviction in the court of public opinion, produces a dubious victory. You show her, but then she takes you down with her, and all that she's said about you, all her attempts to communicate her plight for so many years, are vindicated at last.

So, regarding the blood and how not to have any on him when he left—how to get away "spot-free"—what was his plan? As anyone who read the breaking stories after the murders will recall, one of the most intriguing objects in the case was the small, dark "duffel bag" or "knapsack-like bag" (as it's variously been described by Kato Kaelin and the limo driver, Allan Park) that was sitting on Simpson's lawn not far from where the six-foot-tall, two-hundred-pound African-American emerged into Park's view and then crossed the driveway and went into the house. It's the same one that Simpson later insisted on picking up himself to put in the limo. He must have intended to use it for more than just the murder weapon on the return trip to Rockingham (where, as I'll argue, the weapon was likely transferred to a more compact container, which was then placed in the golf bag that was outside the front door, and which would be checked in at the airport). It must have contained by then his primary murder clothes—meaning the outer layer that did the "dirty" work—which, along with anything else that could incriminate him, he planned to get rid of elsewhere.

That said, the clothes the man was wearing, the guy Park saw crossing the driveway and entering Simpson's home, were also black.

Does that mean that the "duffel" or "knapsack-like bag"—one of the chief indicators, by the way, of premeditation—was virtually empty (because what else would it contain)? Or that Simpson would have chanced driving home in the outfit he wore when committing the murders, one of which, Nicole's, he knew in advance was going to be messy? That's hard to believe. As we'll see, none of the victims' blood in the Bronco was anywhere on the driver's-side seat, so what he wore when he returned *was* blood free, at least where it was in contact with the seat. This set of facts demands a better explanation. What Simpson would have had on when he committed the murders was, in addition to any underwear, *two* layers of clothing: a top or outer layer, the dark sweat suit he was last seen wearing by Kato, which, in addition to helping conceal him, would also, given its close-knit fabric, be relatively impervious to the blood. Then under this he would have worn what he planned to go home in, a second sweat suit, dark just like the first, or, at least, dark clothing of some kind. Based on the published accounts of both Marcia Clark and Mark Fuhrman, it was pretty clearly a sweat suit. But, unfortunately, there's a problem with these accounts that needs to be dealt with: they disagree as to where and by whom these sweats were found.

Competing Versions

Clark's account, which appeared first, describes how she was reviewing some police photographs in August of '94, including a picture of LAPD criminalist Dennis Fung, taken on June 13. He's "crouched near the laundry hamper in Simpson's master bathroom … holding something dark in his hand." She looks closer and thinks it has to be the dark sweatshirt Kato had described. Why hasn't she been told about it? Why haven't these sweats been seized and tested for blood immediately? She summons Fung. He recalls going through the hamper. She shows him the photo. He recalls inspecting the sweats. Why didn't he collect them? she asks. He says that he couldn't see any blood on them, that he thought, "If they'd been used in the murder, the blood would be big and obvious." Clark counters that "if the killer stood behind his victims, he might get only a fine spray on him, if that."[7] Fung feels terrible, but the damage is done. And the sweats have since disappeared—indeed, have never existed, according to Simpson. They've since been spirited out of the house by someone, the likeliest candidate being Simpson's bosom buddy, Robert Kardashian, if not Simpson himself (as I'll later discuss).

Clark's version was soon afterward contradicted, at least circumstantially, by that of Mark Fuhrman, the detective whose reputation and vital testimony in the criminal trial was discredited by the discovery that he had, contrary to his earlier sworn testimony, used the so-called *N*-word to describe African-Americans within the ten years previous to the trial. It didn't matter that this was in the context of a fictional screenplay about a group of rogue cops that he was helping a friend create, and that he was mouthing off for the edification of a relatively sheltered un-streetwise young woman[8] with the kind of dialogue a racist rogue cop would come out with. He had used the word, so he was a racist himself, though nothing in the lengthy record of his police career betrayed any such animus—in fact, often just the reverse. He has since made a profuse and abject apology for his insensitivity, even given this fictional context. For this owning up, I say, he deserves credit. And for him as for all of us, on the matter of sincerity let God be our witness and judge.

Anyway, according to Mark Fuhrman, these sweats were not in the laundry hamper in the bathroom off Simpson's master bedroom, nor were they initially found by Dennis Fung. They were part of

7 *Without a Doubt*, 376–7.

8 Her name was Laura Hart McKinny. They met in 1985 and collaborated over the next few years. For a time they had a romantic relationship as well.

a load of wet wash still in the machine in the main floor laundry room and were found by Fuhrman's partner, Brad Roberts, during the course of the thorough search of Simpson's home on June 13 that followed on the issuance of the first search warrant for Rockingham at around 10:30 or 11:00 that morning. Roberts also found a blood smear a few feet away on the light switch in the half-bath next to the quarters of Simpson's maid Gigi Guarin, who, as mentioned, was away that weekend. He immediately called his partner's attention to these findings. Then two other detectives involved in the search were brought over, as well as the lead criminalist, Dennis Fung, who checked out a possible blood transfer on the washing machine, which turned out to be rust. Finally, the LAPD video photographer was also brought over, and he filmed the sweats inside the machine, a frame of which is included among the photos in Fuhrman's book, *Murder in Brentwood*.[9]

Why the disparity, then, between Clark's and Fuhrman's accounts? The problem is that the sweats, as well as a sample from the blood smear, were never booked as evidence. Then they disappeared or were cleaned up. Furthermore, there was other important evidence that was not picked up from Bundy, even though its existence was mentioned in the scrupulous notes Fuhrman made as the initial detective to arrive at the scene. He gave these notes to detective Phil Vannater when the case was assigned shortly after that to Robbery Homicide and Vannater and Tom Lange were appointed to head it up. Fuhrman accused Clark of covering up for her friend Vannater, with whom she had over the years worked on numerous cases. Moreover, it was Vannater who had called her in on the Simpson case: they were comfortable with each other and liked working together. Fuhrman's probably right about Clark's motivation but

9 Clark's book, as Fuhrman remarks, does not contain the dramatic photo of Fung by the hamper, which you'd think it would, if it really existed (*Murder in Brentwood*, 329).

too vitriolic—if understandably, given all that he went through[10]—in his condemnation of Vannater. Some mistakes were made in a difficult situation, which the celebrity factor—*How could this be O. J.?*—made more difficult still.

A second search warrant for Rockingham was, in fact, issued on June 28, with the in-part express purpose of picking up items that had been earlier mentioned as found but never collected, most notably the pair of black sweats. But, as indicated, they were by then long gone. This allowed Simpson (sort of) to deny that he'd ever owned any and to distance himself from the blue/black fibers found on both Ron's shirt and the Rockingham glove. He's contradicted, of course, by Kato Kaelin's testimony that that's what he last saw him wearing. And then there's the color photo magazine layout that turned up in the civil trial, featuring Simpson in dark sweats, from an issue that appeared just a few weeks before the murder. As well, there's a Playboy exercise video he made at about the same time, which shows him in dark sweats, and which was used as evidence in both trials. Leslie Gardner, the wardrobe stylist on this video, testified that Simpson had been given that sweat suit to keep, along with various others.[11]

I should add that it would not have been part of Simpson's original plan to deny that he owned dark sweats (or even to dispose of *both* of the pairs he wore). Otherwise, why would he wear them when he went to Kato's room? Wouldn't he plan to change into them right after that, as he passed through the house on the way back to the Bronco, or after he'd parked near Nicole's? Once he knew,

---

10 See Chapter 2, note 11 regarding the fresh bloody fingerprint on the knob of the deadbolt on the back gate that he and Roberts discovered, and which he included in his notes, but which was also never booked and then destroyed soon afterward. Had it been booked, the murderer's identity would have been clear and undeniable; and Mark Fuhrman would have been spared his long ordeal—but Fate had other plans.

11 See *Triumph of Justice*, 331–2, 350.

however, that he'd been seen in those sweats by the limo driver when he returned from the murders, he changed his story. And after his struggles with Ron, it probably occurred to him that fibers from his sweat suit would be recovered at the scene. Hence the almost-absurd denial, given the quality of the testimony to the contrary.[12]

There's one other thing to note in connection with Simpson's unwonted visit to Kato's room and what then ensued: the small black bag probably explains why Simpson took the Bentley and not the Bronco on the unplanned return trip to McDonald's (though he would have intended to stop at some fast food restaurant, one that was not on the route to Nicole's, prior to heading her way). Because this bag was likely already sitting in the Bronco, and either empty except for the knife, gloves, and cap, or containing both these and the second sweat suit (which he might not yet have put on if it made him look noticeably bulky).

As for Marcia Clark, in view of the fact that the missing evidence was never recovered, it was pointless from her perspective, both as a lawyer in the course of the trial and as a friend when she wrote her book, to damage Vannater's reputation, something she'd be loath to do anyway, for commendable reasons. Moreover, he was nearing retirement after a long and creditable career with the LAPD. Why tarnish his name now on a case that was blowing everything connected to it out of all proportion? Meanwhile, Clark's "version" of these events, though likely fictional as regards the circumstances, does convey the essence of what occurred: that a potentially major piece of evidence was found but not picked up. But, assuming she knows where the sweats really were found, she's dismayed, apparently, because they may still have borne some of the victim's blood, even

12 You may wonder if the police ever checked to see if anyone at the drive-through McDonald's had recognized Simpson and recalled what it was he had on. They probably did and no one had, but it's not mentioned in any book on the case I've read.

after they'd been washed.[13] I disagree with this, on the basis of the theory already advanced: that Simpson wore two layers of sweats when committing the murders. The sweats in the washing machine were Simpson's undergarments, so to speak, or travel outfit for the journey home. They likely bore no trace, even before they were washed, of transfer evidence from the victims, though they would probably have been stained with *his* blood, a development he had not anticipated—and one that per se would not put him at the crime scene. Still, when he was released after being interrogated the day after the murders, during which interrogation he was asked what he'd been wearing the night before, and when he returned to discover (to his amazement?) that they hadn't been seized, it made sense to dispose of them—in case they did still have traces of blood, and to support the claim he would now be making that he'd never owned dark sweats.

One more thing about the two layers of dark sweats: as his lawyers pointed out at both trials, his accusers' timelines (in the context of their attempts to reconstruct his actions of that night) gave Simpson no chance to clean up after what had to be—nay, was intended to be—a very gory mess. "Intended" both because he wanted to *show* Nicole, and this was part of the statement he needed to make; and because the bloodier the murder the more that supported his alibi, by raising precisely this question: However could he have done so gory a

13 Even if Clark were right about the sweats being in the hamper, there's no way Simpson would have chanced leaving the ones with the victims' blood on them in it, not when he might well be under investigation as a suspect before he returned from Chicago—indeed, even putting them in there to begin with, since this blood might transfer to the hamper. But Clark must have known that the sweats really were found in the washing machine and that any blood evidence was likely long gone. Otherwise, why was the hamper not checked for blood? Her story about the hamper allows her to vent her frustrations, and poor Dennis Fung plays the scapegoat, the idea being, I guess, that after what Barry Scheck did to him in his cross-examination, Fung's reputation couldn't be tarnished any further.

deed, which should have left him spattered all over with blood, and still have had time to get home, clean up, and be ready for the limo driver when he came to pick him up?[14] To give him his due, it was a clever plan—diabolically clever, even—allowing him as it did in one fell swoop both to distance himself still further from the crime *and* to vent to the full his wrath on helpless Nicole.[15]

I return now to where we left Simpson when the murders were done. He would likely be standing at the top of the steps above Nicole's body and pooling blood, his feet planted sideways to her, facing either toward or away from Ron. This way he could keep one eye on the open door to one side, should anyone stir within, and the other on the street as he started to carry out the next phase of his plan: the hasty—and likely well-rehearsed—removal of his bloodied clothes.[16] He had to not only remove them but to dispose of them as well, using the aforementioned small, dark bag that he'd later leave outside on his front lawn. (This he would have set down somewhere near at hand, for instance, just up the walkway alongside the house, or even have thrown to the side at the moment he launched his attack.) And along with his outer garments he would have packed the murder weapon, laid on top of them for swift removal when he got

14 In his fairly recent pseudoconfession (whose listed author is now the Goldman family) he stresses just how drenched he is in blood after the murders (*If I Did It: Confessions of the Killer* [New York: Beaufort Books, 2007]; see especially 132). He's taunting us for our failure to this day to give a credible explanation for how the Bronco, too, wasn't drenched in blood.

15 Daniel Petrocelli tells how jury research showed that the more they emphasized the brutality of the murders the more people couldn't believe that Simpson did it (*Triumph of Justice*, 2). Simpson was surely aware of this further advantage to be gained from butchering, not just killing, Nicole.

16 It's conceivable that he timed himself rehearsing this and other elements of his plan.

back home.[17] There he would transfer it to another bag; most likely the golf bag that he'd left just outside his front door.

Meanwhile, because Simpson had anticipated just about everything, his precautions at Bundy were more intricate still; there was a necessary sequence to how he removed each thing. Since his clothes would likely have blood on them somewhere, and since he would not be able to see it clearly enough to avoid it in the dark, he would have kept his gloves on till he removed his outer sweat suit jacket and pants, to avoid getting blood on his hands that he might then transfer to the Bronco. Thus, as he stuffed the bloody clothes and then the weapon into the bag, the last things to be removed and put in would be the gloves—and the knit cap that was also found at the scene. This cap, by the way, was not an inept attempt at disguise, as Johnnie Cochran so famously mocked in a courtroom scene—his signature moment that was widely replayed in the television coverage following his death in 2005. Cochran, as many will recall, donned the knit cap during his closing arguments and then went on at great length about how he was fooling nobody, that anybody could see he was still Johnnie Cochran. And the same applied to his client: "O. J. Simpson in a knit cap, from two blocks away, is still O. J. Simpson. It's no disguise. It's no disguise. It makes no sense. It doesn't fit. If it doesn't fit, you must acquit." Many were laughing with him, most conspicuously his guilty client, who, in Schiller and

---

17 The Thursday before the murders, Simpson attended a board meeting of the Forschner Company in Connecticut, which makes Swiss Army knives and watches, and he left with a bag full of merchandise. Fuhrman and Roberts saw an empty Swiss Army knife box in Simpson's house the day after the murders, but it wasn't collected as evidence either, and it disappeared soon afterward. Fuhrman makes a good case for the murder weapon being a Victorinox "SAK" lockback knife, a make of Swiss Army knife that the Forschner Company had been importing for years. See his chapter "The Murder Weapon" in *Murder in Brentwood.* All of the victims' knife wounds are consistent with a single-edged blade.

Willwerth's book, is revealed as the source of the "two blocks away" line when his friend Kardashian finds him in his holding cell during preparations for closing arguments, rehearsing that very point aloud, as if he were Cochran himself addressing the jury.[18] Simpson clearly loved how nobody had figured out what the cap was for: it was, along with other unsolved aspects of the case, as if he hadn't done it. And Cochran's virtuoso performance successfully made, or at least insinuated, the point that this cap, on which hairs with Simpson's DNA were found, must have been planted too (or Simpson's hairs planted on it), along with the Rockingham glove and Simpson's blood at Bundy, since it served no apparent purpose.

As stated, however, disguise was not the reason for this cap. Simpson never intended to be seen wearing it by anyone but Nicole, and she'd tell no tales. On the trip over he likely wouldn't have had it on, because it might have made him look like a hood and, in that affluent neighborhood, attract attention. Then, on the trip back, it would be packed away in the small, dark bag. No, he'd put it on when he got there, for a different purpose altogether than anyone has as yet supposed: the role it was to play in his immaculate departure from the crime scene.

Let's return again to where we left him, with his outer garments off and jammed into the bag, the knife deposited on top of them, but the gloves and cap still on. The gloves, or at least one of them, are due off next; these, because they fit so snugly and are the likeliest things to be bloodied, he takes off very carefully, working both of them partly off to where they fit loosely with the fingers and thumbs half emptied—so that he can keep from contacting either with a bare hand. Then he does pull one fully off, the right one, and puts it in the bag on top of the sweats and to the side, perhaps, of the knife.

18 *American Tragedy*, 838. Simpson here, incidentally but tellingly, reveals what pride he takes in his own celebrity, the fact that he is known by one and all, even from two blocks away.

And then, to shield his bare right hand, he slides it under the edge of the woolen cap he still has on, removes it and, in this inverted form, uses it as he would a handkerchief to tug off the other glove, thus taking every precaution to keep the blood off his hands. Or maybe he just takes the cap off in the normal manner and without the extra precaution. In either case, he removes it only when he's got the right glove off and then uses it as described—which is why the cap and left glove fall out together at Bundy, and not the two gloves or all three items together. It's because the left glove and cap are on top, with the right glove underneath, and because they're interlocked with the cap wrapped round the glove—at least till they hit the ground and roll slightly apart, coming to rest by the fence a little beyond Nicole's head and just at the edge of the sidewalk, two of the most dramatic pieces of evidence in the trial.[19]

This is what I think happens next, after he's finished packing. When he goes to close the bag—whether by zipping it up or by buckling or strapping down a top flap—there is a minor problem with the clothes being too bunched up. There is, after all, no time to fold things neatly, especially after the further delay occasioned by Ron, so that the top of the pile is catching in the zipper, or preventing the buckle or strap from being cinched, or he just notes the potential for this. In any case, if he wants to close the bag, he has to compress the pile in some way, either by removing everything, folding the sweat suit neatly, and repacking—which would take time and would certainly transfer blood to his hands and maybe the clothes he still has on—or by jamming or tamping it down, which could also bring

19 Fibers from Ron's shirt were found on the hat, which led Mark Fuhrman, among others, to theorize that this transfer somehow occurred during their struggle (*Murder in Brentwood*, 159). But it's much easier to envision this transfer occurring in the way described here: when Simpson uses the cap to pull off a glove that has been in strenuous contact with Ron's shirt. Fibers from this shirt *were* found on that glove.

his bare hand into contact with blood. So he chooses the second option: because it's quicker, because it limits the area of potential contact to the knuckles of one hand (his left one, naturally, which, since he's right-handed, he can more easily try not to use till he gets home and showers), *and* because the knit cap, the item least likely to have been spattered or smeared with blood—that is, till it made contact with a glove—is lying there at the top of the pile with the left glove enfolded in it or right underneath. It should still be clean on the side facing up and, if he only touches it there when he jams down the pile, then he might hope to avoid any contact with blood altogether. He could, I know, have left the bag open for the time being (he'll have to reopen it if he intends at some point to jam the shoes in there as well, which his footprints show him still wearing when he left); but in its stuffed and unclosed condition it might spill some of its bloody contents during the hurried drive home, while the consequences of this contact seem controllable for the reasons just given.

So he jams down the clothes with his left hand while either supporting the bag from beneath with his right—there's too much blood on the ground to chance setting it there—or gripping it at the top (by a handle or flap) to provide resistance. Also, he tries to make the minimum contact possible even with this procedure. This means he does not make the standard fist (his big open palm is not an option) with all his knuckles leveled into one broad tamp. No, he has a better idea still for reducing the extent of the contact. He curls his fingers at the middle and third, or outermost, knuckles—the thumb is curled below them over the palm—in such a way that the second or middle knuckles jut out beyond the rest, so that they and they alone will make firm contact with the pile, but especially the middle knuckle of his middle finger, which naturally sticks out furthest.

And where does he sustain the most serious wound to his hand, the one he has to bandage, which is still seeping blood when he returns from Chicago the following day? It is right across that very knuckle! And though it veers at an angle midway, it's a fairly deep, essentially straight slice, such as a knife would properly make.[20] This cut he gets from the murder weapon itself, for it, as mentioned, is in the bag as well. It is near or at the top of the pile, for easy removal—either right beneath the gloves and cap or, more likely, right beside them.[21] Thus, as he hurriedly and forcefully drives down his hand knuckles-first to compress the clothes, his hand somehow slides off the cap and into the waiting knife. Or, more likely I think, it's the bag itself, as he holds it in some way to apply resistance, that skews at an angle to one side and sends his hand on its downward plunge into the knife, which is perhaps lodged against the side of the bag and does not give way on contact. Thus, in some such way his fingers are sliced, the middle one first, across the top of the second knuckle as it drives straight into the blade. Perhaps the gash is then made to the adjacent (medial) side of his ring finger, as his hand (or the knife) slides or veers upon contact, or while the clothing or the bag shifts in some way. Or perhaps it is when he recoils in panic, and pulls his hand too quickly from the bag, that he incurs this second more-significant cut, as he encounters the firmly lodged knife again, but at a different angle. Or it could be then that he receives the third cut, the smaller one near the top of the middle finger, on the outer (or lateral) side and thus immediately opposite the fourth-finger cut. Or one (and maybe both) of these additional cuts occur when, after

---

20 The straightness of the edges of the wound to the middle finger would be distorted by the fact that with his knuckle bent the skin around it would be taut when the wound was incurred, but it would be wrinkled or puckered when the finger was straightened, as it was in the police photo taken the following day.

21 If it was a Swiss Army knife, as Fuhrman argues, this scenario requires that the blade had been left open, either by chance or in haste, or because he originally intended to boil it to destroy all blood and tissue evidence on the weapon itself, and he felt the exposed blade would be the more readily cleansed.

the first cut, the knife gets between his middle and ring fingers and then spins like a spit where it is lodged in the bag's fabric.[22]

Meanwhile, as Simpson recoils and the compressed pile of clothes springs back, the cap and the topmost glove, the left one, whether folded together or not, are ejected from the bag. Or perhaps they spill out when the bag skews to one side. Either way, in the darkness and his panicked state of mind, he likely does not notice. His first concern, now that he's been cut, is to get out of there, which he does without any further attempt to close the bag. The right move, perhaps, except that, if this is indeed what happened, he should have kept his hand in or over the open bag, at least until he got into his car. (Remember that the bag was never recovered.) If he'd done that, his blood might not have been found at the crime scene. Instead, however, what we have is the murderer's blood, starting with the drops that land on the walkway at irregular intervals as he departs the scene.

As outlined earlier, the first three drops are to the left of his bloody size-twelve, slightly pigeon-toed, Bruno Magli footprints[23] as they move away from the bodies down the side walkway, right beneath where his left hand would have normally been positioned. These footprints eventually fade out, and there are no blood drops, either, for a space, probably because he's transferred the bag from his right hand to his left or is holding it with both hands, and the

---

22 The knife was likely sharpened recently, if not that same day, which conjures up yet another grim image: the baleful look on Simpson's face as, again and again, he whets the blade.

23 Every one of these adjectives points at him. The Bruno Magli make was identified by FBI footwear expert Bill Bodziak from the rare Silga pattern on its sole (a series of *S*-shaped squiggles). Simpson must have been unaware he'd stepped in blood and, it seems, never looked back to see if he was leaving tracks. Or perhaps he did, but not until the tracks had faded out, and he never checked his soles. As Bodziak says in the criminal trial, criminals never think of their shoes as a possible source of incrimination (*Without a Doubt*, 412).

bag is catching the drops. Though this is not by design, as proved by another drop that falls near the end of the walkway and even more so by a smudge on the latch of the rear gate, which he obviously chooses to open with his left hand, despite knowing that he's been cut. Given the adrenaline rush he's experiencing, he's likely unaware of the seriousness of the cuts and is thinking that if he opens the gate with just his thumb and index finger he'll be okay, forgetting that the blood may have transferred to them. There are also, among the blood samples actually collected, drops on the lower rung and the middle of the gate's center mesh, which probably flew from his hand as he swung it up to the latch. And, of course, there's the bloody fingerprint, "several 'points' in quality," that Fuhrman and Roberts saw on the knob of the brass deadbolt, but which was never booked.[24] Finally, on the driveway just to the rear of the condo there is one more blood drop, as well as a couple of coins, which likely fall from the killer's pocket as he fumbles for his keys in his pants pocket.

The coins were collected by the police but, so far as Mark Fuhrman knows, never fingerprinted. If true, this is one more complaint he has to make concerning the police work that day. Fuhrman also thinks that the location of the coins and the remaining blood drop indicates where the killer entered his car. This well may be, but it is also possible that it was further away, for instance in that parking lot on Dorothy, and that after Simpson transferred the bag to his left hand so that he could reach for his keys with his right, the bag kept any subsequent drops from reaching the ground. And that's all the blood we have at the crime scene—from the murderer, that is—from O. J. Simpson. There's none of his blood on the victims, not even one drop, and for one obvious and only plausible reason—because he didn't start bleeding till after he'd finished with them.

---

24 *Murder in Brentwood*, 17, and see above, Chapter 2, note 11; Chapter 5, note 10.

There is, however, at least one other sample of blood the murderer may have bled there at the crime scene. For the right-hand glove that was found on the walkway at Rockingham has Simpson's blood on it in a number of places, mixed with that of both of his victims. This is the glove that, in the scenario envisaged here, remains in the bag when its mate and the cap spill out. Simpson begins to bleed immediately, of course, while his hand is still in the bag, and perhaps for a moment he holds his extricated hand over the open bag as he ponders what to do next—and as his blood continues to drip. And, at various points thereafter, at Rockingham as well as at Bundy, his left hand, as we shall see, must hold the bag in such a way that, whether deliberately or not, the blood drips to the inside and thus onto what is in there, including this glove.

Meanwhile, if we count the Bronco as part of the extended crime scene, there's the blood found on and in it. On the outside, there was a smudge above the driver-side door handle, which would a few hours later be noticed by Mark Fuhrman when he, Roberts, Vannater, and Ron Phillips (Fuhrman's immediate superior) went to inform Simpson of his ex-wife's death. This would be a main reason for their entering the grounds as a possible crime scene. Fuhrman also saw small brush-like streaks of blood on the door sill, likely caused by one of the Bruno Maglis as Simpson swung his feet into the car when exiting Bundy.[25] However, despite Fuhrman's mentioning them in the notes he turned over, samples of these brush marks were never taken as evidence that day, nor were they photographed, and they had vanished by the time a belated attempt was made to recover them from the by-then-impounded Bronco.

The blood evidence on the inside of the Bronco is more extensive, but not all of it is Simpson's: Nicole's blood and Ron's were found on

---

25 *Sill* here refers not to the horizontal base of the door frame, visible only when the door has been opened, but to that portion of the car's exterior surface that runs like a narrow band beneath the door.

the center console, along with several stains of Simpson's. As well, Nicole's blood showed up mixed with Simpson's on the steering wheel and by itself on a partial print left on the driver's side carpet. Obviously his left foot was kept in one place for a while and on a more absorbent material than the tile or pavement where his tracks had faded out—further proof that he has not yet thought to check the soles of his shoes (see above, note 23). Most of the other bloodstains, however, were Simpson's and were, as befits where he was cut, on the left-hand side of the car's interior, which indicates that he was still at times using that hand. There was a smudge on the door handle notch, on the door wall, and on the headlight button on the instrument panel. Haste—and the hope that his index finger and thumb were still clean—could explain the marks on or near the door handles, both inside and out. Thus he would have had the bag in his right hand as he opened the door so that he could readily deposit it on the passenger-side front seat. And mere carelessness would account for the stain on the door wall; his hand at some point had brushed against it. The light-switch stain could also indicate that he didn't yet realize how seriously he was cut, but also, he likely didn't turn on the lights till the car was in motion and heading away from the scene, so his right hand was busy steering. On the other hand, your own blood in your own car is not by itself incriminating, as he should have realized. And if he knew that his bare left hand had never touched the victims, as I've here argued must be the case, then there was no compelling reason not to use it from time to time for convenience's sake.[26] Meanwhile, let it be noted: though we know from the blood smudges (as opposed to the drips) he left on various objects—at Bundy, in the Bronco, and back at Rockingham—that

---

26 Though it's likely that whatever blood was transferred from his bleeding left hand onto the car was transferred as he got in, or in the initial stages of the trip back, it's possible that some of it wasn't transferred until he arrived home and exited the car and thus had occasion to use his left hand again.

his left hand made contact with these, the only blood left on them was his own. There was no trace evidence from the victims: no blood, no tissue, no fibers, no human hairs—not even dog hair.[27] This despite the fact that the left hand must have been on each of the victims most of the time as they struggled, in order to control them while the right hand did its work. So I repeat: his bare left hand *never* touched the victims, because it wasn't bared till after they were dead.

The presence of his blood on the Bronco's console, to his right, along with that of both victims is more problematic, as is Nicole's blood mixed with his on the steering wheel. Mark Fuhrman surmises that he still had the right glove on and had it on all the way home, and that it's the glove that transferred the victims' blood, and some of his, to where it was found in his car (excluding, of course, what was transferred by his shoes).[28] I obviously disagree with this explanation. Marcia Clark, on the other hand, thinks that the marks, on the console at least, occurred when he dropped the right glove there as he got into the car,[29] meaning, then, that it wasn't yet in the bag, which bag she perhaps assumes had been left behind in the car. I would modify Clark's explanation a bit.

At some point the glove rolls out of the still-unclosed bag and onto the console—when it first is set or plunked down on the passenger side seat, or if Simpson takes a corner too quickly or has to suddenly brake while speeding home. In Robert Heidstra's testimony, he describes how the white Jeep-like car stopped for a moment under a street light on Dorothy and then sped away. If that was indeed Simpson's Bronco, perhaps he was then righting the bag after it had fallen over

27 Contrast this with the left-hand glove itself, on which were found: one hair from Nicole, bloody fibers from Ron's shirt, fibers from Ron's jeans, and dog hair from the Akita.

28 *Murder in Brentwood*, 210.

29 *Without a Doubt*, 471.

and putting the glove back inside. The glove had stains from all three of them, which could explain all the stains on the console. And, if he used his right hand—just the thumb, say, and one finger—to pick up the glove carefully by the cuff and put it back in the bag, he could have come in contact with some mixture of her blood and his, which he would then transfer to the steering wheel.

By this time too, if not sooner, Simpson would be aware of how things have changed, and how his well-laid plans must be modified accordingly. For one thing, he knows he's been cut, though he doesn't know if he's left a bloody trail behind him (he's likely not yet aware that the cap and left glove are still at the crime scene). He will, however, have checked his left hand as soon as it's convenient, or as soon as he has enough light to see by, which could also explain why Heidstra saw the Jeep-like car stop under a street light (if he turned on the interior roof light he'd have risked being seen). And, while he likely realizes he can safely bleed in his own car, he does obviously not want lots of fresh blood there to arouse suspicion; this would be undesirable even in normal circumstances. So, unless there's a cloth handy to wrap around his bloody fingers, the next best thing is to keep his left hand in his lap, so that the blood soaks into his sweat suit. This, too, creates a bit of a problem: a large stain he'd rather not have to explain that accumulates in the four to five minutes it takes to get back home. So he perhaps has to change his plans for these sweats. Originally, he might have intended to leave them in his laundry hamper or tossed on his bed. If found by the police, they would match what Kato last saw him in and would contain no incriminating trace evidence; nay, they would virtually exonerate him. But now they're a cause for suspicion and will definitely need to be washed—which there's precious little time for. So his mind is racing, thinking of how he'll handle this.

Then too, on the issue of time, there's the limo driver. Of course, Simpson has no idea at this point that his regular driver couldn't make it, that his replacement, Allan Park, has come a full twenty-five minutes earlier than the appointed arrival time of 10:45 p.m., and that this has already ruined his alibi. But it makes no difference now, since it's already 10:45, or will be by the time he gets home. For his alibi to hold up, he can't be seen coming back from committing the murders. So on this problem, too, his mind is racing, trying to figure out how he'll deal with an untoward development that could ruin everything.

You will forgive him then, so to speak, if he can't spare a thought for what he's just done, for the carnage he's left in his wake—he's got more pressing issues to take care of. Then again, you wonder: Has what he's done already started to sink in? That parting image of Nicole, the last look in her eyes, or the sight of her near-severed head, should be etched in his mind for eternity. The return journey from Bundy to Rockingham, albeit brief, is still enough time for the realization to dawn of just what he's done; to start wishing he could go back in time and *un*do it. It would be so near and yet so far—so irreversible. Or maybe not; maybe he's still pumped, still focused on the increasingly difficult task at hand, as deaf to any feelings of remorse as he would be to the crowd noise in a hostile stadium, as he hears the quarterback change the play at the line of scrimmage, listens for the snap count, and prepares to take the handoff with the game on the line.

CHAPTER 6

RESURFACING

Let's leave Simpson to his sea of troubles for a while and cut away to where he'll soon arrive: his gated Rockingham estate. There, all is calm, or pretty much so. Kato's on the phone with his girlfriend, Rachel Ferrara, but he's in his semidetached guest room way at the back of this spacious property, and he's soft-spoken; his words don't carry far. Otherwise, except for Chachi, Simpson's old arthritic hound, the grounds proper are deserted; the lights are out, and to a would-be caller it appears that no one's there. And so it would seem to limousine driver Allan Park when he first arrives. As mentioned, Park is very early; though Simpson has asked to be picked up at 10:45 p.m., he's arrived at around 10:20. The reason is that he is unfamiliar with the neighborhood and wants to be extra sure that nothing goes wrong with such a famous client, so he's left himself a large margin for error. It is a bit ironic that the very celebrity that later would help get Simpson off would here help ruin his alibi.

As it happens, Park approaches Simpson's place from the south, which would put the property on his right-hand side. At first he goes quite slowly; he hasn't been given directions, and he's checking out the numbers on the curb, looking for 360. After he sees a couple and gets his numerical bearings, he speeds up a bit. Then he catches sight of the 360 on the curb, just to the north of where the Bronco will later be parked. There's one problem though—at least for Simpson: it's shortly after 10:20 p.m., and the Bronco isn't there. Park continues on. The estate, as he perhaps discovers now, is on a corner lot, so he turns right on Ashford and coasts on by the other driveway entrance on that side; then he does a U-turn, comes back, and parks opposite the Ashford gate, where he'll while away the next fifteen minutes smoking a cigarette and listening to the radio. At about 10:39 he decides to check out the Rockingham entrance once more. The basic layout of the estate's front yard is pretty easy to grasp: the house faces Rockingham to the west, and the driveway runs in a kind of L-shape from the Ashford gate on the north side straight across the front of the house to where it turns at a ninety-degree angle at the southern end of the property and runs west to the Rockingham gate. Park wants to see whether that gate provides easier access for his ungainly white stretch limo. This time, as he approaches he's got the curb on his left and an even clearer view both of the 360 on the curb—and the fact that there's no Bronco anywhere to be seen. He also discovers that the Rockingham entrance is too tight a turn for the limo to negotiate, so he retreats to the Ashford entrance and this time pulls right up to the gate. The result is that when he parks he is facing straight down the driveway, which passes right in front of the main entrance near that north end of the house. Allan Park—so aptly named—an agent unawares of all-seeing Nemesis; predestined destroyer of Simpson's alibi.[1]

---

1 Park's fortuitously appropriate name is something Herodotus would have seized on. A significant name in a situation where a crime is thwarted or requited in some way is always, at least potentially, a calling card of nemesis and demonstration of its all-embracing power—that others, at least, might in future pay heed.

After Park has pulled up to the gate, he does start to disturb the calm a bit, though no one else can hear, by getting out of the car and ringing the buzzer, which makes a loud noise and activates a phone within the house whose ring can be heard all the way out on the street. Then, when no one answers, he calls his boss, Dale St. John, on his pager. The telephone records clearly demonstrate that this occurs at 10:43:44 p.m. He then exits the car and rings the buzzer a few more times, to no avail. Then, from 10:46:30 to 10:48:50 he's on the phone with his mother, trying to get his boss's home number—while his boss is trying to reach him and getting a busy signal. Then he calls St. John again at 10:49:07 and lets the phone ring for fifty-nine seconds, but he gets no answer. Unfortunately, St. John is again getting a busy signal while trying to reach him. It's like a scene from a French farce, except there's nothing farcical about what's just occurred a few miles away. Anyway, Park is back at the gate pressing the buzzer a few more times when he hears his cell phone ring inside the car; it's 10:52:17. So he gets back in and answers; it's his boss, finally, who tells him Simpson frequently runs late and he should wait till 11:15 and then leave if he still hasn't shown up. Then, suddenly, as they talk, Park sees this white male come out from the back of the house and head down the driveway to the far side of the property. He tells St. John "Somebody's here" and then hangs up the phone, at 10:55:12, about thirty seconds after Kato's passed by.

What he sees next we already know. But before I revisit that and then go on to what ensues, I will need to get back to where we left Simpson, on his way back from Bundy, and bring him up to speed. Even prior to that, however, we need a more general break in the action. We will consider what's at issue as regards the second of the two major mysteries I claimed I would solve concerning that night: the three distinct and methodical "thumps" that Kato Kaelin says he heard outside his room. This is a complicated matter too, and various explanations have been proposed that need to be dissected and rejected before I introduce mine. So let's press Pause for a while on the passage of time; that way the action, when it resumes, can run the more smooth and uninterrupted.

Thumps in the Night

Along with Allan Park, Kato Kaelin was the most-key witness for both the State of California and later the plaintiffs in the O. J. Simpson trials. But whereas Park was the straightforward and reliable All-American boy, the ideal witness, Kato Kaelin seemed to be, well, the typical West Coast zoned-out slacker, someone whose powers of observation and recollection you'd have a tendency to doubt.[2] Thus the considerable lengths that Daniel Petrocelli had to go to, in court and in his book, in order to establish Kato's credibility and reliability as a witness despite his beach-boy looks, hanger-on-to-the-rich-and-famous reputation, and tendency to speak in sometimes hard-to-follow sentence fragments. He also, perhaps, had to counter the impression left by Marcia Clark, who, in frustration at Kato's reluctance to be as forthcoming as she thought he could be, had had him declared a hostile witness. Yet even Petrocelli had a problem with Kato as regards the "three thumps" portion of his testimony, because he described the sounds he heard as dull, but heavy, thumps and as occurring at regular or roughly regular intervals. In relating his direct examination of Kato at the civil trial, Petrocelli writes: "The three thumps, Kato said, were 'like someone falling back behind my bedroom wall.' (In fact, I tried to stay away from the term *thump* altogether; it had become an infamous term, and it was misleading, because it didn't describe the actual sound made by the crashing impact.) He hadn't said that in the criminal trial, and I did a little preemptive strike by having Kato pound the witness stand with his

2 In point of fact, Kato does not drink or use drugs—or, at least, he didn't back then.

fist and explain the 'rhythm and volume' of these noises, knowing he would be slammed in Baker's cross-examination due to his several prior testimonies."[3]

Bob Baker, who was Simpson's lead attorney in the civil trial, seems in fact not to have slammed Kato on this point in his cross-examination; at least, Petrocelli does not include it if he did. However, he does describe both Baker and his client as snickering when Kato earlier demonstrated these sounds at his deposition, which he did by crashing his body three times against the wall of the room, as he'd already done for Petrocelli's benefit when they prepared, to illustrate the description he was now providing, that it sounded "like someone falling against the wall."[4] And the point of their snickering, as Petrocelli explains, was the imputation that, what with the marked anti-Simpson reaction after his criminal-trial acquittal, Kato was trying to curry favor with the public by embellishing his testimony with comments like this that would be helpful to the plaintiffs. Indeed, Marcia Clark remarks with some bitterness on how he would later "volunteer" this analogy to a body falling against a wall for the benefit of the plaintiffs when he wouldn't do it for her;[5] meaning, however, that he could have said this all along, not that he was now making it up.

There is also the problem that before the grand jury and at the criminal trial Kato demonstrated how the thumps sounded by knocking three times on the witness box, which produced a thinner and more hollow sound than that of a body hitting a wall or what could be described as a *thump*, which is the word, however, he insisted on using all along. He also insisted all along that the wall was given a series of powerful jolts that made him wonder—as he immediately did out loud to his girlfriend, whom he was talking

3 *Triumph of Justice*, 454.

4 *Ibid*, 204.

5 *Without a Doubt*, 59.

to on the phone, and soon after that to the limo driver—if an earthquake had occurred. And in his deposition to Petrocelli he describes it as a "thick sound" that moved from his right to his left, "as if a body hit the back of the wall."[6] As for the discrepancy, then, in the sounds, he explains in the civil deposition that he thought he was being asked in the criminal trial "to demonstrate the rhythm of the sounds. *Bah, bum-bum*. I just thought they wanted to know, sort of, the pattern, or the rhythm."[7] It sounds like a bit of a lame excuse, just as the knocking was a lame attempt to capture what he'd heard. Perhaps he *was* trying not to appear too blatantly supportive of the prosecution, or perhaps he was just too shy to get up and attempt, before a crowded courtroom, a more vigorous replication of the sound, which would be in keeping with his usual diffident demeanor. Or, perhaps, that *is* what he thought he was doing, reproducing the cadence and assuming that, with the help of his verbal description of a set of jarring thumps, his listeners would supply what he left out: a much heavier version of that beat.

What I want to go back to, however, is Petrocelli's insistence that the word *thump* had to be wrong, that "it was misleading because it didn't describe the actual sound made by the crashing impact." This is a pretty bold claim—that, despite your not having been there, you know better than your witness what sort of sound he actually heard that night. It's based in part, perhaps, on a general tendency to discount the abilities of Kato Kaelin either to remember accurately or to describe adequately what he had witnessed; Petrocelli, albeit understandably, seems to have subscribed to it himself to some degree, despite all that he writes elsewhere in support of this witness. But the main basis for his rejecting the word *thump* is the generally held assumption (by those who think Simpson is guilty) that the

6 *Triumph of Justice*, 204.

7 *Ibid*, 204.

noises Kato heard were the sound of O. J. Simpson somehow either stumbling heavily into the wall or, more probably, colliding by accident with the air conditioner that jutted out from the wall into the walkway space at the approximate point where these noises seemed to come from. This was precisely where the right-hand glove was found, on the ground, about a foot or two in front of the air conditioner. Or it might have been some combination of the previous two explanations as, for instance, in Marcia Clark's summation: "The defendant came back from Bundy in a hurry. Ron Goldman upset his plans, and things took a little longer than anticipated. He ran back behind the house, that dark, narrow south pathway … thinking he could get rid of the glove, the knife, in that dirt area in the back … But he was in a hurry. He was moving quickly down a dark, narrow pathway overhung with trees, strewn with leaves, and in his haste he ran right into that air conditioner … And [that] caused him to fall against the wall, making the wall of Kato's room shake …"[8] Then, of course, he aborted these plans (for concealing the knife and glove) and beat a hasty retreat to the front of the yard, where, on this theory, he'd have had to come up with a different way to get rid of this damning evidence.

Petrocelli certainly assumed much the same about the collision: that it was accidental, that it caused the glove to fall, and that it set in train the sequence of sounds that Kato heard. And he probably assumed the same motivation for Simpson's being back there: to conceal evidence—though, unless I've missed something, he didn't ever come out and say so. Here, as in many other aspects of the case, he didn't explain to the jury precisely how or why something occurred if he didn't think he had to, the intention being to avoid as much as possible the impression that his case was based on speculation and not known facts. When, during Baker's cross-examination, Dr. Spitz

8 *Without a Doubt*, 462.

seemed for a moment in danger of being too confident in his abilities to reconstruct the entire murder sequence blow by blow—rather than merely delivering his opinion on the approximate length of the struggle and the causes of the cuts and gouges on Simpson's hands—Petrocelli and his colleague, Ed Medvene, cringed inside: "We had based our presentation of this case on the credo Less is More. We were not planning to tell the jury exactly how Simpson got to the property; we were not planning to tell them exactly which route he took home. We were not planning to detail how the murders went down, or how he disposed of the murder weapon, or where the murder clothes were. We didn't have to prove any of these things in order to win our case. Those were details that we would never know, details that Simpson was keeping to himself."[9] Clearly it was the wisest course and one vindicated by the verdict in the trial. But, equally clearly, this course was considerably less feasible in the criminal trial where at every turn the prosecution had to fend off the defense's theory of a police conspiracy and the planting of evidence. Any failure to attempt to explain virtually every detail could be seized upon by a predominantly hostile jury as further proof that "something was wrong" and as somehow pointing to the "holes" in the police's diabolically elaborate frame-up.

But, if Petrocelli declined to theorize why Simpson was in the south walkway, he still had the problem he acknowledged of how Kato describes the sounds he heard that night. For, if Simpson had in fact run into the air conditioner, there would not have been a heavy thump, let alone three discrete or methodical heavy thumps; there would have been something more like the crashing sound that Petrocelli took the liberty of insisting Kato actually heard. Interestingly, however, he never spelled out any scenario involving the air conditioner, though he never explicitly excluded it, either. But

9 *Triumph of Justice*, 434.

he seemed to have trouble with the idea that Simpson's accidentally running into it would have produced the series of noises that Kato described and a heavy impact that, again by Kato's testimony, was almost flush against the wall, rather than into the side of the air conditioner with a resulting (and hard to imagine) carom or two off the wall. So, in his book at least, he has floated a suggestion for how Simpson might have acquired the necessary direction and momentum to take him squarely and heavily into the wall: "These three thumps were important; they were the sound of Simpson returning from the murders at Bundy. Directly opposite the back of Kato's room was a five-foot-high wire chain-link fence with enough space between its top and the thick foliage above it for a man to climb through and over. The ground on the property next door was a couple of feet lower than it was on the Simpson side, so if an agitated man were scaling the fence and jumping down in the dark, he might well misjudge the fall, lose his footing, and bump into the building before he righted himself. He could easily drop a glove."[10] I assume he also made this suggestion to the jury, though he doesn't say so in his book. The book, however, conflates such things as his team's collection of evidence, the depositions, the trial, and even his own thought processes in order to minimize repetition.

As for his suggested theory, however, for how these so-called thumps occurred (which the criminal prosecution also entertained, though it was not used in Clark's summation), while it has the merit of recognizing that a better explanation is needed to account for the sounds as Kato describes them, it raises more problems than it tries to resolve. I mean, why would Simpson take the route through his neighbor's yard when he doesn't have to? The limo driver is not going to see him in the dark, and at that distance, from where he's parked on the opposite side of the property, especially with Simpson wearing

---

10 *Ibid*, 204.

dark sweats. And, even if he did use his neighbor's yard, why would he try to climb over the fence right opposite Kato's room, who he has reason to think is still there, and risk being heard? As he approached, he may even have heard Kato talking on the phone, through the two screen windows on that side of the room, which would have been lit up to some degree. Why would he not choose to scale the fence at an earlier or later point? Furthermore, there's the trail of his own blood leading from where he parked the Bronco by the Rockingham gate on up the driveway. Doesn't that tell us the route he took, excluding the return side trip up the walkway that leaves no connecting trail (which I'll later address)? Though his blood is found back there as well, and not just on the glove—it's on the air conditioner and on a nearby cable that runs along the ground near the wall.

If, however, he went through his neighbor's yard, then why is there no blood trail to support this—if not in the yard, then at least on the street, or at the entrance to the driveway, and leading toward his neighbor's property? Or surely there would be some on the fence—seven feet high, in effect—on his neighbor's side? If he hauled his two-hundred-plus pounds over that, he would have had to use both hands, and the blood, you'd think, would have practically spurted out of that one deep cut and onto the fence and ground, where it would have been found. As well, the fence was covered with and closely overhung by foliage, none of which showed damage the following day; nor did he have any scratches. This theory involving the neighbor's yard, then, is unsupported by the evidence; indeed, it is refuted by the unbroken foliage and the want of any blood on the fence. Again, I have a different theory, which does fit all the evidence, but which prima facie might seem strained, in that I think the thumps were deliberate. I'll explain, beginning again with the premeditation factor and its logical implications, which here serve not to suggest why he was back there, but rather to eliminate the usual supposition.

As indicated, the prosecution's explanation in the criminal trial for what Simpson was doing on the walkway is that he was intending to bury such things as the knife and bloody clothes in a dirt area to the rear of his property. Most people who believe him guilty probably subscribe to this theory. But in the prosecution's case, and that of Petrocelli too, perhaps to an even greater extent, this is inconsistent with their portrayal of Simpson as a really smart guy—thus the well-constructed virtual alibi. They color him a truly formidable adversary, who knew the case against him cold as well as all the relevant legal issues, and who was, in fact, the one ultimately calling the shots for the defense. But if they really think that, then they should give him his proper due. A guy that smart, who's planning to murder his wife, who's got Simpson's record of spousal abuse, and who would have obsessed about every detail as regards both the deed and the getting away with it, is not going to be planning to dispose of anything incriminating on his own property—not when he knows (if only from airport departures—his signature activity, thanks to Hertz) what metal detectors can do. So he can't have been heading down the walkway for that reason, unless he was a fool. Nor do the unforeseen delays, with the result that the limo's already there, make a whit of difference, at least as concerns his plans, long since in place, for disposing of the bloody clothes (most likely at the airport in Los Angeles) and the knife (most likely in Chicago). It only endangers his alibi that he was sleeping all the while. In order for it to hold up, he can't be seen coming back from committing the crime.

That said, let's return to where we left him on his drive home from Bundy. As stated, one of the major problems he is facing is that he knows he's running late and that the limo has likely arrived, as ordered, at 10:45 p.m., if not a little earlier. It's the fourth major untoward development of that evening (that he's aware of. The others, in order, are: Kato's inviting himself along, the arrival of Ron Goldman, and the cuts[11]). He also expects the limo to be by the Ashford gate, where it usually picks him up. It's on Ashford as well that he almost always parks the Bronco, including when he'd returned from his golf game that afternoon, the last time he'd used it prior to heading for Bundy. This circumstance will necessitate a convoluted explanation involving his golf clubs, and contradicting what he'd first told the police, for why he went out some time after his daughter's recital and moved it to Rockingham.[12] And it's where, ideally, he would park it when he returns from the scene of the crime, so that the limo driver can see it sitting there innocently and as per usual when he arrives. But conditions aren't ideal: he's late. So instead he goes straight to the Rockingham gate from the direction facing Ashford, with his lights off and then the motor too, perhaps, as he cuts the engine and coasts to a stop to minimize any chance of being noticed. (But in that case, he won't be able, should he want, to correct the slightly awkward angle that he's parked at without restarting the car—which oddity would catch Mark Fuhrman's trained eye a few hours later that night).

Then, when he gets out of the car and enters the grounds,[13] his expectations are confirmed—and in the worst way: the limo's

11 The dog's alarmed and alarming reaction might have been a fifth such untoward development (second in sequence) to delay or alter his plans.

12 It goes as follows, as neatly summarized by Daniel Petrocelli: "His story was that he needed his golf clubs, so he walked to the car, opened the gate, drove into the compound, unloaded, drove out the other way, walked back, and closed the gate behind him. Of course, that was a longer trip than simply going to his Bronco on Ashford and carrying the bags back, and he could easily have backed out and left the car in the more convenient spot where he usually parked, on Ashford" (*Triumph of Justice*, 504).

13 As stated, it's conceivable that some of the blood on the Bronco door, inside and out, was transferred at this point. And the same goes with the headlight button: he may have been turning it off with his left hand as he approached his home.

not just parked on the driveway outside the Ashford gate; it's facing toward the house, right where he has to pass to enter. It's a potential disaster. What he does next is hard to say. But, since he's anticipated this new problem, at least to some degree, he may have already worked out a plan.[14] Even so, it's unlikely that he immediately carries it out. Why not see first what the limo driver is up to? Maybe he's leaning on his car and looking the other way. It's dark, and at the distance he is from the Ashford gate, with various shrubs and trees in between, it's safe to advance up that leg of the driveway past where the Bentley is parked to where it meets the north-south leg. As the blood drops on the driveway indicate, which have trailed him right from where he got out of the Bronco, he doesn't even use the Bentley for cover but passes it on the side facing Ashford and the limo.[15] It's probably at the bend in the driveway that he pauses to take stock of the situation, tries to make out exactly where the limo driver is and what he's up to, or waits in vain to see if he'll turn his back. As we've seen, Park is at this point alternately behind the wheel calling his boss or his mother on his cell phone, or at the gate repeatedly pressing the buzzer, anxious that nothing go wrong. Perhaps a precious minute

---

14 There was a safe and little-known route through the yard of Simpson's neighbor in the back: a path that led to the tennis court gate at the rear of his property. Given the circumstances, however, it was not the option Robert Kardashian once thought (see *American Tragedy*, 145). There was no time to walk around the block and enter from the back—and maybe be seen en route—and he couldn't park the Bronco on the next street over without compromising his alibi. Interestingly, these obstacles are surmounted in his recent "confession," thanks to the aid of imaginary friend and accomplice Charlie, who drops Simpson off on that next street over, then drives back to Rockford and parks the Bronco—and then, of course, vanishes into the same thin air he first emerged from (see *If I Did It: Confessions of the Killer*, 137).

15 The at times irregular spacing of these drops may be accounted for by Dennis Fung's not recovering all the drops Fuhrman and Roberts had discovered and marked; instead, to their considerable dismay, he only recovered every fourth or fifth one (*Murder in Brentwood*, 39).

or two pass in this fashion, with no clear opportunity to enter, or perhaps Simpson can't see clearly enough to be sure. Then, if he hasn't already thought it out on the ride home, he gets an idea for how he might distract the guy's attention. Hopefully Kato is still in his room, where he was headed when Simpson last saw him, just over an hour ago. If he can get him somehow to come to the front where the limo driver is, he'll surely see the guy and let him in, and for a moment they'll be engaged in conversation—Kato with his back to him, O. J.; and the limo driver still facing toward him, to be sure, but not seeing him, because his eyes are focused on the foreground, on Kato, as he explains why he's there and asks where O. J. is. And in that moment he, O. J., will be right in front of him, visible but not seen, as he enters the house. Or maybe it's a moment later, when the driver turns to go back to the car; maybe he waits and enters then.

So O. J. heads down the walkway toward Kato's room with a plan for how he'll get his attention if he's in.[16] This is, as you may have already surmised, by pounding on the wall of his room as heavily as he can, so that Kato will be alarmed enough to try to find out the cause. And though there are windows on that side, it's far too dark in that walkway area. In order to check things out properly, he'll have to go around by the far side of the house (the Ashford side) and enter it from the front, where O. J. did. He, meanwhile, will have returned to the front yard and be lurking

---

16 For the record, there were two doors that led inside the house along the south pathway. But, as Marcia Clark ascertained, neither was operable. "One of them, which led into the garage, had been blocked from the inside by a large dresser that supported a television set. The other, which led into the laundry room, was kept bolted from the inside and blocked by a stepladder and a laundry basket" (*Without a Doubt*, 303–4). Simpson clearly never imagined he'd be running this late, or he might have arranged to give himself the option of one of these doors. But, of course, he'd never have undertaken the operation if he'd thought there was any chance he'd be cutting it this close.

in the shadows, waiting for Kato to notice, or be hailed by, the driver as he passes by the Ashford gate. But right now O. J. is heading down the dark walkway, and with him he's got the still-open bag with the bloody clothes and weapon inside, including the remaining glove, which sits atop the pile. He has also at some point shifted the bag from his right hand to his left, gripping it in such a way—by the edge of its open mouth, perhaps—that his cuts once again bleed into or onto the bag, and thus don't leave a trail (the absence of which would be cited by the defense as one more proof that something was wrong and thus that the glove was planted[17]). Not that he plans it that way, unless it's finally dawned on him that he might be leaving a trail. Most likely he does it at random, or because he's already preparing for how he'll use this bag once he reaches Kato's room.

Now it's quite possible even in this scenario that he, or the bag, does bump into the air conditioner by accident and that this causes the glove to fall out. This would not, however, produce anything at all like the sounds that Kato describes. But again in this scenario, his goal is Kato's room and not the dirt area further back, so he isn't going to be hastening on by. And, even if he can't make out the air conditioner or has forgotten it is there, he should have a rough sense of where he is, especially since a bit of light from Kato's room would be shining out through one or both of the screen windows on that side; and, as mentioned, he might be able to hear him on the phone as he approaches. So, what I think happens is this: As Simpson nears the room, his pace becomes slower and stealthier. He doesn't want to be heard just yet, and he's also listening for signs that Kato is in. Thus, if

17 During the criminal trial the jury was taken on a tour of both Bundy and Rockingham. Schiller and Willwerth describe how eager the defense team was "for the jury to see where the bloody glove was found, far away from Simpson's alleged blood trail at the house" (*American Tragedy*, 470).

there is any contact with the air conditioner, the impact is slight; indeed, he's probably coming to a halt at roughly this point. Then, when he confirms that Kato's there, he makes sure he gets his attention, by driving his shoulder or forearm three times in rapid succession into either the air conditioner's outer facing or the wall right beside it. Most likely it is the wall, as Kato thought he heard—and felt—because I think Simpson wants to produce a jarring thud that will startle Kato but at the same time be a dull, muffled sound that won't reach the limo driver's ears, who might then be the more intent on peering in the direction the sound had come from—and the wall would be better for that. Also, in that narrow walkway, and especially if he uses his shoulder, the wall allows more of a run prior to impact.

Meanwhile, to muffle the sound even more, and perhaps to forestall any bruising he might be asked about later, he positions the bag over one forearm or against an upper arm and shoulder—the right one likely, in either case, since that's his stronger side—gripping it with his left hand as he does by its still-open mouth, so that he continues not to drip any blood on the ground. Then he delivers the three forearm smashes or driving football-style blocks that cause the entire room to shake, including, according to Kato, one of the pictures on the wall. These heavy impacts would also have sent a few blood drops flying from his hand, which would explain why his blood is on the air conditioner and on the cable that runs along the base of the wall.

But, more important, it's then, I suspect, as he pounds the wall, and as Kato reacts with alarm, that the other glove, which wasn't ejected at Bundy and is now at the top of the pile, falls out and to the ground—again, unseen in the dark. It's the most dramatic piece of evidence in the case, both on account of what it really is—an unmistakable, if mute, witness to the murderer's identity (indeed, it amounts to an abstract of all the blood, hair, and fiber evidence[18])—and because of the defense's claim that it's being there was just too pat, too good to be true, *too* inexplicable; so of course it had to have been planted by detective Mark Fuhrman. Which claim, absurd though it may be, benefited from the absence of a more credible explanation on the part of the prosecution for why Simpson was back there and how the three thumps as Kato describes them—heavy, at distinct intervals, and flush against the wall—could have occurred. The jurors, sympathetic as most of them were to the accused, would seize on any weakness, real or imagined, in the prosecution's case as grounds for their claiming to have reasonable doubts. Interestingly, in *American Tragedy*, we learn that the Dream Team *was* theorizing that the thumps were intended as a signal, or designed to get Kato's attention, but dropped the idea when it was ascertained that Mark Fuhrman couldn't possibly have been at 360 Rockingham at 10:51 p.m., the time they occurred.[19]

O. J., when he's finished pounding, heads back quickly to the front to prepare to enter his house as occasion permits. While he waits in the shadows for Kato to arrive, he very carefully removes the knife from the duffel bag, where it sits atop the pile, picking it up with whatever he had with him for this purpose—a handkerchief or maybe some sort of pincers or tongs—and then puts it and what he's removed it with into a smaller, sealable airtight container for

---

18 There are: (forcibly removed) hairs from Nicole, one with her blood on it; hairs from Ron; hairs from Simpson; fibers consistent with hairs from Ron's shirt; hairs from the Akita; fibers from the Bronco's carpet; and blue-black cotton fibers consistent with similar fibers found on Ron's shirt—and, no doubt, with Simpson's long-gone sweats; finally, there's his blood and that of both victims.

19 *American Tragedy*, 527. Fuhrman, who was on backup duty that night, was at home and asleep on the other side of town when he received the call about the murder at 1:05 a.m. He'd been at an officers' party in Palm Springs earlier that evening.

insertion into one of the zippered pockets on his golf bag.[20] He might also remove his Bruno Maglis at this point and jam them into the duffel bag.[21] However, so far as I know, the socks he was wearing, which we'll see were found unwashed on the floor of his master bedroom, did not have any grass stains on them or dirt, as should have been the case had he walked across the grass and driveway in his stocking feet. Either way, after removing the knife, he finally zips up or straps down the mouth of the bag and lays it on the grass near the Bentley. This, of course, is another tactic that would not have been part of his original plan. He'd intended to be home well in advance of the limo driver and to pack this smaller bag inside one of the other bags that are already sitting on his front porch. Now he can't do that without the driver seeing, or at least wondering, what he's up to. Why he doesn't just carry the bag with him into the house isn't clear. Maybe he's worried about some of his victims' blood being on its outer surface and thus a possible transfer.

Kato, meanwhile, does emerge from behind the house some two to three minutes after he hears the thumps, dim flashlight in hand, and on cue as per O. J.'s impromptu plan. But Kato, intent as he is on the thumps—Simpson, if my theory's true, must have just about snapped at this—only waves at the limo driver (who in the meantime has got back in his car to answer his phone and doesn't call out) and then continues along the front of the house to the south walkway, where he starts poking around. O. J., finally, can't wait any longer for his blocking to form. He makes his move, hoping (but not likely praying) he'll catch a break. Which he doesn't—

20 If the plan had been to boil the knife at home as a further precaution, this step was likely abandoned by this point due to time constraints; but possibly not.

21 Petrocelli thinks that when the bag was left on the lawn it probably contained the murder weapon and the shoes (*Ibid*, 518); but it's not clear if he thinks the shoes were removed at this juncture.

the driver, Allan Park, who is still sitting in the limo talking on the phone to his boss, and who has just noticed Kaelin come by, sees—as earlier described—this African American, about six feet tall, two hundred pounds, and wearing dark clothing, walk across the driveway from the direction of the Bentley and into the house. Then the lights come on inside. The driver hangs up, gets out of the car, and buzzes again at the gate. And Simpson finally answers: "I'm sorry; I overslept. I just got out of the shower and I'll be down in a minute." Significantly, he doesn't buzz him in—his normal practice with the regular driver.

Before Simpson can emerge a few minutes later, Kato returns from the walkway area (he only went a few steps up the dark path and then thought better of it) and lets the driver in; then he starts back to check out the walkway, gets scared again, and returns. When Simpson reappears, he is wearing a blue jeans pants-and-shirt outfit and carrying a Louis Vuitton bag, which he sets down on the porch next to his suit bag and grip. He then goes to get his cell phone from the Bronco—according to what he first said to the police. Unfortunately, that would place him in the Bronco at 10:03 p.m. when, as phone records show, he tried to call Paula Barbieri from this cell, so he later "corrected" that to his "cell phone accessories."[22] Meanwhile, as Kato and Park are putting this luggage, including the golf bag, into the limo, Park notices a fifth item, a small, dark bag (or "knapsack-type bag" as Kato describes it) sitting on the grass at the edge of the driveway near where the Bentley is parked, and

---

22 Kato, too, saw Simpson entering the house dressed in a dark sweat suit. Unfortunately, he can't recall whether this was after his first trip up the walkway, when the limo was parked outside, or sometime after the second trip, when the limo had been buzzed in. As Daniel Petrocelli explains, if it was after the first trip, that was incriminating and backed up Park's testimony; but if it was after the second, then Simpson could say that Kato saw him when he was coming back from getting his cell phone accessories from the Bronco and was simply mistaken as to what he was wearing (*Triumph of Justice*, 206).

thus a little back from where he had just seen the six-foot African-American emerge. Kato offers to get it, but (according to both him and Park) Simpson quickly overtakes Kato and says something like, "No, no, no. That's okay, that's okay. I'll get the bag—don't worry about it—I'll get it." He does that and then puts it into the limo.

Kato then tells Simpson about the alarming thumps and asks for a flashlight (presumably with a more powerful beam than the one he already has). They go into the house and are starting to look for one in the kitchen, when Simpson abruptly says it's too late for that; he then gets into the limo and leaves. He also tells Kato not to bother calling either the police or Westec, the private security firm that he employs.

Meanwhile, that's the last we see of this bag. Park doesn't remember exactly where in the limo Simpson put it and at the airport, by the time Park has got hold of a luggage cart, there are only four bags to load, and *it* isn't one of them. Simpson will later claim in his civil trial deposition that he put it in the golf bag while consolidating luggage. But, since the golf bag was in the trunk, he either did that before leaving Rockingham and neither Park nor Kato noticed—which is highly unlikely, especially when he'd called attention to himself by insisting on picking it up—or at the airport, while Park was fetching the cart. Park, meanwhile, has testified that on the trip to the airport Simpson "seemed to be bending down, working with his bags." Was he in fact "consolidating" the small, dark bag into one of the other bags, the ones he still had with him in the back seat? If so, why not say so and be truthful when you can, rather than make up a lie about the golf bag? Unless, of course, you're trying to counter the driver's testimony that would seem to suggest you were up to something in the back seat. Perhaps he was, among other things, checking inside this bag, in better light at last, to see if everything that should be there was there. If that was the case, he may for the first time have noticed that the gloves and knit cap were missing. Not that he could rummage about in the bag to see if they'd slipped or been jammed down the sides, because he might come in contact with blood. But he could be holding it as wide open as possible and turning it round to let in the light on every side. Park also testified that Simpson complained as they drove about being hot, though it was unseasonably cool that night, and that he rolled the window down and turned on the air-conditioning. That he'd just committed a brutal double murder suffices to explain his overheated condition, despite the fact that he'd showered when he got home. But if he's also panicking because he can't see any sign of the gloves and cap, and not breathing properly as his anxiety mounts, that would further overheat him.

In any case, when Park returns with the luggage cart, the small, dark bag is nowhere in sight. It's either packed away to be disposed of in Chicago or, more likely, it's already been discarded in a curbside trash can. The latter would fit with statements made to the police by a certain Ralph Junis. He claims he "saw Simpson arrive at LAX [Los Angeles International Airport] in a limousine, put a travel bag on top of a trash can at the airline terminal entrance, and then reach into the trash can."[23] But when the police check the trash can within a few days of the murders, it's already been emptied.

Junis wasn't called by the prosecution at the criminal trial because, according to detectives Vannater and Lange when they spoke to Petrocelli, "[Marcia] Clark didn't, as a general rule, like 'one-on-one witnesses,' meaning people whose testimony could not be corroborated."[24] Clark did, however, use James Williams, the LAX skycap who checked the bags through. He never saw the small, dark bag. Also, he confirmed that there was a trash can near where he worked. Clark didn't ask anything further, thereby laying a trap

23 *Ibid*, 73.
24 *Ibid*, 74.

for the defense. When Dream Team counsel Carl Douglas asked sarcastically if Williams ever saw Simpson near the trash can, he was told "Yes, he was standing near [it],"[25] thus providing one of the trial's better moments for us fans of the prosecution. Despite that, though, I think the likelier scenario is that Simpson used the outside trash can while the limo driver was busy getting the luggage cart. For, once you're inside at the check-in counter, the circumstances are far harder to control. And the prosecution perhaps thought so too but merely wanted to suggest on the basis of a more unchallengeable witness how the transfer of the bag to an airport trash can might easily have been accomplished at some point.

I would add one thing, though, to these attempts to reconstruct how Simpson got rid of the bag. It goes back to what he was up to in the back seat of the limo when he was bent down doing something with his luggage. What I think he was mainly doing, and according to his original plan, was putting the small, dark bag into a plastic garbage or grocery store-type bag. He wouldn't have wanted an item that might look worth keeping, or as if it might contain something worth keeping, to be spotted when the garbage men emptied the trash can. He would likely have had this plastic bag packed and ready on top of the contents of one of the other bags that he had with him in the back seat. He would then repack this plastic bag, with the small, dark bag now inside it, back into the other (in which sufficient room would have been left), so that the limo driver wouldn't see it when he helped him remove his luggage from the car. Then, when the driver went for the luggage cart, he'd quickly remove it and put it into the trash can, thus getting rid of the bloody clothes (and maybe the shoes).

Ralph Junis, assuming he saw what he claims, made no mention of a plastic bag, or any bag for that matter; he just said he saw

25 *Without a Doubt*, 371.

Simpson reach into the trash can but said nothing about what he put in. He either didn't notice (assuming I'm right on this point) or his view was partially blocked by Simpson's body or by the travel bag he says Simpson placed on top of the trash can.

The weapon, meanwhile, likely goes on to Chicago in the golf bag, which is why, according to James Merrill, the Hertz representative who picked Simpson up at the airport, he insisted on getting it himself from the carousel. And then, as Petrocelli theorizes, once he's retrieved the golf bag, and before he puts it in the trunk of the car that will take him to his hotel, he transfers the knife to one of the other bags, one that he'll take with him to his room. Meanwhile, the golf bag is left in the trunk of the car, which car is to pick him up the next morning for his game.[26] The knife, in all likelihood, next finds itself wrapped in something that masks its shape and feel, stuffed in a plastic bag, and tumbling headlong into a hotel dumpster (perhaps along with the shoes). Or, maybe everything, the small, dark bag as well as the knife, has been disposed of in Chicago: Raymond Kilduff, the Hertz vice-president of sales, who drove Simpson back to the airport the following morning, says his duffel bag seemed "virtually empty," whereas to Merrill, the night before, it had appeared full.

Meanwhile, back at Rockingham, there's some unfinished business. I've covered what he was likely up to as he tried to reenter his home undetected and how the two witnesses say he behaved when he came back out to get in the limo. But I still need to trace as best I can his movements in the few minutes he spent inside; which, among other things, brings me back to the other problem I left him pondering on the drive home: his now bloodied second set of sweats. He needs

---

26 *Triumph of Justice*, 270.

to deal with them—more specifically, to find the time to deal with them, since it's clear they need to be washed.[27]

The first clues as to what he was up to are the blood drops in the foyer inside the front door, which may mean no more than the obvious: he went inside. But it's here, at the latest, that he'd have taken off his shoes and perhaps put them into a waiting plastic bag, for safe insertion in whatever piece of luggage was due to receive the small, dark bag as well. They're loafers, so they're easy to remove, but if he uses his left hand, while his clean right hand holds the bag he's stuffing them into, the exertion, though slight, might yet cause these particular drops. Still, nothing is certain regarding the shoes, and he may have removed them before he entered and disposed of them later in one of the ways I've described. A clearer indicator of his movements is the bloody smudge on the light switch in the maid's ground-floor bathroom and the fresh load of wash, including the dark sweats that Brad Roberts discovered. Simpson likely went straight there from the front door, turned on the light, then took off his sweats and dumped them in the machine. But whether he himself turned on the washing machine at this time is another question, which I'll get to shortly. Either way, he would then go upstairs to his master bedroom to clean up and change. Blood was found in the drains of one of the two master-bedroom sinks and the shower, which confirms what you'd expect—that he showered before getting into the jeans outfit he was wearing when he came back outside.

A pair of dark socks was also found in the bedroom, on the floor at the foot of his bed, in what was otherwise an immaculately tidy room. These were booked as evidence but at first were not thought to be all that significant, since they appeared to be free of blood. Or, as

27 He may have intended to wash them all along but now, due to the delays, did not have the time.

LAPD serologist Greg Matheson wrote at the time regarding blood on the socks: "None obvious." But he also indicated in his notes that they should be tested for blood at a later date, and when they were a few weeks later, they were found to contain several sizable bloodstains, which hadn't been visible under normal light conditions on the dark material. Three of the stains were from Nicole and were on the ankle area of one sock, and three were from Simpson: two on a hem (the upper sock), which he would have gripped to pull the sock down and over the heel, and another on a toe, by which he likely pulled the sock off. Simpson obviously had doffed the socks just prior to entering the shower, and in his haste had left them tossed on the bedroom floor—contrary to what the rest of the room showed to be his normal fastidious habits.

It's odd that he didn't remove the socks with the rest of his clothes and put them in the washing machine; careless haste is probably the best explanation. But he also must have been unaware that his ankle had at some point made contact either with wounded Nicole or with the bloody bottom step she was lying against. Surely if he had noticed some such contact—including her reaching out with a dying hand and touching his ankle—you'd think he would clearly remember and either pack his socks away too in the small, dark bag or at least put them in the wash when he got home—not throw them on the carpet in his own bedroom. Indeed, assuming my theory is right about how he got cut, this transfer to the socks could have occurred when he unexpectedly cut himself on his own knife. Standing, as he would have been, above her on the porch, he might, as he recoiled at the sudden shock, have stumbled backward or sideways down the stairs and brushed against her or the edge of the steps, and, in the rush of alarm he'd be experiencing, not noticed. But also, in his haste and from sheer force of habit, he needlessly got his own blood on these socks by using his left hand. That's not a problem by itself, though it is suspicious, but because her blood is there as well, which he mustn't have known, it's an indelible link between him and her death. And these socks are so poignantly positioned, at the foot of what was once their marriage bed—the final resting place of the last trace of Nicole.

There remains to discuss the wash. As stated, Simpson may or may not have started the machine. If he did, though, he perhaps ran the risk of the churning washer's being heard; the maid's bathroom is at the front of the house, though at the south end, which puts it adjacent to the walkway and away from where the limo is parked. And Kato, who was prowling around in that area after Simpson entered the house, seems to have heard nothing of the sort on a quiet night. The more likely scenario is the one sniffed out by Daniel Petrocelli and his team.[28] When Simpson got to LAX, he called Kato from a pay phone just before midnight, with instructions to turn on the alarm system, which was connected to Westec. Kato had previously never been entrusted with the code, so he wrote down what Simpson recited, went to the front of the house, punched it in on the system's keypad, set the alarm, and then went to bed. Simpson himself admits to making this call.

What's interesting, then, is that the next morning, when the police were by now on the grounds and in possession of a search warrant, Simpson's daughter (from his first marriage) Arnelle let them into the house by the back door—it's just a few steps from her room—and the alarm didn't go off. Or, at least, that's the testimony of the four officers involved, as well as Kato Kaelin, who was with them. Arnelle also lived at Rockingham, in another semidetached guest room just behind Kato's; she had been away since a little after noon on June 12, and didn't return until around 1:30 a.m., when Kato heard her walk by. Arnelle testifies differently, saying that she led detectives Phillips and Lange around the north side to the

28 Cf. *Triumph of Justice*, 277–9.

front of the house, while the other two officers remained behind to question Kato, so that she could turn off the alarm system with the same keypad Kato had used, before she led them in by the front door. There was no such keypad by the back door; you had to go into the bar area for the nearest one, and no one saw Arnelle go there—nor was any alarm registered at Westec.

There was obviously no reason for the four policemen, as well as Kato Kaelin, to lie on so innocuous a point and on a detail they would so distinctly recall (they were entering a potential crime scene where, after Bundy, God knows what horrors awaited). Arnelle was clearly covering up the fact that someone had entered the house after her father had left. We know he called Kato from the airport on a pay phone, so he could easily have called someone else, too—someone who was devoted to him, who was totally loyal, who sided with him completely regarding that "awful" Nicole. Who knows how much he revealed to this person about what he had done, or how he described his predicament. He would, of course, have decided on this course of action, and the need for an accomplice, by the time he got back from Bundy, but the call itself and how he'd *put it*, so to speak, might still have occupied much of his thinking all the way to the airport. My guess is that he said that something really bad had happened but that he otherwise left out a lot, and he asked them to clean up after him, or at least do the wash. It was probably just the latter, though Petrocelli thinks they may have combed the house, wiping up blood spots and picking up strewn garments (though not the socks). But if, as he also argues, they had left the lights off to avoid attracting Kato's attention or maybe the neighbors', there was not enough light to see by—or at least to see blood drops by.

The more likely scenario is someone alone downstairs, in partial possession, at least, of a terrible truth, waiting for the spin cycle to end—or maybe waiting through two agonizing loads of wash. The load of wet laundry that the police found the next day included, besides the dark sweats, some of Arnelle's underwear, and Petrocelli thinks that a second load may have been run after the first as camouflage. But whoever did this wash, it wasn't the maid, Gigi Guarin, who testified in the criminal trial that when she left on Friday all the laundry was dried and folded. She also identified the laundry basket that was visible in the police video of the washing machine as Arnelle's. Arnelle said she hadn't done any laundry since June 9 and hadn't been inside the main house since Saturday night.

Petrocelli suggests three viable candidates for Simpson's accessory after the fact: Arnelle, who was back in her room alone as of 1:30 a.m.; Simpson's longtime friend Al Cowlings, who was also at home and alone after getting back from a party; and Cathy Randa, Simpson's devoted executive assistant, who had served him loyally for over twenty years, who disliked Nicole, and who was also home alone that Sunday night. But it is evident from how he arranges his material whom Petrocelli most suspects: "Who routinely cleans up after Simpson?" he asks at the close of the chapter that details the above; then you turn the page and "Help, Help Me, Randa" is the title of the next. Cathy Randa was a hostile witness to both the prosecution and the plaintiffs in the respective trials. She did, however, admit to getting a message from Simpson sometime Sunday evening on her answering machine (out of fear, thinks Petrocelli, that his or her phone records would confirm it anyway); but she claimed it was afterward taped over. Simpson said he made the call at 7:30 p.m., but there's no record to confirm this. The call might also have been made from the airport, at around 11:30 p.m., on the same pay phone he used to call Kato Kaelin. From all indications, Cathy Randa was a hypercompetent perfectionist, someone Simpson could always rely on to keep the details of his numerous interests and activities in order. But even she—if it was her in the house that night—was too on-edge to wrap things up just right. Whoever it was forgot, in his or her stressed state, to turn the alarm system back on when departing, thus leaving a telltale clue as to his or her involvement. So it's not just O. J. Simpson that the Furies have to visit on their rounds, nor he alone who has good cause to wonder now and then if there's not a higher justice that our crimes cannot elude and if every wrong, no matter how well buried or put behind us, does not somehow resurface in the end.

CHAPTER 7

A CONSTITUENCY OF FOOLS

Once the police had been notified a little after midnight (by Sukru Boztepe, who had a neighbor call 911), events moved swiftly. Clues at Bundy weren't hard to find: the cap and left-hand glove lying between the victims; the large, bloody, slightly pigeon-toed footprints leading away from the body and toward the rear of the property; the telltale blood drops to their left; the blood smudges on the rear gate; the coins in the alley and the blood drop near them, at the point where the killer likely entered his car, or at least where the trail broke off. These were spotted in reasonably short order by the first officers on the scene, Robert Riske and his partner, Miguel Terrazas; later Riske pointed them out to Mark Fuhrman when he arrived at around 2:10 a.m. Others, most notably the bloody fingerprint on the rear gate—never recovered—were discovered by Fuhrman and Brad Roberts, as they combed the premises in search of further clues.

Then, when the group of four detectives—Fuhrman, Ron Phillips, Lange, and Vannater—reached Rockingham just after 5 a.m., where they'd gone to notify Simpson of his ex-wife's death, the trail resumed—the blood trail, that is. While the other three kept ringing in vain at the Ashford gate, Mark Fuhrman strolled over to the Rockingham entrance, where he noticed the Bronco parked slightly askew. This prompted him to take a closer look and, in the predawn light (the sun would rise at 5:42) a reddish-brown spot above the driver's side door handle suddenly caught his eye against the car's clean, white exterior and then three or four vertical brush-like streaks of what also looked like blood on the door sill below.

When this was shown to the others, they decided to enter the grounds; who knew if yet more corpses awaited them there? There was still no response from the main house, but when they went around back they saw signs of life; through a window they could make out a man sleeping in the second of three bungalows (guest houses) on the south side of the property. They pounded on the door, and a sleepy-eyed blond "beach boy" type, about thirty years old, answered the door. He told them Simpson's daughter Arnelle was in the next bungalow (the one furthest from the main dwelling). While the other three roused Arnelle, Fuhrman checked out the "beach boy's" quarters, looking for blood and for shoes with the right kind of sole and asking random questions. "Anything unusual happen last night?" came up in due course, and the answer stopped him cold: several loud and heavy thumps on the wall above the bed at around 10:45 p.m.[1] Leaving the young man with the other detectives, Fuhrman went around to the front to investigate and soon found himself on that dark, narrow walkway, made darker still by overhanging trees. Passing the garage and the main house proper, he was behind what had to be the bungalows when he made that fateful discovery: a dark object on the ground ahead, which he soon saw was a glove, "a right-hand, dark-brown leather glove with something slightly wet-looking on it."[2] It looked very much like the mate of the

1 With the help of the limo driver's cell phone records, this would later be fixed more precisely at 10:51 p.m.

2 *Murder in Brentwood*, 32.

one back at Bundy, as all agreed when they were taken one by one to check it out. By this time, they'd learned too that Simpson was in Chicago, having left for the airport at about 11:00 the previous night. The dog, they knew, had been found wandering the streets at around 10:30 to 10:45 p.m.[3] A viable timeline began to take shape in everyone's mind; they began to think the unthinkable.

Vannater sent Fuhrman back to Bundy, where he confirmed that the two gloves were a likely match—it was around 7:15 a.m. Then he returned with Brad Roberts to Rockingham and parked near the Bronco. While Fuhrman reported to Vannater on the gloves, Roberts checked out the Bronco; by the dawn's early light and by cupping his hands against the window, he saw blood in various places in the interior—specifically, the steering wheel, console, seats, and door panel. He showed Fuhrman and Vannater. Then Roberts, after Vannater had moved away, noticed blood drops on the street, which he and Fuhrman traced from the driver's side of the Bronco right to the gate, then along the driveway to where they stopped just short of the house. They picked up the trail again outside the front door, where Roberts first noticed a drop on the cement outside,[4] and then together they spotted three more drops on the oak floor of the interior foyer. They showed Vannater, who then declared the place a crime scene.[5] What he didn't declare is who the main suspect was

---

3 This time, too, would be adjusted slightly as further information came in. What I'm giving here is what these detectives were working with at the time.

4 The blood drops likely "resume" here because no drops could be recovered from the lawn, which he crossed in the direction of the front door after returning from the walkway and setting the bag down by the Bentley. In any case, he did not walk along the driveway from where it bent to his front door; rather, he took the zigzag route I've described.

5 Marcia Clark attributes the discovery of the blood drops leading from the Bronco along the driveway to the house to Phil Vannater (*Without a Doubt*, 107). She agrees with Fuhrman that it was at this point that he declared the place a crime scene.

at this point. He didn't have to: everyone's thoughts were pretty much in sync.

Simpson, meanwhile, had been notified of his ex-wife's death by Ron Phillips, who called him at his hotel suite in Chicago at around 6:00 a.m. Los Angeles time. Phillips had gotten the number from Cathy Randa (whose name he got from Arnelle). Simpson had left the standard "don't disturb" request with the front desk, but when Phillips explained who he was and the urgent nature of his call, they put him through. Simpson was likely not disturbed by the ring—that is, not woken up. But a chill must have run down his spine as the inevitable suddenly sounded without warning—like the knocking at the gate in *Macbeth*, like the Judgment Day that's to come like a thief in the night. He reacted with appropriate shock and dismay at the news but otherwise, strangely, asked for no further details, such as "How? When? Where?" as most people do in that situation. He then arranged to fly home on the first plane he could catch. When he arrived at Rockingham a little after noon, having been driven from the airport by Cathy Randa and his attorney and business manager, Skip Taft, the place was already surrounded by the various media. They got all they could ask for when Simpson, upon entering on foot through the Ashford gate, was corralled by a uniformed officer and put in handcuffs, mute testimony to the strength of the evidence—what, exactly, the media didn't yet know—that was already pointing at him. To this was added what ought to have been the clincher: "a big old bandage on the middle finger of his left hand," as Phil Vannater would describe the moment to Marcia Clark.[6]

After Simpson was handcuffed, Brad Roberts took control and led him aside by the children's playhouse in the front yard. Simpson wondered why the police were all over his house and grounds (and,

6 *Without a Doubt*, 25.

presumably, not at Bundy solving the crime). So Roberts filled him in: "Where your wife was killed, there was a blood trail. And that blood trail led here."[7] Case closed, or so you'd think. I mean, this was in some ways the nearest thing to the guilty verdict we wanted to hear—and see him hear—but never heard where it really counted: in the criminal trial. He'd been outed, and almost immediately, by a tale writ in fresh blood. What could have been more dramatic?—or more chilling, especially if it was you that had been found out, *and* if you'd enjoyed the stature he had till that moment.

At this point, according to Roberts, Simpson broke into a sweat and started to hyperventilate as he muttered over and over, "Oh man, oh man, oh man." How near he was to confessing we'll never know. Or what was racing through his head at the time. He didn't know about the glove in the walkway by Kato's room, and probably not about the glove and cap at Bundy. But he did know that he'd been bleeding—copiously. Still, was this all they had? In any case, he rallied enough to ask Vannater, who soon took over, to remove the handcuffs—it was embarrassing, what with all the media there and the cameras trained on him. Vannater complied, and by so doing perhaps fanned whatever faint hope Simpson had that he could still pull this off, that his celebrity stature could see him through; and, no doubt, that the evidence was not conclusive. Come on, Juice, you've still got your charm, so use it. You knew at some point it was going to come down to this—that they'd ask some tough questions to see what you'd say and how you'd react. So go with the game plan: be just like you are on TV. They'll eat it up; they always do. Especially these guys, the cops, 'cause they know you're their kind of guy.

Vannater took Simpson down to the Parker Center for questioning; there they were joined by Tom Lange. Howard Weitzman, a one-time criminal defense specialist whom Simpson had contacted on

7 *Murder in Brentwood*, 41.

his way back, and who was present at Rockingham by the time he arrived, went there separately with Skip Taft.[8] Despite Weitzman being there, Simpson waived his right to have him present at his interrogation, lest it look as if he had something to hide, and because he was confident in his abilities to charm the police. And anyway, Weitzman was right outside the door in case he needed him. As it turned out, he didn't, not so much on account of his own abilities, but because Lange and Vannater, (probably out of deference to the fame of their prime suspect) took a very low-key approach. They asked mainly softball questions; they didn't try to pin him down on one version of how and when he got cut or to a specific timeline for his activities after his daughter's recital and until the limo picked him up. They helped him out with answers when he floundered, by interjecting other unrelated questions that let him switch the topic. They didn't confront him when he contradicted himself. Then the interrogation was terminated after a mere—and eerily emblematic—thirty-two minutes (1:35–2:07 p.m.), as Simpson was in the middle of a meandering and essentially noncommittal response to a query about when he last had been at Bundy. The detectives abruptly announced that the interview was over and that they were going to take him to the police photographer to get a shot of, among other things, his cut finger. Amazingly, Simpson got off relatively lightly even here, as he was able, by keeping his fingers pressed together, to conceal two of the three cuts he'd received. The detectives apparently never closely inspected his hands.

There is a tide—a psychological moment—in the affairs of men which, taken at the flood, leads on to such things as a swift resolution of a criminal case; when omitted, that same case is bound in shallows and in miseries. Were Lange and Vannater stranded by

---

8 Weitzman was a former prominent criminal defense attorney who for the prior ten years had been involved with entertainment law. He would soon be replaced by Robert Shapiro.

the ebbing waters? Did they miss their chance to break a vulnerable Simpson? Who can tell? And how many other police officers would have acted that differently? After all, this was the Juice, number thirty-two, a living legend, or what today we'd call a brand or icon. He was a television personality, moreover, someone you thought you knew—not that some celebrities, including some sports stars, aren't jerks. But O. J. wasn't like that. He was always polite in interviews and always had time for the fans; if he said it ain't so, it ain't so. This or, better, some degree of this was almost certainly a contributing factor that day in Simpson's rather tepid interrogation and—more remarkably still—subsequent release; for, after he'd been photographed and a sample'd been taken of his blood, they let him go. He was the prime—nay, the only—suspect in a brutal double homicide; so much for that eloquent blood trail, the gloves and cap, the lack of an alibi, the history of spousal abuse. Marcia Clark, for one, was astounded, as were the rest of the DA's staff. Yes, it was true that he was too famous to try to escape, but she worried about what he'd get up to if he was at large. He now had the opportunity to destroy evidence and intimidate witnesses.[9] Mark Fuhrman was likewise amazed. Vannater and Lange said they wanted to wait forty-eight hours for the results of the DQ alpha DNA tests before they proceeded; he wondered sarcastically how they'd ever arrested anyone before DNA testing came along.[10]

When Simpson was driven home later that day by Robert Kardashian, the place was still surrounded by the media, only more so, to the depth of several blocks. Meanwhile, cops continued to crawl his house and grounds, poking into every nook and cranny, searching

9 Cf. *Without a Doubt*, 25.

10 Cf. *Murder in Brentwood*, 77.

for clues. Incredibly, especially given the seriousness of the crime, the guy who knew where all the eggs were hidden was back in his home, waiting to see what they might overlook. In fact, he was not even waiting; with the police still there, Simpson pulled Kardashian aside into his bedroom walk-in closet and told him, "I want to see if these guys stole anything." He also told him how he kept $8,000 in golf winnings in the closet and, look, now he couldn't find it. This then justified a thorough search of all the drawers to see what was missing, as Simpson kept repeating, "It's not here."

Family, friends and business associates showed up in abundance to lend support. With the police gone, the action centered on the den and its three television screens, all of them turned to coverage of the case. Simpson stared at the screens; for the most part he was sullen and withdrawn, but intermittently he yelled back at the announcers, protesting his innocence, outraged at what they were saying. It's while this was going on that Kato Kaelin arrived back at Rockingham. He had gone to stay with a friend earlier that day, but Cathy Randa had tracked him down, and she and Simpson's attorneys had been pressuring him over the phone, prodding and pulling at his testimony. Then, when that didn't work, they'd literally had him fetched and brought back home, though not to his guest house; instead, he now got to come into Simpson's mansion.

Shortly after Simpson saw that Kato was there, he stated in a strong, clear voice as he stared at the screen, "Kato knows where I was"; then, turning to look at him, he added, "I was home." Kato didn't reply and eventually drifted off to the kitchen. Simpson came in afterward, and they were alone, with O. J. sporting that big, bloody bandage on the one finger that pretty well told you *just* what he'd been up to the previous night. "You saw me go into the house after we got back from McDonald's. Right? You know I was in the house." If Kato caved in, the alibi was restored. It was a terrifying moment for an unassertive, diffident young man. But Kato came through:

"No, O. J., I didn't see you go in." Simpson wheeled and departed, balked yet again in his attempts to quiet a Kato—and maybe for the same reason: their common love for Nicole. Neither the dog nor the man was the aggressive type, but each proved sufficiently true when it came to her. This is one of the ways that nemesis works, one of its channels: the love and devotion that others have for the victim or the wronged. This can help them do what they must to see that justice is done. This was a part of Nicole that Simpson couldn't destroy; one of the ways she could still come back to haunt him.

Kato would be interviewed by Simpson's soon-to-be-new-lead attorney, the smooth and dapper Robert Shapiro, the following day, after which he packed and left Rockingham for good. But the incident above bore out Marcia Clark's fear about the intimidation of witnesses. Though Kato didn't back down, at least on the essential information that he had, there's no doubt many others were contacted regarding any potentially damaging information that they could attest to, especially in the areas of Simpson's past abusive treatment of his wife and his demeanor on that weekend or the weeks leading up to it. And many of them, sadly, would not even need to be pressured; rather, their attitude could be summed up by what Mark Slotkin, a typical Simpson camp follower, yelled at Kato as he departed for his interview with Shapiro: "Get it straight. It's O. J.! It's the Juice, man. Get it straight."[11]

Simpson too had "survived" the night, thanks it seems to a suicide watch mounted by Kardashian and manned by Simpson's sister Shirley Baker and her husband, Benny. Because when he had entered the bathroom around 3 a.m. and she didn't hear the usual sounds, she had called out, "Don't do anything crazy, O. J."—and then, when he didn't respond, "Your kids need you." The silence continued, but then he finally answered. And the next day he told

11 *Triumph of Justice*, 199.

the deeply religious Kardashian that but for what Shirley had said that would have been it; he would have killed himself. He implied that it was a sign from God—and proof of his innocence.

What Simpson really was up to in that bathroom may be readily surmised from his performance the following morning—Tuesday, June 14, day two of his life as a murderer. Kardashian arrived at around 8:30 a.m. to see how he was doing. Simpson was still in bed, sitting up with the television on. He started talking about his interview downtown with the police as if it were only just now sinking in that *he*—can you believe it!—might be a suspect. He then got up and went to the bathroom; Kardashian heard running water. Then Simpson summoned Kardashian, who found him standing in his jockey shorts in a puddle of water, looking bewildered; when he'd turned on the faucet, water had cascaded out onto the floor. In Kardashian's presence, he opened the cabinet under the sink and "discovered" that the elbow pipe was loose. The police had to have done this; they'd been looking for blood! Simpson was horror stricken.

It was quite the act: Simpson knew very well that he was the prime suspect—for good reason—and that the drains in his bathroom were likely to have been checked; the police were looking for someone who they thought, as per his plan, had been covered in blood and who'd had to clean himself off, especially if he was about to board a plane. The reason he'd been in the bathroom during the night was to check things out more thoroughly after the cops and most of his company had left—to try to see what the cops may or may not have found. So he may have discovered that they'd left the elbow pipe loose—or he (re)loosened it himself in preparation for the charade he had in store for the coming morning, when he'd "discover" what they'd been up to and that he was a suspect.[12]

12 My source for this section is Schiller and Willwerth's *American Tragedy*, 32 ff. They do a beautiful job of dryly allowing the facts to speak for themselves.

And that's what Kardashian thought he saw that morning: genuine shock and dismay on Simpson's face. Nor were his suspicions aroused by what came next, when Simpson grabbed the loose pipe, took it to a second sink—which once had been Nicole's and which, as Simpson well knew, had not had its elbow pipe loosened like the other, at least not by him—and started to sluice water through it over and over again, scrubbing as he did so. He was muttering all the while how he couldn't believe the cops had gone this far; he couldn't believe what was going on. With the first sluicing, black sludge poured out from the pipe—something you'd think the cops would have collected to analyze back at the lab (and maybe they did take a sample). But long after that had been removed, he kept scrubbing away and muttering, while Kardashian looked on, alone at first and then with Benny, the brother-in-law. There are stains and then there are stains: the ones you can see and maybe remove, and those "damned" ones that you can never, as Lady Macbeth could attest, rid your mind of—at least by godless means. Simpson by now may have been working on one of the latter kind; if so, it wouldn't go away. In that way, he was stained for life—*and* for afterlife, too, if there is such a thing. Eventually he did stop scrubbing and handed the pipe to Benny to reattach. But meanwhile, the scene spoke volumes for the life that he now had to lead; for what it *felt* like to do what he had done. And, of course, it lets us know where Simpson, when he got back from Bundy, had been trying to control the bleeding on his left hand—running it under the tap till he couldn't wait any longer and had to go down to the limo.

As Simpson dressed, Kardashian repeated his offer of the previous night that Simpson could come and stay with him. And Simpson now liked the idea—in part because he'd done all he could to destroy incriminating evidence in his home or prepare for its removal at such an opportunity as now presented itself. By this I mean items such as the dark sweats that the police never seized and which were thankfully still in the washing machine when he got home; the empty Swiss Army knife box that had been sitting on the side of his bathtub; and a pair of brown gloves that sat atop his dresser and seemed to Fuhrman and Roberts to match the style of the gloves found near the bodies and on the walkway. But also, no doubt, he'd gotten a taste of just how trapped he was by all the cameras and reporters surrounding his home. Who wouldn't want to get away from that? The problem was how to leave and not be followed, and Kardashian had an idea. I've mentioned already the secret route in Simpson's backyard: the path by the tennis courts at the rear of his property that leads through the property of Eric Watts, his neighbor on that side, to Bristol, the next street over. Simpson could slip out by that route while Kardashian left as he came, though the front door, by himself of minor interest to the press and thus not likely to be followed.

First, however, Simpson had to pack. As it happened, Kardashian had brought with him the Louis Vuitton garment bag that Simpson had had with him in Chicago. There is, by the way, a well-known photograph of Kardashian carrying this bag as he departs from Rockingham on the day after the murders, when Simpson was intercepted by the police in his front yard and taken downtown. On the basis of this photograph and the disappearance of the black sweats—which, it was believed, were covered in blood—it was assumed that Kardashian was helping Simpson get rid of this and other evidence. In fact, the Louis Vuitton bag never entered Simpson's home on June 13, nor did Kardashian prior to walking off with the bag. Rather, the bag was in Skip Taft's car when he drove Simpson home from the airport. And when Simpson was arrested, Cathy Randa gave the bag to Kardashian to look after, who then stowed it in the trunk of his Mercedes. The photograph merely showed him transferring the bag from Taft's car to his own.

Simpson now took the Louis Vuitton bag with him into his master bedroom walk-in closet where, out of Kardashian's sight, he was soon very audibly filling it up with various items. He then asked Kardashian to go get something from the Bentley, which was still parked on the driveway where he'd left it when he got back from his trip with Kato to McDonald's. This was a little black, hard-shelled case, which Kardashian duly retrieved—incidentally leaving Simpson alone for a while, though that may have made no difference given how Kardashian took such care anyway to mind his own business and *not* notice what Simpson was putting in his bags. When Kardashian returned, Simpson took the black case into the closet, again out of sight. Kardashian then left by the front door as per the plan; he was carrying the Louis Vuitton bag.[13] Simpson, meanwhile, took the secret route through his neighbor's yard. It worked like a charm; no one from the press corps bothered to follow Kardashian, who doubled back to Bristol where his buddy awaited him, standing on the side of the road like a hitchhiker, with a black duffel bag slung over one shoulder. The little black case, which, as it later turned out, housed a pistol that Simpson had plans for—as a prop in a "made-for-TV movie" he meant to put on—was nowhere in sight.

After leaving Rockingham, they headed for Orenthal Enterprises, Simpson's Brentwood office. Once there Simpson arranged for the highly recommended Robert Shapiro to come by to discuss the possibility of his taking over the case. While they waited for Shapiro, Simpson was on the phone trying to locate his golf clubs, which he did. They were at LAX, where they'd come by a later flight. He was anxious to retrieve them as soon as he could; they were the one remaining piece of evidence, or potential evidence, still in his control that he hadn't yet vetted for possible clues. The meeting with

---

13 So far as I know, there are no photos of Kardashian entering and exiting Simpson's home on Tuesday, the second day after the murders, with the Louis Vuitton bag in tow. It's on this occasion that he may have participated, likely unawares, in the removal of evidence from Rockingham.

Shapiro went well, and it looked as if he would be taking the case; he was already dispensing advice and running the show. On one issue he was adamant: that Simpson not go to the airport himself. He said that it would look bad on him if he were seen worrying about his clubs when his ex-wife had just been killed. Let someone else pick them up. Simpson didn't contest this advice very strongly—he also didn't comply. When Shapiro was gone and they'd gotten in Kardashian's car for the drive to his home, Simpson abruptly said, "Let's go to the airport—I have to get my clubs," which they then did. At this point, Simpson still hadn't seen his now-motherless kids. It's one more clear indication that the bag had been used to convey something to Chicago for disposal—the murder weapon, for sure, and maybe the shoes—hence the need to at least check it and make sure it was clean.

Once they'd retrieved the golf bag, they headed for Kardashian's place in Encino, where Simpson would stay till his Friday arrest. He'd done what he could in person to get rid of evidence—exactly as Clark had feared. Moreover, when a second search warrant was issued for the Rockingham estate on June 28, so that the police could pick up what they now knew they'd missed the first time—the dark sweats were specifically listed in the warrant—they found when they arrived that the place has been meticulously cleaned and the carpet smelled freshly shampooed.[14] Not surprisingly, whatever they hoped to recover from the house had either been disposed of or washed away.

The new warrant also authorized a search of the Bentley for "absence of blood" in order to demonstrate that Simpson *hadn't* been bleeding up to shortly before the murders, when Kato last saw him. I haven't noticed any mention that the Bentley interior had been

---

14 According to Mark Fuhrman, who was one of those detailed to carry out the warrant (*Murder in Brentwood*, 333).

cleaned. No bloodstains were found, of course, since none were there to begin with. But, if the car upholstery had not been cleaned, there would likely have been fiber evidence on the driver's seat—blue-black fibers, that is, from the sweat suit Simpson was wearing—to corroborate Kato's story. Either the police were solely concerned with looking for bloodstains and paid no attention to anything else, or they did retrieve what trace evidence they could find on the seat and no blue-black fibers turned up—because Simpson had already had the upholstery cleaned.

I should add that it's highly unlikely, in my opinion, that any of the evidence that Simpson was able to dispose of or clean up, thanks to his ill-considered release, would have reversed the result in the criminal trial. That jury, as a whole, had an agenda, and there was little to no chance they'd change course. Even if the bloody fingerprint had been recovered, or the Bruno Magli photos had come to light in the course of the trial, I think it unlikely that they'd have voted for conviction; a hung jury was probably the best we could have hoped for. Meanwhile, we'd have seen the Dream Team outdo themselves—no mean feat!—in denying the undeniable or obscuring the plain as day, thus significantly upping the outrage we already felt. So, for the sake of our collective composure, the way that things worked out was probably a mercy. Why the jury, mainly black, was so predisposed to acquit is no great secret: a few hundred years of injustice at white America's hands, much of it dispensed in the very courtrooms where justice should reign, plus, of course, Simpson's sports-star celebrity and very likeable public persona.[15] But

15 A significant portion of the Penn State student body recently gave us fresh proof of the dangerous power of sports celebrity. I'm referring, of course, to the riot that followed on the dismissal of disgraced football coach—and living legend—Joe Paterno. In this case, too, basic values were discarded in shocking fashion, as the mob in effect turned a blind eye to serial child molestation rather than fault their local hero for his failure to stop what he long knew was taking place.

this predisposition was aggravated or inflamed by the events that preceded Simpson's eventual arrest. Marcia Clark, as mentioned, was correct in her apprehensions of what Simpson would be up to if left at large: that he'd destroy evidence and coerce or manipulate witnesses. What she didn't anticipate, and what probably no one could have anticipated, was how he'd engage in jury tampering on a massive scale. But let me rephrase that. There was no jury as yet; this was *jury pool* tampering, a play for the hearts and minds of the public, both the more limited black community and the public at large, from whose ranks would come those with the final say on his guilt or innocence.

Popular "Elections"

That's always been the problem with the public: like King Lear, it's ever known itself but slenderly, which makes it the natural prey for flatterers and schemers of every stamp, for the Gonerils and Regans of this world. Lear, at least, does come to his senses and self-knowledge, and he is reunited in death with Cordelia the true. The public qua public never really learns, for by the time it's seen through the likes of an O. J., some other more topical fraud (or popular frenzy, like Princess Diana) has taken his place (or, after a lull, soon will). It's as if the public has Alzheimer's, at least collectively: those who *do* learn do so as individuals and in so doing escape the general stampede. But they are soon more than replaced by those coming up, who have to learn, if they can, life's lessons all over again. As Barnum said, "There's a sucker born every minute," by virtue of which some O. J. is always at large. On the same principle, there's always some bubble somewhere on some market (stock or real estate, for example), as a new set of fools rush in to be fleeced in their turn.

'Twas ever thus, since history warts and all began to be told—that is, since Herodotus. Tyrants, and Simpson is simply a variation, figure largely in his work (as do their opposites). And if they can't get their way by force, as is often the case when they embark on their careers, they must then resort to treachery and guile. A good example is Pisistratus, in Athens (sixth century BC). With two factions already at odds for control of the city, he champions a third party, the Hillmen, which consists mainly of the poorer classes, though he himself is an aristocrat and comes from a leading clan. Then, with this constituency firmly in place, he devises a ruse. He cuts himself and his mules about the body, then drives his cart into the crowded agora and claims to have barely escaped assassination at the hands of his foes. On this pretext, and relying on the popularity he's earlier earned as a conquering hero in one of Athens wars with a neighboring city-state, he asks for a bodyguard, which the Athenians grant. Not long thereafter, Pisistratus, with the assistance of this guard, captures the Acropolis and takes control of the city.

But if the people seem easy pickings in the foregoing, it's nothing compared to what follows. After a while, Pisistratus is driven from power by the other two parties, who in turn fall out among themselves. Then Megacles, the loser in this contest, makes overtures to Pisistratus, offering to help reinstate him as tyrant if Pisistratus in return will marry his daughter. This agreed on, they then devise what Herodotus calls one of the silliest tricks by far that's ever been pulled—*or* the most cynical, given the appraisal it implies of its intended victims, the Athenians, supposedly the cleverest of the cleverest—that is, the smartest of the Greeks, who in turn have long been reputed the smartest nation going. They find this attractive and strapping young woman, nearly six feet tall, in one of the villages, whom they arm head to toe, mount in a chariot, and instruct in how to strike impressive poses—the dawn of supermodeling, you might call it. Then they drive with her into Athens, where messengers have preceded them, urging the people to welcome Pisistratus back and telling the wondrous tale of how Athena herself has shown him conspicuous favor and is bringing him home to the Acropolis, her temple. The news flies through the city and outlying Attic towns, and soon a throng is assembled: to offer prayers to the pseudo-Athena and receive Pisistratus back with open arms.

Fundamentalism in an age of myth—then as now a principal lever with which to control the crowd. Thus Pisistratus, in preposterous wise, gets back his tyranny and marries Megacles's daughter as per their deal. There's one problem, though: there's a curse on Megacles's clan, for a certain act of sacrilege a few generations back, that Pisistratus does not want passing into his own—as it will, he fears, if he sires children on the daughter (sons he already has from a previous wife). So, in order to skirt the curse, he eschews the normal port of entry and lies with his new bride *ou kata nomon*—"(in a manner) not according to custom (or law)" (1.61). I'll let the tale end here; if you want to know what comes next, go read Herodotus, specifically 1.59–64, where all this is told. But there's a moral to be drawn from the outrage done the daughter: This is what you get—and where you get it—when you stoop to having any truck with tyrants; this is how much they really respect those whose help they sometimes need. Meanwhile, another instance is furnished of a recurring motif in his text, that one of the marks of the tyrant is his mistreatment of women and his breaking the laws designed to secure the rights and dignity of the physically weaker sex. This theme was introduced when Candaules disrespected his wife by proudly displaying her naked beauty to another man.

Let's return to modern times, surely the smartest times ever, thanks mainly to science, and nowhere more so than in America, where in every field they're pretty much state of the art. While we've been away, the DQ alpha blood test results have come in on the Tuesday; the blood that was dripped by the killer on the walkway at Bundy matched Simpson's, but still the police didn't arrest. By Thursday they knew that the blood on the glove at Rockingham contained genetic markers from both victims, and likely from Simpson too; but, though the DA's office was pressuring the police, there still was no arrest. Indeed, Simpson wasn't even under surveillance, though that day, the Thursday, everyone knew where he was: at the funeral mass for Nicole at St. Martin of Tours in Brentwood, then at her graveside in Mission Viejo in Orange County, a hundred miles south of LA. He was in black, of course, and wearing dark glasses, the better to hide his swollen eyes—or avoid eye contact. But, though cameramen in helicopters captured his presence at both locations, even they were given the slip during the return journey. At a brief stop off at the Brown family home in Dana Point, Al Cowlings exchanged clothes and sunglasses with Simpson and left in the limo Simpson had been in; and when the choppers followed him, Simpson went back in Cowlings's Bronco with Kardashian to the latter's Encino home. The media, meanwhile, thought he was back at Rockingham, where Cowlings was dropped off and where they remained encamped.

Finally, early on Friday June 17, the police issued a warrant for O. J. Simpson's arrest on a double homicide charge, and informed his lawyer, Robert Shapiro, (who had by now been formally hired) at around 8:30 a.m. Shapiro then went to Kardashian's place to notify Simpson in person. There he and Kardashian went to Simpson's guest suite, where they found him in bed watching TV. Shapiro told him he had arranged for him to surrender voluntarily at police headquarters by 11 a.m.; little did he know that Simpson already had plans of his own for how he'd surrender, and that his visit would cue a performance such as hadn't been seen since, well, Pisistratus reentered Athens. The police, meanwhile, though it probably didn't occur to them in these terms, were about to learn that allowing Simpson the sports hero and celebrity to be at large was about as smart a move as letting Mark Antony speak at Caesar's funeral. The only differences were that Simpson would play both parts and that the report of (in this case) his guilt would prove greatly exaggerated.

The miracle play that was Simpson's extended suicide attempt had in a sense been underway at least since his sister Shirley had called out to him not to harm himself in the bathroom back on Monday night and then reminded him of his kids and how they'd need him. This, it seems, turned the psychological tide. Maybe that *is* what suggested the idea to him, or maybe it was the fact of the suicide watch that Kardashian had mounted. More likely, though, it was the inevitable cheesy ploy he'd come up with in the circumstances, knowing it was only a matter of time before he was charged. He then had to carry it out either despite the fact most people would see through it (sufficiently content if he could retain his diehard fans) or really believing he'd win most hearts and minds. I tend to think the latter; that he believed he could charm just about anyone he set his mind to. I said before that no one could have anticipated the events I'm about to describe. But maybe I should retract that: Nicole predicted that he would kill her and then would just O. J. his way out of it. She knew him best; she knew how trapped she was. If souls keep an eye on the world they've left behind them, she can't have been surprised at what she saw.

Simpson's first move, after Shapiro had told him the news, was to ask for some privacy so that he could get dressed and have time to think. Then, when the others had left, he got hold of a tape recorder and delivered, after several false starts, a lugubrious, raspy-voiced, self-pitying monologue mainly on the theme of "How did it [his till-then-great life] all go so wrong?" It ended with, "Please remember me as the Juice. Please remember me as a good guy. I don't want you to remember me as whatever negative that might end here." Dead man talking: proof for anyone with a heart who'd hear it later that, but for God's grace, he was as good as gone.

Recording session over, he went downstairs where he was to undergo some medical and psychiatric tests that Shapiro had arranged for with certain high-priced experts he'd brought in. But first he had to make a number of phone calls, including one to Skip Taft; it was to do with his will, which he was now writing out on a yellow pad as they talked, then faxing it back and forth with Taft as the latter corrected and revised. He was also making numerous calls to other friends and even to Nicole's parents, mostly to do with seeing that his kids would be looked after. Clearly these arrangements couldn't be made later, for instance when Taft would visit him in prison, because of course he would be dead by then, as the tenor of each call implied. All in all, they were a still-mounting mountain of evidence as to his state of mind: he was firmly resolved to die. Then, even more letters followed: to his kids, his mother, and "To Whom It May Concern, press or public." He was a martyr to his murdered reputation; a man with a cause—and the cause.

Meanwhile, time wasn't standing still: eleven o'clock had come and gone and the police were impatient. Shapiro told them the address; they were on their way. Simpson said his tearful farewells to Paula Barbieri, who was also part of the large entourage there that day. He told Paula that Cowlings, who'd also arrived, had some cash that would cover her trip back to Florida. In fact, it would do more than that: Cowlings was holding some $8,000 in all in cash and checks; the same $8,000 (in so-called golf winnings) that Simpson had claimed the LAPD had stolen, but which it turned out was all along under a sweater in his closet. Too bad he hadn't recalled where he'd put it back then; it would have spared him having to search through all those drawers.

After Paula had left, he and Cowlings went back to the guest suite where Simpson had been staying, to pick up his stuff for the trip downtown. Kardashian followed shortly thereafter and stumbled upon an at-first-disturbing, then harrowing, sight: his friend sitting alone on a couch with a green towel in his lap and pictures of his ex-wife and kids—of Nicole, Sydney and Justin—spread around. He was bent over staring silently at the pictures, and Kardashian realized there was a pistol wrapped in the towel. Where had O. J. gotten a pistol? It must have been in the black, hard-shelled case he'd had him fetch from the Bentley. It was all but over, or so Kardashian supposed, unless ... unless ... He started to talk religion, tried to get him to pray, reminded him of his children and how they would need him. But it was to no avail. "I'm gonna kill myself," said Simpson. "I just can't live with the pain. I can't go on." Kardashian continued to talk and pray; what else could he do? Then Simpson said, "I'm going to kill myself in this room," which gave Kardashian an idea for how to buy time.

"You can't. This is my daughter's bedroom ... every time I come in here, I'll see your body lying there. Why don't you go outside?" The debate had been deftly shifted: from "to be or not to be" to "where not to be," and Simpson was only too happy to follow along.[16]

Simpson and Kardashian went outside, where they soon found themselves sitting on a retaining wall surrounded by shrubbery near the laundry room door. Simpson still had the towel and gun in his lap, but the issue of locale—where to kill himself?—was now paramount. "I can't kill myself in these bushes," he announced after checking things out. "It's too close to the house." So they went into the backyard, where Kardashian, encouraged by Simpson's unprompted rejection of the last prospective location, suggested he do it out in the yard away from the house. But there was another

---

16 For Simpson's activities this day (indeed for the whole period between the murders and his arrest) I should again express my debt to Schiller and Willwerth's *American Tragedy*, 62 ff., where pretty much every detail I cite may be found. Their understated but fuller treatment of Simpson's extended "suicide attempt" is well worth the read, as is their book as a whole.

snag: "I'd be baking in the sun," said Simpson after looking up. "I don't want to bake in the sun." Next it was outside the living room window, a Simpson suggestion, where an overhanging balcony provided the needed shade.

Kardashian countered, "You can't do it there. Every time I sit in the living room I'm going to see your body there." Simpson then suggested a place on the driveway, paused, then changed his mind again: Cars will later "be parked over where I was." Then a spot by a side entrance was considered and rejected because of some empty cartons in the area; he didn't want to be found in a pile of trash. As Al Cowlings joined them, Kardashian recommended that he go down the street and do it. But no, that wouldn't do, "I don't want to be found in the street." Fastidiouser and fastidiouser, to paraphrase Alice; and the scene was about as real as anything Wonderland has to offer. Then Kardashian had a much better idea. He suggested that Simpson go to the Bel Air Church in Brentwood; it was there that he'd married Nicole. That was perfect! That's what he'd do—Cowlings could drive him. However, though they now had a plan, they didn't act on it right away; final preparations were made as if he'd turn himself in after all. But when the police eventually arrived around 2 p.m.—they'd had trouble with the directions—and Shapiro went to get Simpson, he and Cowlings were nowhere to be found, and Cowlings's Bronco was missing too. The quest for the perfect suicide site had resumed in earnest.

At Kardashian's, the police allowed no one to leave. After a while, his assistant, Nicole Pulvers, brought him the phone and said his sister was on the line and then, when he hesitated, insisted he take it. In fact, the caller was Simpson, who immediately announced, "I shot myself in the head, but I didn't die." Nor, as it turned out, did he even suffer a non-life-threatening wound. Rather, as he explained, the pistol had malfunctioned. He was at the Bel Air Church, but the police had preceded him (having been informed by Kardashian that

Simpson might go there) so *he* was heading elsewhere, to Nicole's. But the police were there as well, as Simpson and Cowlings could see before they were seen, so they moved on.

Back at Kardashian's, Shapiro mentioned in the hearing of the police the sealed letter Simpson had given Kardashian that morning, the one addressed to "To Whom It May Concern, press or public"; perhaps it would give them a clue to where he was going. Kardashian was ordered to hand it over, but he was reluctant. He hadn't read it yet, and Simpson had told him he'd *know* when to read it, and that moment, he felt, wasn't now. They compromised and let him read it out loud. At its outset it was an *apologia* of sorts (or "explanation") *pro vita sua* ("for his life"), or at least for the marital portion and Nicole's death, as well as a deathbed confession, though it turned out there was nothing culpable to confess: "I loved her. Always have and always will. If we had a problem, it's because I loved her so much." But he never mistreated her and certainly didn't kill her; and, as for that 1989 beating when he was charged and had to do community service, he was big enough to confess to "taking the heat" in order to "protect our privacy." The words of a dying man—breathes there a soul so churlish as not to believe them?

The letter, which ran to four handwritten pages, continued in rambling fashion with complaints about how the press had fabricated much of what was being said against him, a plea that the media leave his children alone, and a long list of farewells to a host of friends, business associates, former teammates, family members etc. It closed with, first, a declaration not just of his innocence, but of having lived an admirable life: "I've had a good life. I'm proud of how I lived; my momma taught me to do unto others. I treated people the way I wanted to be treated ..." followed by a suicidal farewell: "I can't go on. No matter what the outcome, people will look and point. I can't take that ... Don't feel sorry for me. I've had a great life, made great friends. Please think of the real O. J. and not this lost person.

Thank you for making my life special. I hope I help yours. Peace & Love, O. J." As a crowning banality, there was a happy face insertion in the O.

While the letter did not provide any clue as to where Simpson might be headed, at least physically, Shapiro immediately grasped its emotional thrust and how best to exploit it even further. He had already scheduled a press conference for 5 p.m., and now he told Kardashian that he wanted him to read the letter there. The shy Kardashian reluctantly agreed, and the police, for some reason—intimidated perhaps by the celebrity aspect of the case—allowed them to leave before they'd finished interviewing them and finding out everything useful they might know as regards Simpson's whereabouts. Kardashian, with Shapiro's assistance—he told him to talk very slowly—read out Simpson's "suicide note" to the assembled media throng, unconsciously enhancing its appeal by his own unassuming and straightforward demeanor. Not everyone bought the performance embedded in the script, far from it. But a significant minority, mainly in the black community (where it formed a landslide majority), did buy into it, including many of the best and the brightest. In Johnnie Cochran's law offices, for instance—where, as Schiller and Willwerth tell us, most in the firm at first thought he was guilty and were convinced that he was when he ran—when they heard his suicidal farewell, as read out by the bluff and honest Kardashian, their feelings changed.[17] Here was the classic black fugitive, not from justice, but from the white man's victimization and exploitation; here was the Underground Railroad all over again.

Not long after the press conference, the Bronco was spotted on the Santa Ana Freeway in Orange County, at first by a couple of ordinary citizens in a Camry, then by Deputy Larry Pool in his

17 *American Tragedy*, 81–2.

patrol car; another patrol car soon joined him. Cowlings had the driver's window down, and Simpson, so far as they could make out through the tinted glass, appeared to be in the back seat. At Grand Avenue, the Bronco came to a halt in heavy traffic and the deputies, their guns drawn, ordered Cowlings to turn off his engine. He refused, vehemently, and drove on when the traffic cleared. The deputies followed; the slow-speed chase had begun. Cowlings, meanwhile, had dialed 911 on his cell phone and told them he had Simpson in the car, who was holding a gun to his own head; he asked them to back off and let him and O. J. go to Simpson's house. The cell phone signal was picked up by the media: a helicopter squadron was soon overhead, while what was by now a freeway-wide fleet of cruiser cars followed behind.

Inside the Bronco, Simpson put down the gun long enough to call his friend Wayne Hughes, a fellow USC alumnus whom he'd known since 1968. He'd already spoken to Hughes more than once that week (including earlier that morning) regarding taking care of his kids when he was gone, and he broached that subject again; he also talked about dying. Hughes knew nothing about the chase and assumed Simpson was alone somewhere and on the verge of ending his life. He recited from memory the forty-first Psalm, while both men wept. When he learned about the chase a little thereafter, he contacted his secretary and had her call the police and give them Simpson's cell phone number.

Meanwhile, Kardashian, who also didn't yet know about the car chase, had made his way to Rockingham, which was once again crawling with cops. After conning his way in by posing as Simpson's therapist, he assembled the near and extended family members that were there, about ten in all, in Simpson's bedroom and started to prepare them for what he felt was the almost inevitable outcome: their father, cousin, or brother-in-law's death by his own hand. While he was talking, someone turned on the television, to see if there was any news, and news there certainly was—the Bronco with all those cop cars in cold pursuit. A TV anchor informed them that Simpson was in the back seat with a gun to his head. Nevertheless, a cheer went up in the room—it was like a slow-motion replay of one of his great runs, with Rockingham the distant end zone, the faraway prize. Everyone felt that if he could only make it back there he'd somehow survive; implied as well is the feeling that if he made it home unscathed it was a symbolic proof of his innocence—and a ray of hope.

Kardashian got Simpson on his cell phone, and immediately was given an update on the suicide mission. "I tried to see her, but they wouldn't let me. I was going to do it at the cemetery." By "they" he meant a police car on watch at the entrance to the cemetery, and when he went around the back to climb the fence, there were people there, which messed up his plans. Then they "drove to an orange field and sat there for a while," but "I couldn't see myself lying in some field. I can't be remembered that way." Sadly, there was no acknowledgment from the Juice that that might also have been too corny. There was, however, one final fallback option: "If I can't do it with Nicole, I want to do it at home," he said in a weepy voice. "But first I want to see Mamma." Kardashian told him his mother, Eunice, had gone back home but that he could call her when he got there. They lost their connection, and when Kardashian got him again, he heard Simpson wail, "Why wouldn't they let me do it, man?" Those meddlesome police, he meant. It was their fault he hadn't killed himself, not his own—which was par for the course, as Nicole could have confirmed.

Kardashian continued talking intermittently with either Simpson or Cowlings—the phone kept cutting out and he had to redial—as the suicide procession slowly wended its way to Rockingham. It was like a vehicular cakewalk, like something out of New Orleans—only the brass band was replaced by the beating blades of the massed media helicopters overhead, and the attendant revelers were not looking down from balconies but from pedestrian overpasses above the freeway. Most were cheering for Simpson and holding up supportive signs with messages like "Go Juice." At Rockingham, the SWAT team had arrived and was taking up positions. Meanwhile, Simpson told Kardashian, "I want to kill myself at home. All I want to do is come home and do that." Soon Simpson and the Bronco were on Rockingham, their moving position now inferable from the house, thanks to the approaching swarm of helicopters above. All but police personnel had by now been moved to the backyard or into the street, except for Simpson's "therapist," Kardashian, who refused to leave and who might after all be of use. Then the Bronco entered the driveway and pulled up before the front door. The dark-tinted glass hindered the view of Simpson in the back, but Cowlings partly opened the door and turned on the roof light, the better to display a piteous tableau: a shadowy Simpson in the back seat, cradling the pictures of Nicole, Justin, and Sydney against his chest with one arm while holding a gun to his head with his other hand. He was hiding his guilt with the ex-wife he'd brutally murdered, palliating his crimes with the kids whose mother he'd killed. It was a kind of *necrostuprum*—"outrage on a corpse"—not to mention on most people's intelligence. At one point he even slid the barrel of the gun into his mouth for a while. This had to be it!—but no, it wasn't. The gun was extracted and placed against the side of his head till the expected pleas for the sake of his children and mother at length persuaded him to remove it from there.

Eventually, of course, they talked him out of the car, on condition that he get to speak with his mother, that he could spend some time with his friend Bob Kardashian, and that they not arrest him until he was inside the house and out of range of the cameras. (Cowlings had already exited the car and been handcuffed and led away out of Simpson's sight.) Simpson emerged very slowly, making it plain all the while that it was truly touch and go. When, finally, he was fully out of the car, he staggered some twenty feet to his friend Kardashian and collapsed into his arms, saying apologetically as he did, "I'm sorry, man, I'm sorry. I just couldn't do it." According to Kardashian, he even seemed oddly embarrassed. If so, it was the one faintly redeeming feature of his performance that day.

Though Simpson *staggered* then, it was only, as Red Riding Hood's wolf might have put it, the better to *walk* in the end—walk free, that is, at the stunning, or so it seemed at the time, end of his criminal trial. For, despite his being in custody from that moment, nonsense remained alive and well and at large. Indeed, his histrionics of that Friday proved but a harbinger of, if not incitement to, things as bad, if not worse, to come. I mean, of course, the antics of the Dream Team which, abetted by the absurd latitude allowed them by judge Lance Ito, turned the trial into what often seemed like a circus, and Simpson, in the eyes of his constituency, into a victim instead of the killer he is.

This, his guilt, was proven by a mountain of uncontradicted evidence that conclusively fingered him. Yet this mountain was itself overtopped by an even bigger mountain of, for the most part, cheap theatrics, baseless innuendo, and unsupported claims and accusations—in other words, a mountain made of air, a mirage, a show almost wholly without substance. Yet, by the grace of the jury, this phantom somehow *weighed* in the scales of justice and brought them swiftly down on Simpson's side. It was blind justice, indeed—not because it was shielded from passion and partisan feeling but because it was plunged in that very element at virtually every turn.

Emotionally, the trial was to a large degree predetermined before it began by, as stated, the history of racial injustice in America, as well as by Simpson's huge popularity and impeccable public image.

But these forces, semilatent at the outset, were whipped into a frenzy by the melodramatics of that slow-speed chase with all its suicidal theatrics. It was this above all that gave his supporters—the black community (or most of it); his true-blue fans of no one race; plus the sad legions of conspiracy-theory devotees (who've never met a state-run plot they didn't like)—all the emotional ammunition they would need to ignore the manifest truth conveyed by the evidence.

So you wonder—or at least I do—what Herodotus would have said had he seen Simpson's slow-speed flight and its aftermath. I mean, if there were a fake-off, so-to-speak, between Past and Present, would Herodotus still give the prize to Pisistratus and Megacles for the outrageous ruse they put over on the ancient Athenians? Or would Simpson's pseudo-suicide procession, along with the eventual verdict, take the cake? We'll never know, of course, but of this much I am certain: had he seen Simpson's act, he would not have been surprised. There's one thing all our science hasn't altered one iota: the more things change, the more they stay the same.[18]

---

[18] Let me put this another way: There's never a shortage of Dream Teams of one stripe or another. If the black community was the principal dupe of the Simpson crew, it's the white community in America that's been the main constituency of the Dream Teams that have gotten them mired in Iraq and Afghanistan.

CHAPTER 8

THE AFTERLIFE

As everyone knows, Simpson was eventually acquitted—resoundingly so—after a long, unruly, and melodramatic criminal trial. Then he was convicted in the civil trial and assessed damages, which he has by and large avoided having to pay.[1] So I guess, taking the half-full view of things and leaving aside the question of whether his October 3, 2008 conviction on other charges constitutes payback in some degree for his earlier crimes, you could call it a draw. But from the strict or measure-for-measure point of view, you've got to be quite the optimist if that made you feel good or gave you true satisfaction—because in both trials, in point of fact, he escaped: the first time technically, the second de facto. If justice is confined to what the courts mete out, if it's a mere material thing, such as (in descending order of severity) execution, imprisonment, or damages, then Simpson, in connection with the murders of Ron and Nicole, has dodged all three bullets (the first one

---

1 See my discussion of how he really came out ahead on *If I Did It* (chapter one, note 14).

when the prosecution, for strategic reasons, declined to ask for the death penalty). But I said at the outset that I'd here apply a different perspective and try to look at things through Herodotus's eyes. In his world, too, the patently guilty often got off, thanks to their wealth and connections, or because, like many a tyrant, they were simply too powerful to bring to account. But, secure as he was in his trust in a higher power, and in its law-enforcement arm, which he called nemesis, Herodotus never doubted that the guilty would one day pay in some way, and in a way that cut to the quick and hit them where they lived, where it hurt most.

The mills of the gods grind slowly, but they grind exceedingly fine: heaven is patient *and* thorough, and when all is said and done, it's settled every score. Hipparchus, a son of the aforementioned Pisistratus and brother to Hippias, who's succeeded their father as tyrant, has a vivid dream on the eve of the Panathenaean festival:[2] a tall and well-shaped figure of a man stands over his bed and, in verse, "riddles" him the following:

Endure, O lion, as you suffer the unendurable with spirit enduring;
None, who's mortal, wrongs' requital shall not requite. (5.56)

The next morning he is seen consulting with the dream interpreters, but whatever they tell him, he goes ahead anyway and takes part in the festival procession, during which he is assassinated. This assassination is prelude to the eventual, and final, ouster of the Pisistratids some four years later. The "riddle" in what the dream figure said refers to the ambiguity of who has committed the wrongs that are to be requited; for the murderers of Hipparchus, though they're punished with death,

2 The great national festival of the Athenians celebrated annually as the Lesser Panathenaea, but in grand style every fifth year as the Greater Panathenaea. It commemorated the original union of Attica, the region of which Athens was the capital, by the hero Theseus.

are ever after revered as tyrant-slayers and as heroes by the Athenian people. In other words, they achieve a consummation (that is for a Greek of that, or any, time) devoutly wished; and what they do is regarded as no wrong.[3] The key to the riddle is to recall—from that passage halfway across Herodotus's text, which this picks up, where he last was discussing political events in Athens—Pisistratus's sacrilegious use of the country girl dressed up as Athena to help him enslave her own city. Hipparchus is to pay, on the symbolically appropriate day, both for paternal wrongs and for his own (he is part of the tyrant regime). As Herodotus tells us at the outset of his text, through Solon's advice to Croesus, we should always look to the end, or long term, and count no man blessed until he reaches the end with all his good fortune intact. This "end," in more ways than one, may not just be the end of his mortal life. (Tellus, after all, was blessed in that, among other things, he saw his sons thriving with families of their own.) In this spirit, then, I'll take a look at Simpson's situation since the murder trials concluded—and prior to his stunning screw-up in Las Vegas—in search of intimations of a higher justice or of indications that nemesis has been busy all the while: slowly tightening its grip upon a killer, steadily driving O. J. Simpson mad.

In retrospect, one of the most remarkable aspects of the whole Simpson saga—the mounting evidence against him, his arrest, and then the subsequent trials—was the extreme swings in fortune that took place, sometimes in the course of one day. At first his guilt seemed obvious and confession and plea bargaining a foregone conclusion. Then the Dream Team started weaving their courtroom magic, aided above all by the revelations of Mark Fuhrman's apparent racist background,

3 Recall how Solon pronounced Tellus the most blessed of men for, among other things, having died heroically in battle defending his homeland.

the ethnic makeup of the jury, and the recent Rodney King affair. In addition, there was the odd and inexplicable aspect of key portions of the evidence, which I have dealt with here—especially, the cuts to his fingers, the lack of cuts to the glove worn on that hand, and the absence of any of his blood on the manhandled victims—how did that all fit together? Armed with things like this, the defense was able to make unreasonable doubt seem reasonable, thus inducing the jury to turn a blind eye to a mountain of uncontested evidence. Lead was turned into gold, at least superficially—and for as long a time as it took to get Simpson off.

Equally amazing, however, was how some of the most damning evidence didn't emerge until the civil trial. This included such things as his message manager records, which showed he did retrieve the break-up message left by Paula Barbieri, despite his many denials; also, the authoritative testimony of Dr. Werner Spitz—not new evidence as such, but a new and compelling interpretation of the evidence—which convincingly demonstrated that both victims were likely dispatched in very short order. Most spectacular, however, were the photos of him in the Bruno Magli shoes, which exploded all his lies and funky, down-home posturing on that score ("I would have never owned those ugly-ass shoes"). The first set of photos to appear, in April of 1996, had been shot by a certain Harry Scull at a Buffalo Bills home game on September 26, 1993. They were dismissed by Simpson and his new lawyers as a forgery, and "expert" witness Robert Groden was secured to testify to that effect in the civil trial. Then, eight months later, with the trial in progress and with the "expert" witness's testimony already on the record, another thirty photos of Simpson in the Bruno Maglis, shot that same September day by one E. J. Flammer, also turned up. Moreover, one of them had appeared in a team newsletter, the *Bills Report*, months before the murders occurred in June of 1994. The photos, or at least eight of them, were introduced to the discomfiture of the defense's "expert" and then handed to the jurors: tangible evidence—not some airy-faerie DNA—that readily evoked a mental image of Simpson at the crime scene, astride the blood-soaked bodies of his victims.

I've said that even these photos would likely not have gotten him convicted with the sympathetic jury he had in the criminal trial. They would, though, have stiffened the resolve of a few of them and perhaps produced a hung jury and a retrial, with who knows what result. But what happened, happened, and in the sequence that it did. The photos came too late to secure, for most of us, *real* justice in the courts: some tangible and quantifiable form of punishment proportionate in severity to the crime (for only the criminal court really had the power to do that). What they did do, however, was make plain his manifest guilt to all but a few. "If the shoe fits, you can't acquit," partial though you may be to O. J. Simpson, or averse though you may be to the LAPD. This Simpson knew. Lawrence Schiller reports that a friend of Simpson's and member of his entourage, whom he does not name, said that "all the air went out of O. J.'s balloon that day … [that] that day [Simpson's] friend saw a broken man."[4] In other words, that was the day that made it plain, to him and to everyone, that even some limited form of his former celebrity would never again be attainable.

When Delphi first speaks directly in Herodotus, it is in answer to a test question simultaneously put via messengers to it and every other oracle he knows of by Croesus, who wants to be sure of their authenticity before he asks what's really on his mind. Delphi's dactylic response,[5] quoted in full, begins with what amounts to a programmatic claim as to the scope of its powers:

---

4 *American Tragedy*, 951.

5 The oracle usually delivered its response in dactylic hexameters (the same meter as was used in epic verse), but other meters also occurred. The dactyls (long, short, short) are not reproduced in my translation, in case some wonder.

I know the sands in their number and take the measures of the sea
The mute I comprehend and I hear him who speaks not. (1.47)[6]

In other words, it not only knows every material detail, it knows our every thought and inclination, where all our buttons are, what we most fear and what most prize, wherein we most presume—*and* the blind spots thence ensuing. Croesus is only concerned with the oracle's command of the facts, of which it gives a demonstration by correctly describing what Croesus is secretly up to (boiling tortoise and lamb's flesh in a bronze cauldron) at that precise and prearranged moment in time in faraway Lydia. Thus assured of Delphi's powers (only one of the other oracles answered right), Croesus then asks if he should march against the rising power of Persia, and he is assured that if he does so he will destroy a great empire. So he attacks Persia and does, indeed, destroy a great empire—his own, the possibility of which had never occurred to him.

O. J. Simpson loved celebrity, loved the adulation of the crowd, and basked in its glow; he assumed it was his due and that he'd have it all his life. So it's ironic that the net effect of his combined murder *agons* ("trials," in this context, you'll recall) was to let him go scot-free, or virtually so, of any formal punishment, to leave him at large and with enough money to live well on, but to strip him of virtually all reputation and respect. It's as if he had one wish granted him by a leprechaun that he had to phrase just right or, better, a pact with the devil. It was his soul in exchange for what he desired most—to be rid of his ex-wife, so that she could no longer hurt him by showing him that she didn't need him and by getting on with her life—and, of course, to get away with it. And he did get his wish. The devil

6 It also understands those who speak no matter what language, as indicated by an oracle to the founder-to-be of the Greek colony of Cyrene in as-yet-unknown-to-Greeks Libya, wherein it cryptically uses *battus*, the Libyan word for "king" (4.156). A comparable tale is told at 8.135.

kept his bargain—after his fashion. Literally, he satisfied the terms of their agreement, but qualitatively, what he delivered was a wasteland. The proffered apple turned to ashes when Simpson bit in. He's a byword now for "killer" and a pariah for life, the butt of countless jokes. While still at large he could make money, if needed, from his name, but only by appearing as a sort of freak, as in that pay-per-view candid-camera program *Juiced*, broadcast in the summer of 2006, wherein, among other things, he pretended to sell the infamous slow-speed-chase Bronco at a used-car lot. Or on that website, *JudgeOJ.com*, where we got, or were to get, eventually, eighty hours' footage of him at various locales, such as a bus stop or a strip club, living out his life just like the rest of us, and ostensibly not undergoing the tortures of the damned. It was a "new lowest low" as some wag called it at the time,[7] but of course, it was since superseded—or should I say *sub*-seded—by his instantaneously infamous "confession," *If I Did It*. And this, in turn, was challenged soon after that (for disgrace of place) by what happened in Vegas.

To expand on the book: as anyone that's read it ought to know, it's no confession. Its alleged description of almost all the gory details of that night—he blacks out for the actual onslaught on Ron and Nicole—the details that only the killer would know is, as he says, hypothetical, if not imaginary, like his clearly imaginary friend and accomplice, Charlie. Or worse, it's a thinly veiled attempt to float the suggestion that he was having dreams of a violent and ("justifiably") angry nature at the time Nicole was killed. Thus, after Kato leaves him in the front yard, he closes his eyes to try to stop thinking about her, her "loose lifestyle," and the "threat" it poses to their kids. He then opens them and sees forever-last-nameless Charlie approach with "news" of even "*more* sordid conduct" by Nicole; "news" that

7 It's spoken by an "unidentified male" in one of the videos from the *JudgeOJ.com* website, which was shown on CNN's *The Nancy Grace Show* (August 7, 2006).

in essence replicates what he says he had just been told at Sydney's recital by Ron Fishman, the husband of Nicole's friend Cora. And, on three different occasions in his narration of what follows, he has this strange sensation that it's all just "one of those crazy crime-of-passion dreams," or "a nightmare"[8] he'll awake from. Later on in that same chapter, "The Night in Question," when we're back in a world there are other witnesses to, he protests how it's been misrepresented how he responded when he was notified in his Chicago hotel room of his ex-wife's death. He claims that he did keep asking for further information because, of course, back in reality, he didn't know. And at its end he makes this telling comment: "Half of you [the public] *think* I did it ... The other half *know* I didn't ..."[9]

The payoff for all this, or so I suggest, comes in the next chapter, which is for the most part a verbatim transcript of his interrogation by Vannater and Lange the day after the murders. Near the end, they ask him his thoughts on taking a polygraph, and he replies: "... sure, eventually ... but it's like I've got some weird thoughts now ... when you've been with a person for seventeen years, you think everything"[10]—including, I guess, acting out violent fantasies in your dreams. So, it's no wonder he failed that polygraph test (the one Shapiro had him take shortly after the murders). By a bizarre twist of fate, his dreams at or around that time, in which he was subconsciously venting his "righteous" wrath on Nicole, coincided with her *actually* being butchered by persons unknown. Poor O. J.!

8 *If I Did It*, 135, 138–9. The other dream reference is at 132–3. Meanwhile, a number of the details in the "Charlie" section strangely reverse the well-known facts: the *right* glove, not the left, is removed, by him, at the crime scene *prior* to his attack (131); the air conditioner he bumps into is on the *front* of Kato's guest house, not the back (138), and the light that soon afterward flashes on his bedroom phone as the limo driver rings places the driver at the *Rockingham* gate, not the Ashford.

9 *Ibid*, 148 (italics mine).

10 *Ibid*, 169.

Was anyone ever more misunderstood? And by a polygraph, too! He bombed on that test for being too nice a guy: for beating *himself* up and taking the blame for something he didn't do; for something Nicole, by her "loose conduct," had likely brought on herself.

The book was originally slated to be published by ReganBooks, an imprint of HarperCollins, in November 2006, but publication was halted and two FOX TV specials featuring Simpson interviews scrapped (by order of Rupert Murdoch) due to mounting public outrage. This was despite Simpson's having been paid an advance (through a dummy company set up in the name of his kids) of, reportedly, upward of a million dollars.[11] Subsequently, the Goldman family sued for and won the rights to publish the book as a means of recovering some of the damages they were awarded in the civil trial. As a result, it was published in the fall of 2007, under the expanded title *If I Did It: Confessions of the Killer*,[12] and it carried the assurance that most of the proceeds were to go to the Ron Goldman Foundation for Justice, a victims' rights group. The Brown family tried to stop its publication—understandably, given that it whitewashed all Simpson's history of abuse with Nicole and trashed her severely in the process. But they were not successful. As a result, Simpson got paid, handsomely, to abuse and maul their sister and daughter all over again—in the full public eye—*and* to paint himself as the victim. Not many believed him, but there were still remnants of his original constituency who continued to buy his act. If there

---

11 Simpson dictated the material for the text to unaccredited ghost-writer Pablo Fenjves, who was, by yet another odd twist of fate, the primary witness in both trials for establishing when it was the Akita began to howl. A screenwriter by profession, he lived on the next street over from Nicole and shared a back alley with her. Fenjves still firmly believes that Simpson did it.

12 On the cover and title page the "*If*" is reduced to one seventh the size of the rest of the title. It's also superimposed on the upper end of the following "*I*," to make the point that this hypothetical overlay is a figment of Simpson's unrepentant imagination.

was any satisfaction for the rest of us—the vast majority, not the half that Simpson fondly claims—it was in seeing how badly he wanted to be liked as before, in seeing his puppy-dog wriggle, and seeing him try yet again to O. J. his way (as Nicole said he would) back into our affections. But he was now to be rebuffed by almost everyone, to be reminded just how much he was despised and how the animus against him had not abated in the least—more than thirteen years later. So you would think that with each passing year the grim reality of what he is, and the mark he indelibly bears would, finally, have started to sink in.

In Shakespeare's *The Tempest*, Ariel, the magician Prospero's familiar spirit, confronts the villains of the piece with just what it is they're up against on Prospero's island:

> You are three men of sin, whom Destiny,
> That hath to instrument this lower world
> And what is in't, the never-surfeited sea
> Hath caused to belch up you;[13] and on this island
> Where man doth not inhabit; you 'mongst men
> Being most unfit to live. (III, iii, 53–8)

Nemesis, as explained in the first chapter, is simply an aspect or dimension of Destiny/Fate and, like it, "hath to [hand as] instrument this lower world and what is in't." As such, and given its intimate knowledge of our psyches, it needs must be—assuming that such there be—the most refined of punishers, all our legal systems being but rough justice by comparison. As regards O. J. Simpson, one of

13 So that there's no misunderstanding due to inversion, *the never-surfeited sea* is the object of *caused*: "Destiny ... hath caused ... the never-surfeited [thus normally all-swallowing] sea to belch up you."

the instruments of this lower world that nemesis had to work with was his own much-prized celebrity, of which, by a most perfect irony, he's ever since the original trial been made a prisoner. Most men, in a similar situation—patently guilty but beyond the reach of the law—could have lost themselves in the crowd.[14] Simpson, despite his wealth, never could. No matter where he went, everyone knew his story and could recognize him on sight. And no matter how straight a face they'd keep, he'd always have to wonder what they were really thinking. What were they going to say the moment he was gone? Meanwhile, to make it worse, he was growing uglier—not because of age, which ought to bring a beauty all its own, but because the truth was slowly but steadily oozing out into his very features, rendering them crueler and more malevolent—or, by turns, more impudent and smirking—every day and turning him into a living caricature of himself. It's just one more illustration of the old adage "murder will out"; or, as Hamlet puts it: "Foul deeds will rise, though all the earth o'erwhelm them, to men's eyes" (I, ii, 257–8).

To return to the murder trials: obviously they accomplished something in the way of payback, though it was more obvious in the second case because it gave us the satisfaction of a formal conviction, and because new evidence and testimony made his guilt even plainer than day. But the first one, as well, accomplished a lot *by* the very failure to convict—for that increased our outrage and disgust all the more. What's even more interesting, though, is their combined result, which as engineered by fate, has in effect sentenced Simpson to a kind a limbo for the rest of his life. He's on an island of sorts of his own making (a condition his now being jailed only renders explicit), branded as a killer and cut off from any genuine intercourse

14 *Celebrity*, should you care to know, literally means "a crowd" or "multitude." The adjective *celeber*, from which it derives, means "filled, crowded" or (of places) "frequented." Then, by extension, it means "celebrated" or "famous" when applied to people who, for whatever reason, are lionized by others.

with most of humankind. In this regard, it's worth resuming Ariel's speech a few lines further on when he apprises the villains—among them Prospero's brother, Alonso, who'd usurped his throne and left him to die—of the future that awaits them:

> The powers delaying, not forgetting, have
> Incensed the seas and shores, yea, all the creatures,
> Against your peace. Thee of thy son, Alonso,
> They have bereft; and do pronounce by me
> Lingering perdition, worse than any death
> Can be at once, shall step by step attend
> You and your ways … (III, iii, 73–9)

This, then, is Simpson's state: a lingering perdition—literally "loss"—of all that he holds dear. And every day, wherever he goes, whoever he sees, with few exceptions, he's reminded of this: he is no longer welcome in our world.

Oh, I know I need to qualify some of what I've just said, albeit less and less as time goes by. Yes, there are some who still believe him innocent of the murders, like close family members (whom you can't fault, unless they perjure themselves on his behalf), and the most intensely committed of his original constituency, among them those who simply can't admit that they were wrong. But even some of his most loyal supporters have quietly slipped away, like Robert Kardashian, a few years after the trials had concluded, after he himself was shunned by many former friends, and after his fiancée, Denice, had broken off their engagement. Or there's Al Cowlings, whose friendship with Simpson went back to their boyhood days in Oakland, but who also loved Nicole like a sister. And most of those who were still with him (while he remained at large) were morally bankrupt opportunists (like the supporting cast in Vegas), taking advantage of his need for flattery and companionship and for keeping up appearances as best he could. I mean, what real satisfaction can he get from such as these—so many varieties of prostitute that neither love nor respect him? As for the black community as a whole, can you think of any black comedian who tells (or has told) Simpson jokes that hinge on the assumption of his innocence? I can't recall ever hearing such a joke. This says a lot: comedians have their finger on the pulse of popular opinion and they know what's really going on; they trade on being hip. Naivety, unless it's ironic and they're deliberately playing the fool, would be fatal to their professional reputation.

The perfect illustration of this point for me is a scene in *Undercover Brother* (okay, I do go to such films), a popular movie which came out in 2002, some six years after the trials. The hero, a private detective played by Eddie Griffin, is a throwback to the so-called blaxploitation movies of the seventies; he has the cocky strut, big Afro, tight and shiny leather duds, the nonstop layin' down da funk. Unbeknownst to him, what he stands for, which the movie refers to tongue in cheek as the heyday of real black culture, has been systematically undermined and watered down by the Man, a.k.a. Whitey, who it turns out *is* an actual person with a secret organization dedicated to (and succeeding in) making black people bland. The Undercover Brother is clued in to all of this in the scene I'm referring to, when the BROTHERHOOD, a black organization dedicated to stopping the Man, brings him to their secret headquarters to conscript him. He's wide-eyed at what they tell him, but then it all makes sense. "So the conspiracies we believed for all these years are really true? The NBA really instituted the three-point shot to give white boys a chance?"

"Absolutely!" says Smart Brother (the science guy).

"So," adds Griffin, "the entertainment industry really is out to get Spike Lee?"

C'mon, man," says Conspiracy Brother (the total paranoid, who not long before was claiming George Washington Carver was denied credit for inventing the computer—from a peanut!), "even Cher got an Oscar!—Cher!"

Then comes the topper, as Griffin's character asks with a hopeful look, "And O. J. really didn't do it?" No one responds; all you get is nervous coughing, the averting of eyes, and a quick change of topic.

Most black people, I suspect, know what went down at that first trial: it was in part a payback for past injustices inflicted on them, with Simpson the undeserving beneficiary. Passion isn't principle: the latter abides and has stamina; the former wanes and eventually fades away. Many of Simpson's most impassioned and sincere believers, with the passage of time and without their daily fix of Dream Team rhetoric, have long since sobered up and come to their senses. It's comparable to the collective paroxysms of grief and rage that followed on the admittedly tragic death of Princess Diana. There was a mass mania of dangerous proportions fuelling wild conspiracy theories and demanding a witch hunt. But this, too, has now largely subsided and even some of those who most succumbed, who most were in its throes, are now privately sheepish at the recollection.

Meanwhile, there is still the possibility of defections from the innermost circle of the Simpson camp—I mean, from among his closest kin. Despite all the rejection he endured, despite the social pariah he'd become, he still had custody of Justin and Sydney, his children by Nicole, until they turned eighteen, and he still has the consolation, presumably, that both of them, at least, believe in him. But who knows? Maybe one or both are harboring some doubts. It has now (February, 2012) been more than seventeen years since their mother's murder, which would make Sydney twenty-six and Justin twenty-three.[15] Has either one secretly read any of the main books

15 She was born October 17, 1985; he, August 6, 1988.

written about the case, like the ones I've cited here? Or have they just read their father's ludicrous *I Want to Tell You* (though not on the witness stand)? Or have they deliberately tried to shut out everything connected with the horror of that night—at least so far as life will let them? Because there must have been cruel taunts from time to time from other kids or, equally painful, the furtive looks and whispers when they entered and realized they'd been the topic of the conversation just cut short. Hopefully there have been friendships, too, with kids who took them for themselves and disregarded their father, or maybe pitied them on that score. But if they do have close friends, you further wonder: do they ever confide in them about that night, or their thoughts since, or confess how hard it is to balance grieving for their mother and making the best of the family situation that remains? Or, if not with a friend at some sleepover, did one of them ever talk to the other as they lay in bed before falling asleep, recalling, perhaps what he or she had heard, if anything, on that cruel, childhood-world-destroying, watershed June night? Did the younger Justin ever ask his sister what she really thought, and did she then tell him to stop bothering her and go to sleep, that the criminal court had said their father was innocent, which settled it once and for all? And did she then lie there wide awake and wonder? So one of the emotional instruments fate still has at its disposal is his relationship with his children by Nicole: Will one, or both, reject him? And if they do, how crushing will that be?

The Unkindest Cut

Periander, the tyrant of Corinth, provides an object lesson in this kind of retribution—and in other kinds as well. He inherits his position from his father, Cypselus, who seizes power in Corinth after consulting Delphi. Delphi promises him success—up to a point, for his sons will succeed him in authority but not the sons of his sons. In other words, his line will be of short duration—not a happy outcome for a Greek paterfamilias. Nevertheless, Cypselus captures Corinth and rules it harshly. And his son, Periander, rules likewise in his turn, especially after getting some cryptic advice from Thrasybulus, the tyrant of Miletus, in Asia Minor. Periander asks him through a messenger how he may most safely preserve his rule. Thrasybulus makes no overt response but instead takes the messenger on a walk through a wheat field where, as he plies the man with questions about Corinth, he keeps cutting down all the tallest stalks. When the messenger returns and Periander asks what advice Thrasybulus gave, he says he gave none; moreover, he thinks the man mad for destroying his best possessions, and he describes what he's seen him do in the wheat field. Periander at once takes the point and immediately begins to execute or banish any Corinthians who are conspicuous for influence or ability.

Periander's crowning outrage upon his subjects, however, comes about as a result of a domestic crime, the murder of his wife, Melissa, though it comes about in a roundabout way. A friend has left something in his keeping and when, several years later, he asks for it back, Periander cannot recall where he has put it. So he sends a messenger to enquire of Melissa at the Oracle of the Dead (the Necromanteion), which was situated in Epirus, in northwest Greece, by the river Acheron.[16] But when Melissa's phantom appears, she says she will not tell, for she is cold and naked, since the clothes in which she was robed on her funeral bier had not been consumed in the fire. Then, as clinching proof that she is speaking true, she adds that Periander had cast his loaves into a cold oven. This convinces her husband for, as he alone knows, he laid with Melissa after he had slain her.[17] So Periander summons all the women in Corinth to

16 It was regarded as being a branch of that Acheron, the river of *achos* ("pain" or "distress"), which was one of the four rivers of Hades or the Lower World.
17 Had Simpson had "world enough and time" the night he killed Nicole, what would he not have done to assert his control?

the temple of Hera, where they arrive as to a festival, in their finest robes. Then he has them all stripped naked by his guards and their clothes burnt as he says a prayer to Melissa. This done, he sends again to the Oracle of the Dead, and Melissa, now appeased by her ample new wardrobe, tells him where he had placed his friend's deposit. Meanwhile, she has her revenge on him for her murder and the violation of her corpse by prompting him to an action that provokes in the Corinthians a substitute indignation for what he is owed for the undivulged offenses he'd done her.

The foregoing, however, does not directly bring an end to Cypselid rule. That is set in train when Periander's two teenaged sons visit their maternal grandfather, Procles, where he rules in Epidaurus. As they're about to leave, Procles asks them if they know who killed their mother. The elder, but less capable, takes no hint from the remark, but the younger, Lycophron, who has his father's acuteness, is deeply disturbed and from that day forward refuses to talk to his father. Eventually Periander, in a rage, turns him out of the house and, when others put him up, keeps forcing them to turn him out as well. Finally, he issues a proclamation that no one is to give his son shelter, or even speak with him, on pain of being fined a certain sum, to be dedicated to the service of Apollo. So Lycophron, the son of Corinth's lord, is reduced to sleeping outside under whatever shelter he can find. A few days later, when Periander comes upon him dirty and hungry, he feels pity for the boy and begs him to return, citing all the advantages that await him, including the eventual takeover of rule of the city. But Lycophron's only reply is to tell his father that he owes the fine to Apollo for having spoken with him. So Periander gives up and sends the boy away to live in Corcyra (the present-day Corfu), a colony of Corinth he also rules. Much later, when Periander is an old man and feels himself no longer up to managing his affairs, he sends to Corcyra asking Lycophron to return home and take over his rule (he had no confidence in the older brother). But Lycophron makes no reply and, when his sister comes, too, to plead their father's case, his only response is that he will never set foot in Corinth while his father is still alive. Periander then makes one final offer: for the sake of their dynasty he will step down and move to Corcyra, and Lycophron can come to Corinth and rule in his place. Lycophron accepts, but the Corcyreans, alarmed at the prospect of the dreaded Periander in their midst, murder Lycophron in order to keep him away. Thus all the father's crimes come home to roost in indirect and unforeseen wise in the death of his son and the consequent end-to-come of the Cypselid dynasty in Corinth. Periander had, by the odium he'd incurred, cut down the finest and most able member of his own household and rendered it too weak to maintain its rule after his death.

Simpson, likewise, still has this in prospect: his potential repudiation by one or both of the children of his murdered wife. Or it may already be more than a possibility; there may be signs of suppressed anger and resentment finding vent. Certainly Sydney has had a reputation for displays of temper that have made their way into the news. Still, you never know how much even this, his rejection by one or both of his children, might hurt him. According to certain associates, while Nicole was still alive he used to put his own amusements, chiefly golf, ahead of being there for his kids when it most mattered. Not that this necessarily means he doesn't love them; he treated Nicole shabbily but still loved (or obsessed over) her. But you can't be sure—unless you're blessed with Delphic insight—if the loss of their affection would be emotionally devastating, would be for him the hardest (remaining) blow he could incur this side of the grave. He might be so shallow and self-absorbed that even this wouldn't faze him all that much, or so resolute and proud that, if ever he's back on the outside, he'll simply go on with his golf and hired friends for the remainder of his days, smirking all the while at the rest of us, making it plain, at least on the outside, that our general condemnation doesn't hurt him.

That still leaves, of course, the inside to which we're not witness, and the question—public outrage, or even his kids' potential defection, aside—what about remorse per se for the crimes that he's committed? What about this mode of nemesis, the third and final one that I discussed—the most important one of all? I mean, what if he *had* really gotten away with it, had not been cut at the crime scene or seen by Allan Park, so that there was no hint of suspicion as to his involvement?[18] Indeed, what if someone else had been wrongly accused and convicted or even been executed for the crime? How would he have taken that, were it the case? Would he have been comfortable accepting condolences, maybe even appearing, if requested, at some victims-of-violence fundraiser?[19] Or would remorse relentlessly have asserted itself? Would he have been haunted, especially in his dreams and private moments, by what he had done?

There are people who kill and are driven mad by shame and remorse; they later come forward and confess of their own volition, so that they can once again live with themselves and find some peace of mind. In January of 2004, in Fort Bend, Texas, a teenage girl, Ashley Nicole Wilson, was found hanged in her apartment with a suicide note nearby. The medical examiner and the police concluded she had died by her own hand. That March, however, Ashley's boyfriend, Dan Leach, after seeing Mel Gibson's *The Passion of the Christ*, came

18 And no need to be in that Vegas hotel room thirteen years later.

19 Such a possibility is in fact the starting point for Plato's *Republic* (written about two generations after Herodotus). Socrates is asked by two young acolytes to prove that the life of the consummate villain, who attains all his earthly goals and is never detected in his crimes, is still of all lives the least happy—and this without any reference to rewards and punishments in some putative afterlife.

forward and admitted to her murder, that he might seek redemption. He had killed her because she was pregnant and he wanted her altogether out of his life. The murder, by the way, was very cleverly disguised. Stealing a ploy from some *CSI* episode, he had persuaded her, as an exercise in psychotherapy, to write a letter detailing all that was wrong with her life; hence the apparently genuine suicide note. He also wore gloves and succeeded in leaving no DNA at the crime scene. Similarly, in Ottawa, Ontario, on June 6, 2006, a man was found wandering the streets stark naked and under the influence of hallucinogenic mushrooms, screaming that he was the murderer of Jennifer Teague, a fast-food restaurant worker who'd been raped and murdered the prior September. When sober he denied it, but then a few weeks later he approached a few neighbors, confessed again, and said that he needed help. He then repeated this confession to an off-duty police officer and described the killing, including details known only to the police. In this particular case, a boyfriend who had been under suspicion was finally cleared.

Does Simpson have that in him? Apparently not, or not sufficiently, at least up until now. He is, I think, too big an egomaniac; he's been spoiled too much by all the fuss that's been made over him, all the adulation directed his way for most of his life. He still doesn't think of what he's done as murder, because "Nicole had it coming," because *she* had wronged *him*. Her crime was a kind of *lèse-majesté* or injury to the Periander-like "greatness" that was him; in other words, a kind of treason, for which she died the death. That being the case, that is, if he really is that arrogant and that blind to what he has done, *and* if there really is a Nemesis (which of course you can't prove), and It (or rather, She) saw all of this—saw it with that same Delphic insight that sees right though us and understands all our stops and starts (Delphi and Nemesis being but different functions of one entity, *to theion* or the Divine)—then it's worth noting how remarkably well that accords with the way he was tripped up. I mean, if you were looking to humble his pride at its most exultant and wipe that smirk from off his face for a while, how better than in a way he never saw coming, one that would both shake him to the core when it first happened and plant a permanent seed of doubt in his mind. In this context, then, I'd like to revisit my explanation for how the cuts to his hand occurred and to suggest how the reconstruction offered here might also best explain why it is that of all the evidence against him he might be asked about, it is the cuts that far and away irk him the most.

Daniel Petrocelli says: "Simpson hated the cuts. He had broken down or gotten extremely agitated every time I had grilled him on them …"[20] This was evident from his testimony at both his deposition and the civil trial. But it is not only Petrocelli, a hostile observer, who confirms this. There is also the incident I've already mentioned that Schiller and Willwerth relate, the charged encounter between Johnnie Cochran and his client in Simpson's cell, which I'll here revisit.[21] It was near the end of the trial, and Cochran was preparing his summation. He wanted to go over a few things again with O. J., especially his explanation for how the cuts occurred, since it was the one piece of evidence that even the defense attorneys were having difficulty dismissing (or blaming on the cops). So he raised the issue again as tactfully as he could: "You know, O. J., look, you've never been clear about the cuts, the blood, the various cuts. You remember every detail of everything else. But about the cuts you say, 'I don't know exactly when I got them.'" And Simpson suddenly snapped and raged at Cochran: "I'm paying you guys! You guys listen to me, listen to me!" Indeed, his manner was so vehement and threatening that Cochran, in relating the incident to fellow Dream Team members, admitted that he was scared.

20 *Triumph of Justice*, 608.

21 See *American Tragedy*, 842.

Why is it, then, that Simpson is so unnerved by any mention of these cuts? Maybe it *is* just because he has no good explanation. But that applies to a lot of things, so I venture to suggest that it may also be because of the *way* that they happened, which has of itself—and in addition to the *fact* that they happened—severely shaken his confidence. Let me put it this way: no one has a greater stake in there being no God, in the traditional sense of the word, with its attendant notion of divine retribution or Day of Judgment, than someone who has committed a crime such as this. I'm not arguing for or against God's existence, only for there being a psychology, in some form or other, contingent on this notion. Simpson, no doubt, had no such qualms when he plotted the murder. Indeed, the mere concept of right and wrong likely never occurred to him, except so far as he felt wronged by Nicole. And he probably presumed on his own ability to stomach what he would do, that is, to be able to live with himself afterward. After all, there had been frequent violence in the past, and lying to cover it up, and he was comfortable with that. So why not live with this, too—quantum leap though it would be in degree. *And* there was the ego gratification of pulling it off, of putting Nicole in her place and duping most everyone else; it was not that jealousy wasn't the primary motive, but presumption and hubris also factored in. One can only guess at his state of mind when the murders were finished. There would be apprehension, to be sure, but likely exultation, too. His heart is pounding, but he's trying to be methodical, to carry out his plan for leaving no trail. Then, just when he thinks that he's succeeded, when he's all but ready to leave, he has it all confounded in that way—when least expected, when he thinks it's all but "in the bag" and is maybe dropping his guard. And for it to come from that quarter, the very knife with which he's slain his former wife—for it to recoil on him, her killer, and mark him out as such—why, it's almost uncanny! It's as if it were revenging itself for the vile and heinous use to which it's been put.

A Classic Case in Point

In Herodotus, as mentioned, one of the hallmarks of nemesis and its intrusions in the course of mortal affairs is, if you know how to look, an observable element of poetic justice, or a certain symbolic symmetry connecting a given crime and the comeuppance of its perpetrator. It is as if it, nemesis, were an artist, forever accomplishing its ends with a kind of trademark flourish—not for vanity's sake, for vanity is excluded from that realm, but in order that the exquisite irony of one's own or another's downfall may hit home and register all the more tellingly on men. The fear of God, it's been said, is the beginning of wisdom, and this is what nemesis teaches—or, better, implants. By the calling card it leaves it gives men pause, when they realize that the old wives' tales may essentially be true; that there, indeed, may be a witness to all their crimes that they can't elude; and that appropriate punishment of some kind awaits all mortal hubris.

The most egregious tyrant in all of the *Histories* is the mad Cambyses, who succeeds his father, Cyrus the Great, as Persia's king. His downfall, too, hinges in part on a cut that is "accidentally" incurred. He is on campaign in Syria, when he learns that a Magian usurper (from the priestly caste of the Medes, a kindred people who once ruled the Persians, but whom the Persians have overthrown and now rule in their turn) has seized the throne in his absence, under the guise of being his brother Smerdis. Now Cambyses, while residing in Egypt, has already had this brother secretly slain, thanks to a misleading dream in which he was warned by a messenger from home that Smerdis was sitting on his throne and that his head touched the sky. And he has slain his sister-wife (one of two sisters that he had compelled the Persian courts to allow him to marry in violation of ancestral law and custom) when she obliquely chided him for their brother's death. Realizing then the true state of affairs back home, and keenly regretting the needless death of his brother due to the misunderstood dream, he leaps on his horse, intending to lead his army against his capital, Susa, and reclaim his throne. But as he leaps on the steed, the cap falls off the sheath of his sword, and the exposed blade pierces his thigh, *right* where he, in resentment at the worship it received, had struck and killed the Apis bull. This had been his greatest sacrilege, for this was the bull that the Egyptians (whom he'd conquered) regarded as the manifestation of a god.[22] At once sensing that the wound is mortal, he enquires after the name of the adjacent town and is told it is Ecbatana. Thus prophecy is fulfilled, for the oracle at Buto[23] has said he will die at Ecbatana, which he had naturally taken to mean in ripe old age, in the Median Ecbatana, the former capital that is now the summer residence of the Persian kings. The double shock of the wound and the unexpected outcome of the prophecy brings him fully to his senses, and after brooding in silence for some twenty days, he summons the leading Persians to his side and remorsefully confesses "that of all things that I'd most sought to conceal," his crime against his brother and how he's been the fool of fate: "Mistaken as to all that was to be, a brother-slayer I needlessly became and was bereft my kingship nonetheless."[24] In so confessing he acts generously and patriotically, for he is thereby able to explain who this Smerdis really is that sits on his throne and to urge the Persians on pain of a curse to regain their

22 Apis, or Epaphus, would appear among the Egyptians only after long intervals and would be greeted with general rejoicing when it did. It was the calf of a cow that would never calve thereafter, and it was said it was begotten by a flash of light from heaven. Its markings were what revealed it to be Apis: black, with a white diamond on its forehead, with the image of an eagle on its back, the hairs of its tail double in number, and a scarab under its tongue. It was originally regarded as a manifestation of Ptah, the supreme god, but by Herodotus's day it was connected with Osiris.

23 The name both of a city in the Nile Delta and of the cobra goddess worshipped there.

24 For Cambyses's death and these quotations, see the *Histories* 3.65. For Cambyses generally in Herodotus, see 3.1–38, 61–5.

patrimony and overthrow the Median usurpers. A few days later, as gangrene and mortification of the thigh set in, he dies.

According to Greek myth, Astrea, the goddess of Justice, quit this lower world in disgust at the advent of the Iron Age[25] and its better-made knives—in disgust, that is, at the ever-more-rampant violence here below. Poetic justice may be said to have likewise quit the world in relatively recent times, in disgust at the ever-more-iron-headed outlook of modern man: our unremitting materialism, pragmatism, and commercialism. Of course it does survive in (mainly mass appeal) movies—in not-to-be-taken-seriously escapist entertainment—as a melodramatic or sentimental vestige of a simpler time; but as a real force it's largely long gone, along with, by no coincidence, a true understanding of what the word *nemesis* properly means.

O. J. Simpson, meanwhile (and to further compound things), is hardly the literary type. I doubt that he's read Herodotus, or the Greek tragedians, or even much Shakespeare.[26] He's thus your all-too-typical modern man, a complacent materialist (and lifelong jock, to boot), whose notions of poetic justice and nemesis prior to that fateful night were, respectively, dismissive and vague at best. So it's unlikely that when that contretemps occurred—his chance encounter with his own bloody knife—that a man like him, in an age

---

25 The last and worst of the four ages (from the standpoint of our ever-worsening moral and intellectual caliber, as the ancients saw it); the one we're still in now.

26 I've referenced Shakespeare a lot, and it should by now be obvious why. He and Herodotus have essentially the same outlook on the issues of hubris and crime and the punishment or chastisement they inevitably incur thanks to the workings of an indignant and inescapable Nemesis/Fate. Delphi and Nemesis rule in *The Winter's Tale* (see especially III, ii, 115–73) as much as in the *Histories*. And what's explicit in that play is implicit in all his mature output (that is, roughly from *Hamlet* on).

like ours, would have framed his thoughts in these terms. Moreover, there was no prophecy to the apparent effect he'd die in ripe old age, still in possession of his good name and fame. Nonetheless, I expect he had, to some degree, a Cambyses-like moment of sudden recognition—the *anagnorisis* of Greek tragedy—of his own all-too-human fallibility, which the *peripeteia* or "reversal of [one's] fortunes" ushers in. He had thought he was home free: at first, when the game plan all fell into place, when he'd figured out just how he'd pull it off; and then again briefly, but triumphantly, when his victims were disposed of and the coast still looked to be clear.

I said, "to some degree a Cambyses-like moment" because he wasn't and, so far as I can see, still isn't repentant. What he was was shocked—and humbled. It was as if he in his heyday, the fastest back in the NFL and a former first alternate of the 1968 US four by one hundred meter relay team,[27] having broken free of the field, with the end zone in sight and a touchdown an as-good-as-done deal, were suddenly brought down from behind by a phantom opponent faster than he. At that moment, then—or at some combination of that moment with the revelation the next day of the extent of the blood evidence linking him to the crime scene, along with the fallen cap and glove—even he, with his towering ego, must have been shaken. And mixed with that chagrin, he would have had an intimation, if only at a very visceral level (and without ever using the terms that I've used here), of the operations of a higher power. He would even have had, if dimly, the sense that he was getting his just desserts.

Of course as things turned out, he didn't, at least originally, get those just desserts in anything like the form of punishment most of us would assign. But, as I've suggested, nemesis, assuming there is such a thing, may have had an even more fitting fate in store, may

---

27 He was a member of the USC 4 x 110 yard sprint relay team that set a world record in 1967. Which record still stands for this distance as it's no longer run, the 4 x 100 meters having since taken its place.

have been implementing a more refined form of justice all along. I've described his foreseeable situation for the rest of his life, whether incarcerated or not, as a kind of limbo. In this respect, it's eerily like the slow-speed Bronco chase: he's caught, but he's not caught; he can't escape, but neither has he been fully called to account. And he can prolong it, apparently, for as long as there's gas in the tank. In other words, it's not a limbo without end. What that end will be none of us knows for certain. Many of us hope or have faith that a heaven awaits and that we'll make the cut and those that we love along with us. Some even claim to have intimations of that state. This is not a hope Simpson can have. Indeed, just the opposite: he (with Macbeth) has to hope that there's nothing hereafter, that *this* is it. As for intimations, he's had one, too, as I've described: that moment when all his best-laid plans came suddenly undone. He'd like to dismiss it as bad luck that could have been worse—he could have been convicted or even put to death. But there are nagging doubts that just won't go away, try as he might to allay them, *as* proved by the nerve that's struck whenever he's questioned closely on these cuts. It's as if he's been given a token similar to what Croesus was by Delphi, and Periander by his dead wife, Melissa, to assure the respective questioner that its or her power is real. It's not as explicit as these, admittedly, but it's as vivid nonetheless. He's had a close encounter with something he'd *like* to forget but *can't*—if anything, as he gets older it only gets harder to put from his mind. And it's left him with the fear of God—in the form of the fear that there is One.

That having been said, let's look again at Simpson's more recent history—by which I mean the increasingly impudent and erratic behavior that culminated in the Vegas fiasco—to see if this seed of doubt's been bearing fruit. Prior to that, we hadn't heard a lot about him since the trials, try though the media might to make as much as they could out of relatively minor incidents, like that Florida road-rage case or his daughter's anger-management issues. Then, suddenly and in rapid fashion, we were getting a series of ever-more-aberrant escapades, which—besides making him money—seem designed to taunt us with his shameless want of all contrition and to rub our face in his getting away scot-free. Up to a point, there was at least some method to his madness. The car-dealer sketch, the *JudgeOJ* website, and *If I Did It* all made money—in the latter instance, plenty—and didn't put him in jeopardy with the law. But there was no sufficient reason for that monumental misstep in Las Vegas, where he gave his enemies the very opening they'd long sought. It truly was insane.

If protesting too much is tantamount to confession, then Simpson's actions leading up to his arrest, with their gratuitous and escalating impudence and defiance, spoke volumes about his real internal state. And what they bespoke, you would have to conclude, was a man being hounded by something, a soul that knew no peace and had been steadily worn down over time by the awful truth that it must live with—*and* by the seed of doubt first planted the night of the murders. Damned man walking—that was the spectacle Simpson now afforded and thus the irrational and self-destructive behavior as he fought ever more desperately to maintain, in his own eyes as much as in others', the illusion that he had won.[28]

It's not inconceivable that Simpson could win on an appeal of his Vegas conviction and see his sentence reduced as, for instance, a

28 To complete note 19 from this chapter: Socrates does eventually prove, to his interlocutors' satisfaction, that villainy is its own sufficient requital, even without an afterlife to fear; and that the most absolute of villains, the unalloyed tyrant, is himself the most tyrannized over of all men—by his own unbridled ruling passion. He is at constant war with the better part of himself, as he perforce must suppress and deny at all times every finer feeling. Moreover, even if undetected, he has to live in perpetual fear that he somehow one day will be.

different jury is allowed to consider lesser charges than kidnapping (as broadly defined in Nevada). So he could be back among us after less than the minimum nine years he now faces, with a potential life expectancy of many more years thereafter. But for the majority of us that should no longer be cause for concern. He'll still be in that—now so patent—hell of his own creation, whether it ends with our earthly existence or not.

CHAPTER 9

COMING CLEAN

So where do we go from here? Or, rather, where does Simpson go? I said in the opening chapter that I'd point the way to redemption as Herodotus sees it. Not that I thought it likely Simpson would take this advice, but in order to complete the lost perspective, or all-but-forgotten world view, I'm claiming to revive. In the *Histories*, the possibility of redemption—or reversal of ill fortune, including the removal of a curse—by a change of heart and the requisite sacrifice or act of atonement that that changed heart sees it must make, is introduced somewhat obliquely early on by one of those beguiling digressions that dot his narrative. This one, in fact, occurs during his otherwise brief survey of the reigns, and signal deeds, of the successive Mermnad kings in Lydia, the ones who follow Gyges to the throne after he overthrows Candaules. And it illustrates well why it is we lose track of the Delphic prophecy that Gyges's line will fail in the fifth generation and thus requite in the fullness of time the wrong involved in the ouster and slaying of Candaules.

In the reign of Croesus's father, Alyattes, the Lydians' war with Miletus, a Greek city in Asia Minor, is brought to a peaceful close in the twelfth year, thanks to a strange chain of events. For the Lydians, during their annual harvest-time invasion, accidentally burn down the temple of Athena at Assesus with the fires that they set to destroy the crops, and shortly thereafter Alyattes falls ill. When the disease lingers, he sends to Delphi for advice, but the priestess of the shrine refuses him any answer until he rebuilds the temple. Word of this exchange comes to Periander of Corinth, who in turn passes the information on to his good friend Thrasybulus (he of the cryptic wheat-stalk-whacking message), who then rules Miletus. And when Alyattes sends a messenger to seek a truce for as long as it will take to rebuild the temple, Thrasybulus is ready with a ruse: he has all the grain he can muster piled in the public square, and when the messenger arrives, the townsfolk are all drinking and making merry. When word of this gets back to Alyattes, he can only assume that the Milesians are by no means reduced to extremities by famine, as he'd supposed. So he concludes not just a truce but a permanent peace and builds not one but two temples for Athena—and, of course, recovers from his illness (1.19–22).

Having finished with this tale and the reign of Alyattes, and before he moves on to Croesus's reign, Herodotus, since he's mentioned Periander, thinks it a fit moment to insert (1.23–4) a remarkable tale that occurs in connection with him—on the face of it for no other reason than that it *is* remarkable and strange. There is a poet-musician, Arion of Methymna (in Lesbos), the most renowned of that era, who dwells at Periander's court. He it is who gave the world the dithyramb, the hymn to Dionysus, and first trained choirs to perform it. After a long time spent with Periander in Corinth, he has the urge to travel to Italy (the southern portion of which was largely colonized by Greeks). This he does and, thanks to his talent and fame, there makes a great deal of money performing for hire. At length he decides to come home, and he books passage on a Corinthian vessel sailing from Tarentum. But the wicked crew, seeing the great wealth he brings on board, plot to kill him and steal his money. When Arion becomes aware of their intent, he begs them to take his money but spare his life—to no avail. So he makes a second request: that he be permitted to stand on the afterdeck dressed in the robes of his calling and sing them a song, after which he promises to kill himself. This request the sailors grant, delighted at the prospect of hearing so famous a singer. Arion then dons his bardic robes, takes up his lute, and sings *ton nomon ton orthion* (or "shrill strain"), after which he leaps into the sea. The sailors then continue on to Corinth.

Meanwhile, a dolphin comes to Arion's aid and carries him on its back to Taenarum, a cape in the eastern Peloponnese (in the south of Greece). Thence, still dressed in his singer's robes, he makes his way to Corinth and to Periander, who is little inclined to believe the strange tale he is told. So he keeps Arion under guard and awaits the sailors' return. Once they arrive, he has them brought into his presence and enquires after Arion. They reply that they left him alive and well in Tarentum. At these words, Arion himself steps forth, dressed just as he was when he leapt into the sea, and the lie is exposed. As to the sailors' fate, it's left to the imagination, but since they'd crossed the tyrant Periander, it must have been grim. Herodotus only tells us that an offering of Arion's still may be seen in a temple at Taenarum; it's a small bronze figure of a man on a dolphin. The digression concluded, he resumes where he'd left off, by telling us of the costly presents sent to Delphi by Alyattes as thank offerings for his recovery. Then the lengthy tale of Croesus gets underway.

As I said, on the face of it this is simply a remarkable tale, two dimensional in the telling and with a neat, happy ending. But Herodotus's original readers would have readily sensed something more beneath its pleasant surface. They would have known that that was no mere dolphin that came to the rescue but rather an agent of Apollo, if not the god himself—Apollo Delphinius—in a guise he was wont to assume. And they would have recognized too that the "shrill strain"

Arion sang, *ton nomon ton orthion*,[1] was a set phrase for a certain hymn to Lord Apollo, so that his coming to the rescue was, in fact, a response to a prayer. The more thoughtful might also have reflected that it was in his dolphin guise that Apollo served as a *psychopompos* or "soul conductor" through the waters of the other world, through which the souls of the dead had to pass to obtain purification; and Arion was as good as dead when he leapt into the sea. Virtually everyone, though, would have sensed the allusion to Delphi. The shrine's etymology is debated, but one of the main candidates has always been *delphis*, the Greek word for "dolphin," which etymology was reinforced in antiquity by various founding myths that tell how someone in distress at sea is carried to the adjacent coastline by a dolphin, whereupon Apollo bids them build a sanctuary and name it for their watery savior.[2]

Still, you might ask, what does Arion's life's being saved have to do with redemption? What did he do wrong? The answer, as the pious would have known, is that he should not have been so concerned with worldly wealth, and in particular should not, as it were, have prostituted his sacred calling. Thus it is only when he divests himself of all his newfound wealth and dons the robes of that calling that he is saved, the ensuing physical salvation mirroring or symbolizing the change in attitude or spirit that precedes. He becomes himself again; which, in a context framed by Delphic references—Alyattes's consultation concerning his illness and the thank offerings he eventually sends—conjures up what Delphi stands for above all: the precept/panacea at its entrance: "Know thyself." And Alyattes too, you'll note, does much the same, in that he recognizes that the priestess's refusal to answer his query regarding his health until

---

1 One of the extended meanings of *nomos*, "law" or "ordering principle," is "musical mode."

2 For a detailed discussion of Apollo Delphinius and the legends associated with his cult, see Eunice Burr Stebbins, *The Dolphin in the Literature and Art of Greece and Rome* (Menasha WI: Banta, 1929) 77–82.

he has rebuilt the temple is in fact the prescription for his cure, which prescription also sets in train the end of the war of aggression he is waging and the resumption of peace. More important still, this tale and its morals, both overt and implied, is prelude to the *Histories'* most complete case study in redemption: namely, the tale of overweening Croesus (1.26–92) and how he is chastened by fate and made a better man. Especially, however, it anticipates the conclusion of that tale, when Apollo intervenes to save his life.

In the opening chapter, I described the incident in which fabulously wealthy Croesus is visited by the Athenian lawgiver Solon, and how he dismisses Solon as a man of no great account when he fails to name him as the most blessed of all men he has seen—reserving the epithet "blessed" for those only who've reached the end with their good name and good fortune intact. At this and the attitude it implies, nemesis took dead aim at Croesus, first depriving him of his eldest son and then, as later discussed, inducing him by an ambiguously phrased oracle to initiate a war against the rising power of Persia. When at length Croesus has been defeated, and his capital Sardis is being sacked, his conqueror, Cyrus the Great, has him bound in chains and placed upon a huge pyre to be burnt alive. Croesus, meanwhile, stunned and depressed as he is at the sudden and utter downturn of his fortunes, has not spoken a word since his capture. But now, as he stands amid the flames, it occurs to him how divinely inspired was Solon's advice, and heaving a bitter sigh, he thrice calls out his name. This catches Cyrus's attention, and he sends interpreters to enquire after what Croesus has just said. Croesus explains that Solon was a man whom he fervently wishes all kings might have had converse with; then he tells of their encounter years before and how all that Solon said has turned out true, but especially as concerns those who think themselves the favored of Fortune. These words produce a change of heart in Cyrus, for he reflects that he, too, is a mere mortal like Croesus, and this, along with a newly aroused fear of retribution and a sense of the instability of all earthly affairs, makes him repent of his purpose and order that Croesus be removed from the flames. By now, however, the fire is beyond all human control. Whereupon Croesus, his will to live revived, calls out to Lord Apollo, bidding him, if any of his many offerings has ever pleased him, to come to his aid. Then suddenly, on a "clear and windless day," clouds form in the sky, and a violent storm bursts forth with such heavy rainfall that the flames are quenched and Croesus's life is spared (1.87).

The tale of Croesus then winds to a close as he becomes the trusted, Solon-like, counselor of Cyrus—but not before he is allowed by his new master to send messengers to Delphi to expostulate against the ingratitude of the god and the "deceitful" oracles that have brought him to this pass. The shrine, however, reminds him of the vengeance owed Candaules in the fifth generation of Gyges's line, and how his overthrow is the fated expiation of his forbear's crime. It also explains the true meaning of the misleading oracle[3] and how it had been Croesus's responsibility to enquire again as to exactly what empire was meant. When Croesus hears the reply, he absolves the god of all blame and recognizes that he alone is responsible for his errors and his fate. His salvation *and* self-knowledge are complete. Indeed, it's almost like a posthumous experience or state translated

3 Or oracles, to be precise, for Croesus consulted with Delphi a third time as to whether his reign would be long, and the priestess replied that when a mule should come to sit on the Median throne, he should fear for his life (1.55). Croesus thought such a prospect absurd and became the more confident that he and his line would rule forever. But now the priestess explains that that "mule" was Cyrus, who was of doubly "mixed" descent (both class and race), being the son of a Median princess and a Persian of (at the time of Cyrus's birth) lower rank. The reader, by the way, is being taught by this as well: there is a Delphic-like dimension to Herodotus's text that he must be cognizant of to read it aright.

into the realm of the here and now. In essence, he has a retroactive clarification of his whole life, and he emerges from this cleansed of all presumption and at peace. What's also important to note is the convergence of human contrition and divine intercession, for it's when Croesus is humbled and sees the wisdom of Solon's counsel that heaven steps in to save him from the flames.

Meanwhile, his salvation hearkens back to the essential elements in the barebones tale of Arion. Both men are first divested of all their worldly possessions and then, at their fortune's lowest ebb, they call out to Apollo to come to their aid. And both are rescued in a way connected with water, which symbolizes the purification or catharsis they undergo. Indeed, the dolphin and the rainstorm might be said to function somewhat like the deus ex machina of Greek tragedy, the convention whereby at a critical juncture a god is brought out on stage on some kind of device to resolve or untangle an apparently hopeless situation. Just as soliloquies serve to make thoughts audible, so the "god from the machine" (among other things) serves to allow spiritual awakenings or profound changes of heart—that is, purely internal and ineffable psychological events—to be made both audible *and* visible. It thus allows what might be called the ultimate purpose behind the tribulations that are tragedy's stock in trade[4] to be shown dramatically or staged. It is only *in extremis* that humility and self-

---

4 I've referred to *The Tempest* several times already. Though the play is not a tragedy but a romance, it still amounts to a kind of abstract or compendium of Shakespeare's own deployment of the former genre. The *tempest* in the title stands for all "the slings and arrows"—or adverse fortune—ever sent anyone's way. By means of this device, Prospero has his enemies cast upon the shore of his enchanted island, there to be made aware of their sins and the "lingering perdition" that "the powers" have prescribed if they fail to repent. As Ariel says at the close of this same speech, "whose [the powers'] wraths to guard you from … is nothing but heart-sorrow and a clear life ensuing" (III, iii, 79–82). The water symbolism should be noted too, for the storm also stands for the cleansing or catharsis that both the characters and, through them, the audience, undergo.

knowledge are perfected, as we finally turn toward heaven in the wholehearted way it requires. At this point, and not before, heaven turns toward us or, rather, turns toward us in merciful mode, for the tribulations, too, were heaven sent. Catharsis and realization, two sides of the same coin, are made manifest and dramatic; they are thereby imparted in varying degree to the spectators as well, to the extent that they are engaged by, or feel for, what the protagonist undergoes. It should not be forgotten that Greek drama grew out of religious ritual, which is always in some fashion a renewal of the link beneath heaven and earth—or God and man.

O. J. Simpson, even supposing he read this, would, I expect, not be impressed. For one thing, I doubt if he'd identify much with a poet-musician like Arion, even though he, Simpson, was an artist too—sort of. But his film career was itself a kind of prostitution of his real gifts, which were athletic. He was trading on a name he'd made in football and taking work that others were far more qualified to do. As for Croesus, he might resonate a bit, seeing that he had all that money. But still, he was more like an owner than a player, or like one of those rich guys that always sought out Simpson's company, wanted to play golf with him, and wanted to be his friend. They're fine in their way, but they're not players, or warriors, as he was. They can buy a championship, but that doesn't make them champions.

Meanwhile, the stories themselves sound pretty far-fetched—a dolphin swimming to the rescue! A cloudburst coming in response to a prayer! Does anyone believe such things today? Not likely. And, frankly, I suspect Herodotus didn't believe them either—these particular miraculous bits—*in* their literal sense. But he did, I'm sure, believe in what these miracles represented or symbolized, which is that heaven does come to the aid of whoever turns to it with a pure, or purified, heart. And that potentially means *anyone*. No one in his text outdoes Cambyses in madness and murder; but even he, as I've recounted, does come to his senses in the end and express remorse. (Then again, not everyone learns before it's too late; there are some, like Cleomenes, who stay lost souls until they die.) Moreover, in telling such stories as these of Croesus and Arion in more distant times, Herodotus is preparing his readers for very real events of not-so-distant date to come later on in his *Histories* and for what we may call the divine dimension, or backdrop, that he wants them to sense in all that occurs. Of course, all that occurs, even in Herodotus, is far too much to treat of here: there are so many strands in his narrative and so many peoples or ethnic groups. Fortunately, however, selection is made easy. No strand is more stirring, or more infused with the divine, than that which deals with the Spartans, and conveniently, none more suits the fallen "hero" of this *History* of mine.

Sparta—this is a name that Simpson should readily recognize; he should both know basically who the Spartans were and what, to this day, they and their state connote. He's probably seen that Tom Cruise movie *The Last Samurai*, which makes frequent reference to the Spartans and their famous stand at Thermopylae; it's a fair comparison, since the Samurai, like the Zulus and Plains Indians, to cite other examples, share much the same warrior ethos as the Spartans. Then there's that mega-hit *300* from a few summers ago (2007); he's likely seen that too; it's his kind of film.[5] Moreover, Spartans is in modern times a popular name for sports teams of all sorts, though especially fitting in the macho world of American-style football, where heroic or formidable names are usually a part of the motivational mystique. The Michigan State Spartans most obviously come to mind. Michigan State did play Simpson's USC once during

5 Viewer beware: though the basic scenario resembles the facts, the movie is otherwise riddled with distortions of Herodotus, most of which pander to either the modern secular-humanist bias, or to an adolescent need to demonize the enemy, in this case the Persians.

his illustrious college career (USC won 21 to 17), but it was not for all the marbles; thus it was not an *epic* encounter. Instead, it was their Big 10 rivals, the Ohio State Buckeyes, who met USC and Simpson in a Rose Bowl (on New Year's Day, 1969) with the national Division I title on the line.[6] The Buckeyes won 27 to 16. But the highlight of the game was a Simpson touchdown run, one of his greatest: an eighty-yard gallop to glory that featured a sudden surging cut to his right, about fifteen yards downfield, which eluded the entire defensive backfield and bought him some space, and then a sprint to the far corner of the distant end zone as, with Olympian strides, he outran the angles the Buckeye deep backs still had.

Simpson, meanwhile, though not a Spartan, *was* a Trojan, the name of the Southern Cal teams. The Trojans, the original ones, weren't Greeks, as everyone (hopefully) knows. But no matter: it's the same classical world, same gods, *same* language even (because in the *Iliad* there are no translators; thanks to poetic license, both Trojans and Greeks speak Greek). And, of course, they lived by the same warrior ethos, which is why a few thousand years later football teams who call themselves Trojans intend by that the same heroic associations as those who opt for Spartans as their name. Such names are not just *names*, they're also *slogans*—in the original sense: they're battle cries, the *cause* these teams espouse. Interestingly, given the topic of this text, the cause of the Trojan War was a Spartan woman named Helen, who deserted her older husband, Menelaus, for Paris, a young and handsome Trojan prince. This essentially mirrors the scenario Simpson was in, for, whether Ron and Nicole were actually lovers is no matter; in Simpson's mind they *were*. But I stray from my point, which is to introduce, succinctly, the Spartans and what they stood for

---

6 USC defeated Indiana 16 to 3 in the previous Rose Bowl, but it was not for the national title. Simpson was only at USC for two years, since he'd been in a two-year junior college program prior to that. Notably, he led the Trojans to the Rose Bowl both years he was there.

in more depth—indeed, thanks mainly to Herodotus, what they still stand for today. Because I then intend to hold them up to Simpson, as a standard or a bar that has been set *and*, more important, as an object lesson in how even he might yet retrieve his situation. Failing this, he ought to give back his Heisman Trophy and concede thereby that he's no Trojan or Spartan—that he can't play in their league.

Though Sparta's mixed government was headed, as indicated, by a twin kingship or diarchy, their polity would most accurately be described by a term that has virtually disappeared from the modern political lexicon: *timocracy*. It signifies a state in which the governing class is restricted to those who by nature (character type) and training are emulous above all of *timē* (honor) and *aretē* (the cultivation of martial excellence)[7]—in other words, a hereditary governing warrior caste. Herodotus, though he describes the reality, does not use the term; instead he uses such phrases as "released to freedom" (7.103), "released to war" (2.167), or "to the warrior-hood" (2.165) to describe the Spartans and their like in other states. What he means by this is that they were released from all menial activities (supported by an ancestral estate or allotment of land that was largely worked by a serf-like caste, the helots) in order that they could devote themselves solely to the pursuit of martial skills,[8] both individual and, above

7 It was for Plato the second-best form of government, the best being rule by philosopher-kings.

8 The Spartans were debarred from pursuing any craft or trade; they were to devote *all* their time to military readiness. Xenophon, another Greek historian who flourished two generations after Herodotus, called them "master craftsmen in war" (*The Constitution of the Lacedaimonians*, 13.5), in pointed reference, perhaps, to this restriction on their activities. Compared to them, he said, all others were but "slapdash improvisers." As an Athenian exile living among them as their guest, and renowned military hero in his own right, he would have known whereof he spoke.

all, collective. The Spartans were, in battle, cohesion incarnate. Meanwhile, the excellence they attained to was the chief guarantor that their country remain free.

It's hard to find anything to compare them precisely to today, though obviously an elite military unit is the nearest candidate. Another partial comparison, though, could be made to top-flight Olympic athletes that the state supports on condition that they devote themselves wholly to being the best that they can be in their events. But there was this difference: the Spartans were to do so virtually all their lives. A further difference—no endorsements! Spartan law forbade the private possession of gold or any luxuries; they stayed tough by, quite literally, religiously preserving the hardy and disciplined lifestyle that their divinely sanctioned lawgiver, Lycurgus, had given them. Thus qualified, the comparison to an Olympian is one that Herodotus would have endorsed. The Spartans, in particular, excelled at the ancient games, and generally speaking, the athletes then—victors and also-rans—were soldiers as well, either lifelong or part-time.

It is, moreover, a comparison he virtually makes himself in his narration of the events of Thermopylae, the Spartans' finest hour, and the one for which they're most remembered to this day. For, when the battle is over and the three hundred Spartans have been slaughtered to the last man,[9] Xerxes, through an interpreter, enquires of a few Arcadian deserters the following day what the rest of the Greeks are up to. He's told that they are celebrating the Olympic

---

[9] One Spartan, Aristodemos, survived due to his being away in a nearby town for treatment of acute inflammation of the eyes. But a second one, Eurytus, who was there for the same reason, had his servant lead him to the battlefield, where he plunged blindly into the fray to die with his comrades. Aristodemos was then shunned in Sparta for not doing likewise; he would die at Plataea the following year as he hurled himself madly at the foe to retrieve his good name (7.229–31, 9.71). The three hundredth slain Spartan is furnished by Leonidas.

festival, which they do by holding athletic contests. They're then asked, "For what prize (*athlon*)?" and they reply that it's for an olive wreath, the symbol of victory. At this, Tritantaechmēs, a Persian general, exclaims: "Good heavens, Mardonius [the chief commander of the army and the man who most had Xerxes's ear], what kind of men are these you've brought us to fight with, who compete [literally 'engage in *agons*'] for no material reward, but solely for excellence's sake (*peri aretēs*)!" (8.26).[10] Xerxes, who has sought to conceal from his troops how many men he has lost at the hands of the Spartans (some twenty thousand), is angered at the reply. And the reader senses why—because all the honor of the prior day belongs to the Spartans, and the real and lasting victory is theirs.

Meanwhile, it is not just Sparta's bravery and prowess that shine through: there is her piety as well and her close relationship with heaven. For the Greek reader would have made a further connection at this juncture; he would have known that the Olympics were founded by Hercules himself and were held in his honor.[11] And the Spartans *were* Heraclids; that is, they traced their lineage back to the deified hero Hercules in the genealogies of both their kings (which are recited in the text). Moreover, Herodotus has explained why he thinks Leonidas, the Spartan king who led them that day, chose to stay and perish, when it was quite possible for him along with the rest, with no loss of honor, to beat a tactical retreat. For when the

10 The Olympic Games were mainly an athletic event, but the three other Panhellenic games gave equal precedence to poetic and musical contests for a similar symbolic and ethereal prize, such as the laurel wreath awarded at the Pythian Games. This is the context in which Arion's artistic apostasy would have been seen. Herodotus, it should be added, is romanticizing somewhat (about the Games): some victors got ample material rewards from their proud countrymen when they returned.

11 There were competing mythic explanations, but the favorite version is that Hercules built Olympia and instituted the games to celebrate his cleansing of the Augean stables.

Spartans first got word that the Persian was coming, they consulted at Delphi. They were told that one of two bitter fates was in store: either a king "of Hercules's line" must perish or Sparta herself be annihilated (7.220). *Why* they faced this dilemma I'll not get into, except to say that nemesis and what might be called the "wrath of Hercules" so required.

In brief, Leonidas—who as a Spartan priest-king was custodian, and student, of all the oracles she received—knows in advance that he must die—he and the three hundred with him, all of whom have been chosen (in part) because they have male heirs and their family line can continue on without them. Thermopylae, then, *is* Sparta's Olympics this year, her event or *agon*, and her requisite offering to Hercules. As Herodotus points out, seemingly in passing, the narrow "gateway" at Thermopylae (between the mountains and the sea) is at the foot of a spur of Mount Oeta (7.176.3), on whose summit—as everyone knew—the mortal Hercules died in agony at the end of all his labors and was thence apotheosized, or translated into heaven.[12] And you have a sense, a most palpable intimation as it were, that the Spartans achieve a like consummation, or translation into glory, on this day.[13]

The foregoing was to give a taste of what Sparta was about. But it's not exactly imitable today, at any rate not by O. J. Simpson. The

---

12 A little later he mentions another feature of the vicinity, "the river Duras, that's said to have sprung forth to come to Hercules's aid as he was being consumed by flames" (7.198). He is referring to the funeral pyre atop Mount Oeta, on which Hercules was burnt alive, at his own command, to release him from the agonies inflicted by the poisoned shirt of the centaur Nessus, which he'd been tricked into putting on.

13 Herodotus twice intimates that he is an initiate into the mysteries of the Cabiri, a religious order dedicated to the cult of Hercules (2.51, 3.37). The reader would not do amiss then to be alert to the inner, or spiritual, applications of that myth in appropriate sections of his text.

following Spartan tale, however, illustrates the same standard of conduct as the foregoing *and* in a way that Simpson could replicate, given his peculiar legal situation and even given his incarcerated condition. It concerns a remarkable act of self-sacrifice undertaken by two Spartans of the highest rank in the years following the Persian invasion, and thus, strictly speaking, after the events that Herodotus has set out to record. He inserts it, allegedly, simply because it is remarkable, but it's also, I'd say, to give a timely foretaste of how the Spartans are about to perform at Thermopylae and, more important, as a clue to why it is that nemesis requires a Spartan king to die.

The occasion for its insertion (7.133–7) is this: Xerxes, prior to his invasion of Greece in 480 BC, sent heralds to the various Greek states to demand earth and water, the tokens of submission. Many submitted, especially in the north where they were more exposed to attack; most didn't. Then Herodotus adds that no heralds were sent to Athens and Sparta, since those sent a decade earlier by Xerxes's father, Darius, with this same demand had been slain by the outraged recipients. In Sparta they were thrown into a well and told to fetch their earth and water thence.

Despite the provocation, such conduct was grossly reprehensible in the eyes of everyone; for it was accepted as an unwritten law, by both Greek and barbarian, that the persons of heralds were sacrosanct and inviolate. As a consequence, says Herodotus, the "wrath of Talthybius," the herald of Agamemnon (in the *Iliad*), and thus the figurative representative or personification of the principle transgressed, descended on the Spartans in this wise: for many years thereafter, try as they might, they could not obtain any favorable omens from their sacrifices. Greatly concerned by this, they held frequent assemblies, at which the question was put by a public crier: "Would any of the Lacedaimonians [another name they went by] be willing to die for Sparta?" The (normally) pious Spartans knew, of course, wherein they had offended; they knew, as well, the price they had to pay. As to this there was no debate. Finally, a pair of Spartans came to their country's rescue. There was in the city a temple to Talthybius, and a family—the Talthybiadae—said to descend from him that had, by inherited right, the sole privilege of serving as Sparta's heralds. Noblesse oblige: with privilege come attendant obligations. And it was clear what was called for in this case: "an eye for an eye, a herald for a herald." Accordingly, two men of this clan, Sperthias and Boulis, stepped forward to offer their lives in exchange for the murdered Persian heralds, that Sparta might be reconciled with heaven.

The commitment made, they then set forth for distant Susa, Xerxes's capital,[14] where few Greeks from the European homeland had ever been before. And the Xerxes they were to present themselves to was by now, as you would expect, a bitter man, for this incident occurred several years after his debacle at the hands of the Greeks. Herodotus does not record much of the journey itself, except for an exchange with a Persian *satrap*, whose guests they were for a night and who wondered why men of their caliber didn't submit to the Great King's authority and rule over Greece as his agents—which advice they disdained as connoting slavery. But he earlier (5.52–4) described at length the Royal Road leading from Sardis, Croesus's capital in Lydia (not far from the Mediterranean coast in present-day Turkey) to Persian Susa. From Lydia it wound through various ancient lands: first Phrygia, Cappadocia, and Cilicia (also in Turkey), then through Armenia, then Matiene (now in northwestern Iran), and thence down into Cissia, the land immediately east of the Persian homeland proper, but now the heart of her empire.[15] Along the way they passed many guard posts; wended through lands now arable, now rugged; forded,

14 There was another capital, Persepolis, but it is not mentioned in Herodotus. Susa is thought to have been the more splendid of the two, thanks to the magnificent palace built there by Darius, to which Xerxes made significant additions.

15 Cissia is the Elam of the Bible.

or were ferried across, numerous streams and rivers, among them the Tigris and Euphrates, until finally, on the banks of the Choaspes, magnificent Susa heaved into view. The total distance is some 450 Persian *parasangs* or about 1700 miles; all in all a ninety days' journey for a mounted traveler at that time (to which should be added the roughly five or six days spent at sea crossing from Greece to, likely, Ephesus on the Turkish coast and the three days' journey thence by land to Sardis, where the Royal Road began).

This, then, is the journey that these heralds made—for the most part among *xenoi*, "strangers," many of warlike breed—protected all the while by the badges of their office and steeled by their commitment to remove the blemish that had sullied Sparta's name and cut her off from all propitious intercourse with heaven. When they reached Susa and were ushered into Xerxes's august presence—likely in the vast thirty-six-pillared *apadana* or audience hall (about 120 meters square), filled with soldiers and high-ranking courtiers of every sort—his bodyguards at first tried to force them to prostrate themselves before the Great King. But this they refused to do, saying it was not the custom in Sparta to worship a mere man like themselves.[16] Then they declared their mission: "O king of the Medes, the Lacedaimonians have sent us to render satisfaction for the slaying of the heralds in Sparta." But Xerxes, even if further irked by their refusal to kowtow, replied magnanimously, saying he would not, by slaying the Spartan heralds, transgress a law the entire world held sacred. Moreover, he had no intention of releasing the Spartans from the consequences their atrocity had incurred.

16 The historicity of the *Book of Esther* is debated, as is the identity of Ahasuerus, the Persian Emperor who takes her to wife. But this Xerxes is the primary candidate. Conceivably, then, Queen Esther lived, was in the palace at the time, and at least heard tell of the noble conduct of these Spartan heralds, men every bit as devout and anchored in principle as the heroes of her tribe.

So the heralds returned unscathed, and despite Xerxes's refusal to exact revenge, the wrath of Talthybius was appeased to the extent that Sparta's sacrifices again met with favorable omens. It was, however, not fully slaked till the next generation and the tragic conflict that raged toward the end of Herodotus's life: the Peloponnesian War between Sparta and Athens. At least, that's what the Spartans believed, and so did Herodotus. For he finds it *theiotaton*—"most divine" or "characteristic in the extreme of how heaven operates"—that this wrath did not finally work itself out until it had descended upon the sons of these same heralds, Aneristus and Nicolaüs, who, in 430 BC, were captured on an embassy to Asia, handed over to the Athenians, and then summarily slain.[17]

What, then, has this to do with O. J. Simpson? He's not an ambassador, of good will or otherwise, and will certainly never become one: diplomatic immunity is not something he'll ever enjoy. Thanks to the Fifth Amendment of the US Constitution, however, he does enjoy what amounts to much the same thing: "nor shall any person be subject for the same offense to be twice put in jeopardy of life or limb." It's more commonly called double jeopardy, and it is a procedural defense (it doesn't per se dispute the facts) designed to prevent potential prosecutorial abuse by the government through repeated prosecutions used as a means of harassment or oppression. No doubt it's a wise measure for the most part, which is why in various forms it's in effect throughout most of Europe and the English-speaking world. Leaving aside, however, whether there are wiser versions of it, it is obvious that double jeopardy as it exists in

17 This whole story *can't* have occurred, if we're to believe the film *300*. There the killing of the Persian heralds by them feisty neither-god-nor-man-fearing Spartans (*led* by Leonidas) is justified, 'cause I mean, like, they totally asked for it. Call it the adolescentification of history—and morality.

America cannot be an unalloyed good if it lets an O. J. Simpson go unpunished. For not only was the original verdict partisan and dubious, additional evidence later emerged that conclusively put to rest *all* reasonable doubt as to his guilt. That said, it's still all water under the bridge. It's what has been dealt and therefore what was meant to be, with the result that Simpson is immune from further criminal prosecution for the murders of Ron and Nicole. In this respect his person is inviolate, just like the heralds of old. I was going to say "sacrosanct" but then choked on the word. But that's what he is, or rather, that's what the law is that he's hiding behind. And fairly so: a law, even if flawed to some extent, deserves respect. Meanwhile, you never know, a present outrage may serve a long-term purpose that we shortsighted mortals cannot—yet—comprehend.

It's an ill wind that blows nobody good. And, with Fate at the helm, that Fate that "hath to instrument this lower world and what is in't," there is in principle nothing that can't be turned to some account, including the unholy sanctuary Simpson still enjoys on the score of the murders and will enjoy for the remainder of his life. Though double jeopardy preserves him *from* punishment, it also preserves *for* him a unique opportunity. As things (still) stand, he's like the Spartan heralds on their mission in another way, as well, in that he's surrounded by "strangers" virtually everywhere he goes. This is not because he's in a foreign land but because he's alienated just about everybody—at least everybody whose good opinion matters (I exclude those parasites who exploit his needs for companionship and adulation). He's an outcast—for all eternity perhaps—and his double jeopardy protection is as much a curse as it is a blessing. The Spartan heralds earned the admiration of all who met them; Simpson, the inviolate, yet transparent, killer who walked among us, and likely will again, his full debt to society still unpaid, earns disgust. But this he can reverse.

As the Supreme Court has determined, "double jeopardy is a personal constitutional right that can be waived. Where there is an opportunity to oppose the action and the defendant decides to forego that opportunity, there is no functional equivalent of a successive prosecution for the same offense."[18] So, O. J., if you want once more to be a hero, here's how you do it: waive your right not to be tried again, admit your guilt, and accept unconditionally whatever punishment is assigned. In short, sue for justice against yourself. Granted, this may not be as simple as it sounds: from what I've read further to the foregoing, you may still be prevented by the niceties of the law from harassing yourself with a second criminal trial—in which case, fight it. You fought against what at first seemed hopeless odds before, in an unjust cause, so why not do so now when your cause is just (and you've got so much time on your hands). Try everything, as if you were seeking a cure for cancer, which is pretty much the case. Be as ardent as widowed Orpheus when he sought Eurydicē. Assemble another Dream Team—there are many, I'm sure, who would take you on pro bono—and make the whole operation a kind of crusade. You could plead, perhaps, that you'd perjured yourself when you pled "not guilty" and that that should nullify the original trial. Likewise when you pretended the glove didn't fit, when you didn't make your best effort to put it on. Or, if perjury doesn't fit in the latter instance, try obstruction of justice. By failing to cooperate fully you, in effect, tampered with the physical evidence, thereby compromising the outcome of the trial.

Are you collapsing with laughter, O. J.? I hope not. Because this really is the only way you'll ever regain something not just like, but even superior to, the respect that you once had. Not from everyone, of course. Family members and close friends of the victims may

---

18 See http://www.kessleronforfeiture.com/crime.html, especially the section entitled "Waiver." Steven Kessler is an attorney who has written extensively on the double-jeopardy clause of the Fifth Amendment.

understandably never forgive wrongs done to a loved one. But even some of them might relent if they saw you take responsibility for your actions, saw you truly regret what you have done. And the sort of people you hang out with (are now confined with) might think you're a fool, might hate you for making them uncomfortably aware that the conscience does exist. The small do hate the great with a vengeance; they always have and always will. But the rest of us will be reminded that, differences of scale aside, we've all done things we regret and not had the courage to make amends for, to say the heartfelt sorry that needed to be heard while there was still time. I know that that's a far cry from running the risk of execution, but what can I say—you've dug yourself such a deep hole. I think, however, that the thing you most fear is the shame and disgrace. But what else is your life about now? Pretend as you may, you can't escape it; it is *forever* staring you right in the face. So why not face your fears instead, and defeat them? Facing what you most fear can bring relief.

In *American Tragedy*, Lawrence Schiller explains how he deals with the question of whether he thinks you're guilty or not by saying, "If [you] did it, it doesn't exist in [your] mind."[19] But what he really thinks is hardly in doubt, as is made quite clear in a brief, but haunting final chapter (a briefer epilogue ensues). It concerns Ed Medvene and some impressions he'd recorded prior to the Simpson case after visiting a client in San Quentin on death row. What had struck him was the simple dignity of the men that he'd met there: "In the death-row waiting room there was resignation, there was peace, there was an inescapable sense that no matter how antisocial the behavior, how horrendous the crime had been, there

19 437.

was humanity. No one in that room was the center of his own world. [Medvene] saw growth in those convicted and condemned men."[20] Reading this, I was reminded of a story told me by my father when I was a boy. He had been a newspaper reporter for the *Winnipeg Tribune* (now defunct) and had been a witness at the hanging of a certain Henry Malanik, the last man ever hanged in Manitoba (1952). He related the story in great detail, including how Malanik had undergone a radical transformation during the interval between his conviction and his death, thanks mainly to the assiduous ministrations of a Catholic priest. He told me that the angry and defiant man who had shot an unarmed police detective point-blank with a twelve-gauge shotgun as he tried to talk him into surrendering peacefully—Malanik had just stabbed and wounded his girlfriend's husband—went to his death with a dignity and calm he had never before shown he possessed.

Dignity is the last thing anyone would associate with you, O. J. Or as Schiller reports of Medvene: "(He) had never seen any growth in O. J. No insight. No change. He sees no humanity in Simpson … O. J. Simpson is a whole different kind of man from those guys in San Quentin." From all indications, this is still your situation, the state your soul is in. Its *agon*, or struggle, in the only arena that really counts, is all but lost—*unless* you can rise to the occasion and grow into someone you've never yet shown you can be. No one can do this for you, certainly no psychiatrist of the modern stamp. Dignity in the traditional sense, honor that's either unblemished or redeemed, is not what psychiatry deals in, much less the heroic—and nothing short of heroic is called for here. So steel yourself, as the Spartans did, for the task. They were prepared from birth to deal with trials this demanding, so much so that bravery was a kind of ritual with them, as the following incident illustrates:

---

20 *American Tragedy*, 967

When Xerxes was approaching Thermopylae, he sent a rider on ahead to see if the Greeks were at the pass as reported. The rider happened to find the Spartans posted in plain sight and either exercising or combing their hair. When this was related to Xerxes, he was amazed, and he sent for the wrongfully deposed Spartan king, Demaratus, whom he had in his entourage—and whose deposition and humiliation at the hands of Leonidas's mad half-brother, Cleomenes (whose fatal self-mutilation I related), was part of the reason the "wrath of Hercules," or wronged principle of kingship, demanded a royal death. In debate with Xerxes, Demaratus had already foretold that the Spartans would not retreat from their post (7.104). And now, vindicated by the scout's report,[21] he explained to the Persian how "it is the *nomos* [or common practice] of the Spartans to pay careful attention to their hair [which custom required they wear long] when they are about to put their lives in jeopardy" (7.209). The Spartans, for all their prowess, did not swagger or hurl boasts—far from it. They were the Laconians (the country of which Sparta was the capital), from which we get *laconic*: they were "terse of speech," the proverbial strong-and-silent types. This hair-combing ritual is meant to sum them up. It, and other rituals like it, served to help them focus calmly and resolutely on whatever trials were to come and to gather all their inner strength for release when battle began.

This, their preparation, is something you can identify with, O. J., at least in part. You've put your game face on more times than you can count, ever since you were a kid and started to play organized

---

21 He tells Xerxes at this point that it is his own "greatest *agon*" or challenge (7.209) to speak nothing but the truth. When the Spartans at Thermopylae, as led by Leonidas, make good all he says about them, you have the sense that the two royal households are reconciled around the same principle and that the breach between them is healed, symbolically, by the *agon* that they share in their separate ways.

football, though no doubt you got better at it as time went by and the stakes increased. Well, the stakes couldn't be greater than they are right now; yet, strangely, you're not focused at all. It's as if you don't know how badly you're losing, or as if the final standings are set and all that's left is a meaningless game. But, of course, the season in this instance *is* one game; it's all or nothing, and the contest is your life. That's the downside. But the upside is that they keep score a little differently, so no matter how lopsided things seem, and how little time's left, the game's never totally out of reach. It's not the fact that you've trailed throughout and played poorly that counts but the sincerity with which you commit to a winning game plan, if only for the contest's final play. Thus did the good thief, and thus did the first Thane of Cawdor in *Macbeth* (the rebel whom Macbeth defeats and then succeeds), whose "deep repentance" on the point of death for all his treasons earned him this immortal accolade: "nothing in his life / Became him like the leaving it" (I, iv, 7–8).

What else it earned we can never know for certain, at least not this side of the grave. So reason tells us, and if we were just rational creatures, that would be it. But imagination, after its fashion, knows no bounds, and what it conjures up is a tremendous sense of relief or of being released: the final catharsis that's our ultimate aim in life. To compare great with little, it might be the way you felt that day when you broke free from the pack on that brilliant Rose Bowl run, when you knew for sure that, with your speed and strength, you'd outdistance all pursuit—like that, but ten thousandfold more so, and once and for all. Of course, in your case, there's no telling what the sentence would be if you pled guilty in a second criminal trial (not that that should concern you), so the answer as regards your eternal state might have to wait. But, even in this world, you'd finally find relief and feel clean again as you haven't felt for a long time. You'd be able to look no-matter-who straight in the eye—a rehearsal perhaps for an encounter yet to come.

What was it like when you first met her? Was it love at first sight? Did you catch your breath? Did she make you go weak in the knees? When did your *eyes* meet, really meet, for the first time? If not right away, then it was not long after, I think. No one knows better than you, I suspect, that she was the one, and now that she's gone, there won't be another. She can never be replaced. And this is perhaps the bitterest aspect of your situation, like the loss of the public's respect, but even worse: a happiness and intimacy that once was yours you will never have again. If there only were a way! A second chance! If you could undo, or at least atone, *all* the harm that you've done!

What's in a name? It's a question the Greeks often asked. That's partly because their names all clearly meant something, like Hercules, "Hera's Glory." But they also paid attention to names as potential omens, the idea being that in a given (critical) situation, the significance of the name of a person you encounter may be heaven's subtle way of guiding your steps.[22] Thus, when Hegesistratus of Samos accosted Leutychidēs, the Spartan commander of the Greek fleet, and beseeched him to attack the Persian fleet at Mycalē and free the Ionian Greeks of Asia Minor, the Spartan suddenly interrupted and asked his name, either "by chance," says Herodotus, or in "the hope of a propitious sign." And when he learned that his interlocutor was "Leader [of the] Host,"[23] he cut conversation short, saying, he "accepted the omen" and would come to Ionia's aid (9.90–2).

Nicole's a Greek name too, at least etymologically, though its use as a woman's name (in various forms) likely started long after classical times. It's the feminine form of Nicholas, or anciently Nicolaüs,

22 This is the forward-looking complement to what I said earlier (chapter six, note 1) about how Herodotus looks for significant names as potentially indicative of the workings of nemesis in a given prior situation.

23 *Hege-* is the base of *hegemon* ("leader" or "guide"). From *stratos*, "something spread out or deployed" (think of "strata"), you get *strategos*, "general," and from that "strategy."

which we just met with earlier on in this chapter as the name of one of the sons of the Spartan heralds. It's comprised of *nikē*, or "victory," with which most of us are familiar, thanks to the famous sporting-goods manufacturer, and *laös*, "the people" (or "laity"). Combined, it means "[The] People's Victory" or "Victory [of the] People." This, I suppose, assuming there's anything to this, can only be Fate's way of being ironic, of wryly mocking the outcome of the criminal trial, because "the people" were ignominiously defeated, not on the evidence, but thanks to the Dream Team's dubious tactics and a jury all too predisposed to acquit. So, Mr. Simpson, here's your chance to vindicate Nicole and give the "victory to the people," where it belongs; to be a champion again; to hear the crowd's applause for deeds well done *and* perhaps, you never know, a sound more welcome still.

In the months before she died, before you killed her, you were trying to reconcile your differences and see if you could get back together again. It didn't work out, mainly because she saw you hadn't changed; she saw that she was just being sweet-talked back into the same intolerable situation as before. So, change! Become what she lost hope in your ever being. Shakespeare's Cleopatra, at the close, with Antony dead and Rome again triumphant, weighs what her earthly future holds and chooses noble death. It is catharsis pure and simple: she washes her hands of all the world, in the sense of all that's mean and paltry, and commits herself heart and soul to Antony for all time: "Husband, I come: Now to that name my courage prove my title" (II, ii, 290–1). Your life as it stands now, Mr. Simpson, is even more paltry, and less worth preserving, than was hers. So, change! And by so doing renew your marriage vows—indeed, truly affirm them for the very first time. "Character is destiny," said the Greeks, as I mentioned early on. That statement, however, is open-ended: it could refer solely to the here and now, the course our life takes in this world, or it could encompass our final *destination*, our just desserts, the terms on which we'll pass the life to come. *You* still have a chance to change your character, your life, and, if in fact there is one, your final destination. You have a chance to *earn* a better fate.

So there you are, where you always have been: in the arena, on the stage, of life. You're an *agonistes* if there ever was one, in every sense of the term. Your challenge is to retrieve your situation, to win the game and become a hero in the final act. It's either that or die an object lesson in disgrace, as despised a man as any on this earth. The outcome is all in your hands. I mean, it's always all in anyone's hands, but in your case it's so public and clear cut—it's that immunity that you possess and you alone can voluntarily surrender or circumvent. You're not just the protagonist of this drama; you're the author as well. You're not condemned to play the part as written; the pen that writes the ending is yourself. To revert again to the language of your true vocation, the world where once you were its greatest star: you're not just the running back in this situation. You're the coach, and you're the quarterback, as well. The game's on the line, and time is about to expire. You're calling the play, and there's only this one designed to go *all the way.* Do you want the ball? Have you got what it takes to win it? Can you hear the cheers in those end zone stands? *Can you hear her call your name?*

What if …

Select Bibliography

The Simpson Case

Clark, Marcia, with Teresa Carpenter. *Without a Doubt*. New York: Penguin Books, 1997.

Fuhrman, Mark. *Murder in Brentwood*. New York: Kensington Publishing Corp., 1997.

Kessler, Steven. "Crime and Punishment … and Punishment: Civil Forfeiture and the Double Jeopardy Clause." Last modified May 26, 1996. Accessed November 22, 2011. http://www.kessleronforfeiture.com/crime.html.

Petrocelli, Daniel. *Triumph of Justice: The Final Judgment on the Simpson Saga*. New York: Crown Publishers, Inc., 1998.

Schiller, Lawrence, and James Willwerth. *American Tragedy*. New York: HarperCollins, 1996.

Spitz, Werner U., and Russell S. Fisher, eds, *Spitz and Fisher's Medicolegal Investigation of Death: Guidelines for the Application of Pathology to Crime Investigation*, 2nd edition. Springfield IL: Charles C. Thomas, 1980.

The Goldman Family. *If I Did It: Confessions of the Killer*. New York: Beaufort Books, 2007

Wagner, Richard. "The Left Hand Glove." Last modified July 28, 2002. Accessed November 22, 2011. http://www.wagnerandson.com/oj/lefthand.htm

Walraven, Jack. "The Simpson Trial Transcripts." Accessed November 22, 2011. http://walraven.org/simpson/

Herodotus et Alia

Brown, T. S. "Herodotus' Views on Athletics." *The Ancient World* 7 (1983): 17–29.

Chiasson, Charles. C. "The Herodotean Solon." *Greek, Roman and Byzantine Studies* 27 (1986): 249–62.

Finley, M. I., and H. W. Pleket. *The Olympic Games: The First Thousand Years*. New York: The Viking Press, 1976.

Flory, Stewart. "Arion's Leap: Brave Gestures in Herodotus." *American Journal of Philology* 99 (1978): 411–21.

Forrest, W. G. *A History of Sparta 950–192 B.C.* London: W. W. Norton, 1968.

Gardiner, E. N. *Greek Athletic Sports and Festivals*. London: MacMillan, 1910.

Goodman, M. D., and A. J. Holladay. "Religious Scruples in Ancient Warfare." *Classical Quarterly* 36 (1986): 151–71.

Grene, D. "The Historian as Dramatist." *Journal of Philology* 58 (1961): 477–88.

Herodotus. *The Histories.* Translated by A. de Sélincourt. Edited with notes and introduction by John Marincola. London: Penguin, 2003.

How, W. W., and J. Wells. *A Commentary on Herodotus.* 2 vols. 1912. Oxford: Clarendon Press, 1964.

Hude, C., ed. *Herodoti Historiae.* 3rd ed. 2 vols. Oxford, 1926. Corrected reprint. Oxford: Clarendon Press, 1986.

Huxley, G. L. *Early Sparta.* Cambridge: Harvard University Press, 1962.

Kapuściński, Ryszard. *Travels with Herodotus.* Translated by Klara Glowczewska. New York: Alfred A. Knopf, 2007.

Lattimore, R. "The Wise Adviser in Herodotus." *Classical Philology* 34 (1939): 24–35.

Lings, Martin. *Shakespeare's Window into the Soul.* Rochester NY: Inner Traditions, 2006.

Marozzi, Justin. *The Way of Herodotus: Travels with the Man Who Invented History.* Cambridge MA: Da Capo Press, 2010.

Miller, M. "The Herodotean Croesus." *Klio* 41 (1963): 89–92.

Ondaatje, Michael. *The English Patient.* Toronto: Vintage Canada, 1993.

Parke, H. W., and D. E. W. Wormell. *A History of the Delphic Oracle.* Oxford: Clarendon Press, 1956.

Segal, C. "Croesus on the Pyre: Herodotus and Bacchylides." *Wiener Studien* 5 (1970): 39–51.

Stebbins, Eunice Burr. *The Dolphin in the Literature and Art of Greece and Rome.* Menasha WI, Banta, 1929.

Young, D. C. *The Olympic Myth of Greek Amateur Athletics.* Chicago: Ares Publishers, 1985.

Robert Metcalfe was born in Winnipeg, Manitoba. He earned a master's degree in English from the University of Manitoba and a doctorate in classics from the University of Toronto. His dissertation focused on Herodotus. Metcalfe lives in Toronto, Ontario, and works in advertising sales.

CPSIA information can be obtained at www.ICGtesting.com
Printed in the USA
LVOW08s0709240114

370726LV00001B/3/P